THE COMPLETE

Children's
Liturgy

BOOK

THE COMPLETE
Children's Liturgy
BOOK

A comprehensive programme for every Sunday
of the Lectionary by KATIE THOMPSON

Illustrated by
Jennifer Carter

Kevin
Mayhew

First published in 1995 by
KEVIN MAYHEW LTD
Rattlesden
Bury St Edmunds
Suffolk IP30 0SZ

ISBN 0 86209 636 7
Catalogue No 1500022

Front cover: *'Portiere'* designed c.1890 by John Dearle for
Morris and Co. Embroidery on silk. Reproduced by courtesy of
Victoria and Albert Museum, London/Bridgeman Art Library, London.

Editor: Shona Clark
Cover design by Juliette Clarke and Graham Johnstone
Typesetting and page creation by Vicky Brown
Printed and bound in Great Britain.

Contents

Introduction

This book provides a complete but flexible scheme for celebrating the Liturgy of the Word with children. It offers a framework for every Sunday of the Year and the major Feast days, which can be adapted to suit the age and needs of a particular group. It provides a step by step guide for the liturgist, and can be used as a valuable resource to stimulate new ideas.

WHAT IS CHILDREN'S LITURGY?

It is the Liturgy of the Word suitably adapted to make it relevant to the lives and experiences of young children. It gives them the opportunity to understand the Gospel message and participate in the Eucharistic celebration at their own level.

WHERE DOES IT TAKE PLACE?

The children celebrate the Liturgy of the Word in a room set apart from the main congregation. The setting should be relaxed and comfortable, with some carpet for the children to sit on, or an informal arrangement of chairs. A simple altar with candles and a special place set aside for proclaiming the Word of God, help the children to appreciate that Christ himself speaks to us through the words of the Gospel. The leader and helper(s) are responsible for preparing the room and making sure that everything is in the right place before the beginning of Mass, and for rearranging the room afterwards.

WHEN DOES IT TAKE PLACE?

The children should be present at the beginning of the Mass until the end of the Introductory Rites, when the Priest invites them to leave with the liturgists for their own celebration. They are recalled immediately after the prayers of the Faithful by a member of the liturgy team or the congregation, when they return to the main assembly with the offertory procession, to celebrate the Liturgy of the Eucharist. The time available depends on many factors, including the length of the individual homily, and how much of the adult celebration is sung instead of spoken. Getting the timing right comes with practice and experience. Each suggested scheme takes approximately 25 minutes from the introduction to the closing prayer, but the liturgists should adapt these to meet individual circumstances and needs.

WHO ARE THE LITURGISTS AND WHAT DO THEY DO?

What it takes to be a liturgist is a desire to help children to take a more active part in the celebration of their faith. Many young parents are eager to make attendance at Mass as enjoyable and meaningful an experience as they can for their children. Often they are willing to volunteer to help with children's liturgy, which benefits all the younger children in their worshipping community. Teenagers or older parishioners can become involved, as well as anyone with experience in teaching or leading groups of young people.

Ideally each session should have at least two liturgists, one to lead the children in prayer and discussion, with a suitable number of 'helpers' according to the group size, who assist with the activity, the singing and any general organisation. The liturgy team should meet regularly to discuss and prepare liturgies, and to organise activities and artwork.

A TYPICAL SCHEME FOR THE CHILDREN'S LITURGY OF THE WORD IS AS FOLLOWS:

WELCOME

Greet the children warmly and introduce yourself to anyone who might be new, or visiting the group. The atmosphere should be as relaxed and friendly as possible, so that the children feel happy and at home. To set newcomers at ease, it is sometimes helpful to explain briefly, that the children have gathered to listen to God's word and to praise him in their own special way.

INTRODUCTION

This allows you to set the scene and to introduce each liturgy to the children. Often it provides an opportunity for some initial discussion and to make any explanations which might be necessary to help the children understand the Gospel of the day.

SIGN OF THE CROSS

Blessing ourselves reminds us of being welcomed into God's family at our baptism. Making the sign of the Cross helps us to remember that we are all brothers and sisters in the one family of God, which has gathered together to worship and praise him. A small dish of holy water can be passed around for the children to bless themselves.

LIGHT THE CANDLES

Providing a simple altar helps to make both the room and the liturgy special, and fosters an attitude of prayer and respect. A white cloth, a crucifix and some candles are sufficient, and the children can be encouraged to bring flowers to decorate their altar. For reasons of safety, the candles should be lit by an adult while the children listen to a reading, sing a song or say a prayer (suggestions are given for each liturgy). Use this time to settle the group and to remind them that Jesus is the 'light of the world', who speaks to us all through the Gospel or scripture readings which they will listen to. We can be like 'candles' who share the light and warmth of God's love with everyone we meet.

SAYING SORRY

Children first learn the importance of forgiving, and being forgiven, in their own families. 'Sorry' is a word which is familiar to even the youngest child. Reconciliation with God, and with each other, is a cause for celebration in the whole community. As members of God's family we depend on each other, because whatever we do or say, affects everyone who is united by God's love. It is important to try to build a sense of trust in Jesus, and confidence in his boundless mercy and forgiveness. We all have a need to admit the mistakes we have made, and to ask for forgiveness, but do not dwell on negative feelings of guilt or failure.

To help the children learn to reflect and to ask for God's forgiveness, a variety of prayers, readings, and simple songs set to familiar tunes are suggested. The children can also choose a 'sorry colour': write out the word 'SORRY' on a large piece of paper, using a different colour for each letter, and display this in the liturgy room. Then write out the words of the sorry prayers, which can be found on page 343, each in a different colour, corresponding to one of the letters of the word 'sorry'. When a child chooses a 'sorry colour', by referring to the large word 'SORRY' displayed, the corresponding prayer can then be said.

GLORIA

Every Sunday we gather together as one family to celebrate the Resurrection of Christ. The Gloria is a prayer of praise which can be spoken or sung, but whatever format is used, it should always be joyful. You can vary the form of the Gloria from week to week using the different prayers and songs suggested. The Gloria is not normally said during the seasons of Advent or Lent.

GOSPEL ACCLAMATION

The Liturgy of the Word is, by its nature, an occasion of worship. To mark the proclamation of God's word, the children joyfully sing or say an acclamation together. (This can be done with the children sitting or standing according to choice, or the practicalities of space!)

GOSPEL

This book provides a Gospel or reading for every Sunday and major Feast day of the Church's year. These follow the Lectionary, which details the Gospel and readings which are to be used for a particular Sunday or Feast day. The Lectionary follows a three year cycle, Years A, B and C, and each new liturgical year begins on the first Sunday of Advent.

A copy of your Diocesan Yearbook, Ordo or Almanac will contain a liturgical calendar, which is the easiest way to find out which Sundays of the Year or Feast days are celebrated on which dates. The texts provided are adapted for children, who will enjoy listening to the word of God, and will understand its meaning more fully. Occasionally, a reading is used if the Gospel is difficult for children to understand, and it makes the message clearer or conveys the theme better. The Gospel can be read by an adult or one of the older children in the group. The important thing to remember is that the reader should proclaim God's word, and proclaim it well. This requires preparation and practice. To help the children to appreciate that Christ himself speaks to us through the Gospel, a special place should be set aside for proclaiming the word of God. This might be as simple as a specially designated place to stand, or a particular chair to sit on. The end of the Gospel should be marked by a final response, to tie in with the format of the adult liturgy.

DISCUSSION

After every Gospel, a series of questions are provided to help prompt a brief discussion, and to encourage the children to share their understanding of the word of God. These questions and answers are there to guide and help the liturgist to direct the children's thoughts, and to clarify the Gospel message. The level of discussion can be pitched appropriately, depending on the age range of the group, appreciating that older children may gain more from this part of the liturgy than younger children. Good preparation of the discussion, and enthusiastic delivery, are essential to encourage the children to participate and respond in a lively and enjoyable way. It is important to give every child an opportunity to participate in the discussion, and to appreciate whatever they might say, never forgetting that everyone's contribution is valuable.

ACTIVITY

The activities suggested, aim to help the children to retain the stories, understand the various themes, and remember the Gospel message. The activities are intended to be a joyful expression of worship, and can be adapted to suit the needs of individual groups. The time available for completing the activity is often very short, so it is important to be well organised and to have as much as possible prepared in advance.

Appreciate the children's efforts and don't expect perfection. Allow them to make the artwork their own special gift to God, which is presented to him at the Offertory procession.

Their work can then be displayed in the church and shared with the whole community.

CREED

Our faith is expressed in the words of the Creed, and it is important to say it with the children, to confirm their faith, and to unite the children's celebration with that of the adult congregation. A simplified version of the creed has been included, which uses language more appropriate for young children, although older children may prefer to use the adult version.

CLOSING PRAYER

A closing prayer which is linked with the theme of the day is included at the end of each liturgy. The children should be encouraged to sit quietly for a few moments of prayer and reflection, in preparation for rejoining the adult congregation to celebrate the gift of Jesus in the Eucharist.

Year A

First Sunday of Advent
Be ready

INTRODUCTION
The word 'Advent' means coming. During Advent the readings tell us how God's people longed for the arrival of the Saviour promised by God. During this season we think about when Jesus will return and remember the first coming of Christ as a baby.

SIGN OF THE CROSS

LIGHT THE CANDLES
Light the candles and then read:
Jesus said, 'Let your goodness shine out like a light in the darkness, so that through you, the love of our heavenly Father will touch the lives of others.' (cf Matthew 5:16-17)

SORRY
Encourage the children to close their eyes and to listen carefully to the words of this prayer:
Dear God,
help us to forgive anyone who has hurt us.
We must be ready to forgive others,
just as you forgive us.
If we have done wrong,
by our words or actions,
we want to say we are sorry
and we will try to be good.

GOSPEL ACCLAMATION
To welcome today's Gospel sing the Advent Song.

GOSPEL (cf Matthew 24:37-40, 44-45)
One day Jesus said: 'Long ago, there was a great flood, and it swept all the people away, except for Noah. No-one had prepared for the flood, for they had not listened to Noah's warnings. In the same way, you will not know when the Son of God will return, for only my heavenly Father knows this. Lead good lives so that when the time comes you are ready!'

DISCUSSION
We all know that the first coming of Jesus was as a tiny baby at Christmas. We also know that one day Jesus will return, although we have no idea when. During Advent we spend some time thinking about this second 'coming', and whether we will be ready when it happens.

Who knows when the world will end? – Only God knows the day and time, so we must always be prepared. Today's Gospel reminds us that we should always be ready for the second coming of Jesus, at the end of time.

What sort of lives did Jesus tell us to lead? – Jesus told us that we should all lead good lives so that when God calls us to be with him in heaven we shall really be ready for the happiness which he has promised us.

The Advent wreath is a German custom, which celebrates the coming of Christ, the 'Light of the World'. The circle represents God's unending love, just as a circle has no end and no beginning. Evergreen leaves represent God's everlasting love, which never dies. The candles represent Jesus, the 'light' of the world. There is one for each Sunday of Advent and one for Christmas day itself. We light them in the following order:

1. Purple – This is the traditional colour of Advent and Lent, a symbol of our longing for forgiveness.
2. Purple
3. Pink –   The traditional colour of the third Sunday of Advent (originally called Gaudete), a symbol of rejoicing as we await the Saviour's coming.
4. Purple
5. White – This candle is lit on Christmas Day itself to signify the Birth of Jesus.

ACTIVITY
It may not be practical to prepare a real Advent Wreath for the childrens' liturgy, especially in view of the fire hazard. Your parish may have one in the main Church anyway. A good suggestion is to make an Advent wreath decoration as shown here. The children can cut out the leaves, candles and the flames and fill in the appropriate colours. These are glued into place on a circle cut out from card. The first candle is 'lit' today by gluing the first flame in place and then one for each Sunday as Christmas draws closer.

CREED

CLOSING PRAYER
Our friend Jesus,
we ask you to send your Spirit to guide us,
so that we will lead good lives,
and be ready to greet you when you return.

Second Sunday of Advent
John the Baptist

INTRODUCTION
John the Baptist was the son of Elizabeth and Zechariah. He was chosen by God to prepare the people for the coming of Jesus. He told them that they must be sorry for all the things that they had done wrong,and try to live better lives. Today we will hear how and where he lived, and about the message he shared.

SIGN OF THE CROSS

LIGHT THE CANDLES
As we light our candles and sing our Advent Song, we try to prepare, like John the Baptist, for the coming of the promised one. Sing the Advent Song.

SORRY
Help us to be sorry for anything we have done wrong, and to try hard to be good.
Sing Sorry Song 4: *When we say that we are sorry.*

GOSPEL ACCLAMATION
To welcome today's Gospel we sing Acclamation 5: *We have come to hear you Lord.*

GOSPEL *(cf Matthew 3:1-12)*
John the Baptist went to live in the desert in Judaea. He wore a coat made from camel hair, tied around the middle with a belt. The desert was too hot and dry for many things to grow, so John lived on wild honey and locusts. God had told him that he was sending someone special to save the world. He wanted John to tell everyone that they must change their ways and try to become good. People came from far and wide to be baptised by John in the River Jordan. They wanted to say sorry for all their sins. One day John told them, 'I can wash you with water, but a very special person is coming who will baptise you with God's Spirit and wash away all your sins.'

DISCUSSION
Where did John the Baptist go to live? – In the desert in Judaea. *(Discuss what a desert is like. Show pictures if possible.)*

What did he wear? Do you think his coat was very comfortable?

Can anyone remember what John had to eat in the desert? – *(Make sure the children know what a locust is!)*

What was the message that God wanted John to tell the people and how should they prepare? –

God wanted John to tell all the people to change their ways and become good.

ACTIVITY
'Light' the second candle on the Advent wreath decoration. Photocopy the picture of John in the desert and ask the children to colour this in.
OR
In advance prepare a large picture of John the Baptist. Make copies of locusts and the honey pot. Using glue-sticks, glue John's coat, and encourage the children to sprinkle on sawdust, sand, porridge oats or any other material to represent the rough camel hair. Alternatively glue patches of coarse material or fabric into place. The remainder of the group can colour the honey pots and locusts which complete the picture.

CREED

CLOSING PRAYER
Heavenly Father,
you sent John the Baptist to prepare
the people for the coming of your Son.
As Christmas draws closer,
help us to prepare too,
so that we may be ready
for Christmas day.

Third Sunday of Advent
Jesus is the promised one

INTRODUCTION
King Herod had John the Baptist put in prison. Now John knew that Jesus was the 'Promised One', sent by God, but some of his friends were still unsure. So, from from behind his prison bars, John sent his followers to ask Jesus a very important question.

SIGN OF THE CROSS

LIGHT THE CANDLES
As we light the candles, we say together:
Fill our hearts with the light of Jesus.

SORRY
John the Baptist knew that Jesus was the Saviour promised by God. As we prepare to celebrate his birth, we ask our Saviour to forgive us if we have done wrong.
Choose a sorry colour.

GOSPEL ACCLAMATION
To welcome today's Gospel sing the Advent Song.

GOSPEL (cf Matthew 11:2-11)
While John the Baptist was in prison, he heard about the things that Jesus was doing, and sent some of his followers to find Jesus. 'Tell us, are you the one sent by God, that John has told us about?' they asked.

Jesus said 'Go and tell John what you have seen and heard: the blind can see, the lame can walk, lepers are cured, the deaf hear, and the dead are brought back to life. The Good News is being shared so that everyone can believe in me.' As John's friends hurried away to tell him what they had heard, Jesus said to the crowds, 'God sent John to prepare for my coming. He is a truly great man, and will be remembered for all time.'

DISCUSSION
How many candles will be lit on the Advent wreath today? – Three.

Today is called the third Sunday of Advent, but in past times it was called 'Gaudete Sunday'. Can anyone remember what 'Gaudete' means, and why our candle is pink today? – Gaudete means 'joy', and our candle is pink as a symbol of rejoicing as we await the birth of our Saviour and Lord.

As Christmas gets closer, the light is getting brighter, and the feeling of excitement is growing.

John the Baptist was excited to learn of the marvellous things that Jesus was doing. Why did he send his followers to Jesus? – He sent his followers to find out if Jesus really was the promised one.

When they found Jesus, what did they see and hear? – Many marvellous miracles which Jesus was performing, showing that he truly was the promised one of God.

How do you think they felt on seeing these miracles? – They were probably amazed to see all these things and filled with joy as they realised that they had met God's chosen one.

The 'light' of the world was already filling the lives of those he met with love, life and hope!

ACTIVITY
'Light' the third candle on the Advent wreath decoration.

Photocopy the picture for the children to colour in or draw a picture of John's face onto a large sheet of paper. Cut out some bars to 'imprison' him. Add the figure of Jesus preaching to the scene.

CREED

CLOSING PRAYER
God our Father,
as we look forward to Christmas
the excitement is growing.
Just as the light from the Advent wreath
grows brighter,
we pray that the light of Jesus
will grow brighter in our lives too.

Fourth Sunday of Advent
The angel's visit

INTRODUCTION
Before Mary and Joseph were married, the angel Gabriel appeared to Mary and told her that through the power of the Holy Spirit, she was going to have a child. This child would be the Son of God.

SIGN OF THE CROSS

LIGHT THE CANDLES
As we light our candles today, we remember that Jesus is the light of the world. Together sing the Candle Song.

SORRY
A reading (cf Matthew 17:3-5.)
If someone does anything to harm or hurt you, you can tell them so, but if they say sorry, you must forgive them. Even if they hurt you over and over again, if they say sorry and truly mean it, then you must forgive them over and over again. Just as God our Father forgives us, so we must forgive others, not once, but many times.

GOSPEL ACCLAMATION
To welcome today's Gospel sing the Advent Song.

GOSPEL (cf Matthew 1.18-25)
Before Joseph and Mary were married, Mary told Joseph that she was expecting a baby. Joseph was a kind and loving man and felt confused and unsure of what to do, for he did not want to upset Mary. One night, an angel came to visit Joseph in a dream. 'Joseph, do not worry. Take Mary home with you and marry her. The child within her is of the Holy Spirit. She will have a son, and you will call him Jesus. He has been sent to save the world.' So Joseph did what the angel had told him, and he and Mary were married.

DISCUSSION
No one knows exactly what an angel looks like, but how do we usually imagine them ?

When the angel Gabriel appeared to Mary, and told her that she would have a child, do you think that she felt afraid? – She trusted in God completely, and relied on him to explain this happening to Joseph.

What messenger did God send to Joseph in a dream?

Like Mary, Joseph trusted in God and did what was asked of him.

ACTIVITY
'Light' the fourth candle on the Advent wreath decoration.
Copy and colour the scene of the angel appearing to Joseph in a dream
OR
Get the children to draw pictures of what they imagine angels might look like.

CREED

CLOSING PRAYER
God sends an angel to watch over each of us – our guardian angel. Listen carefully to the words of this prayer:

Lord keep your angel by my side,
To care for me and be my guide,
To be my friend throughout the years,
And keep me safe from harm and fears,
To stay with me each night and day,
So from your love I never stray.

Christmas Day
Jesus is born

INTRODUCTION
The Roman emperor Augustus wanted to know how many people lived in his empire so he ordered a count to be made of all the people in the land. This meant that Joseph and Mary had to travel from Nazareth to Bethlehem, because Joseph had been born there. The journey was long and difficult and the time was coming for Mary to have her baby.

SIGN OF THE CROSS

LIGHT THE CANDLES
As we light our candles today, we remember that Jesus is the light of the world.
Read the following:
The world was full of darkness and shadows, but now it is filled with light so everyone can see. God has sent a tiny baby, his only son, and he will fill our world with peace and love. (cf Isaiah 9:2-3,6-7.)

SORRY
God loves us so much that he sent his only son Jesus to save us from our mistakes. Jesus told a story about a loving father whose son left home and lived a wicked and selfish life. This made his father very sad. One day the son came back and was truly sorry for all his mistakes. His father hugged him and forgave him for everything. God is our loving Father and he will always forgive us if we are truly sorry.

GLORIA

GOSPEL ACCLAMATION
To welcome today's Gospel sing Acclamation 3: 'Alleluia, Alleluia.'

GOSPEL (cf Luke 2:1-20)
Joseph and Mary arrived in Bethlehem to register for the census ordered by Augustus. The time came for Mary to have her baby, and he was born in a stable, because there was no room at the inn. She wrapped him in strips of cloth and laid him in a manger. On a hillside near the town, some shepherds were watching over their sheep. Suddenly, an angel appeared and the sky was filled with God's glory. The shepherds were terrified, but the angel said, 'Do not be afraid, for I have great news for you. Today a baby has been born in Bethlehem, he is Christ the Lord. You will find him lying in a manger.' The sky was filled with the sound of angels singing, 'Glory to God in the highest, and peace to all people on earth!' The shepherds hurried to Bethlehem and soon found the stable. There in the manger lay a tiny baby. They told Mary and Joseph what they had seen and heard that night, and they shared their amazement. Mary listened carefully and cherished all these things in her heart. The shepherds went back to their sheep on the hillside, singing God's praises for everything had been as the angel had said.

DISCUSSION
Use a prepared christingle as a visual aid for the discussion and ask the children if they know what the different parts of the christingle symbolise.
The christingle comprises:
1. An orange – this represents our world.
2. A candle pushed into the top – this represents the 'light' of the world.
3. A red ribbon around the orange – this represents the Blood of Christ.
4. Four cocktail sticks with dried fruit stuck on – these represent the fruits of the earth, and the abundance of the four seasons.
The points to emphasise are:
1. That Jesus came to save the whole world and everyone in it.
2. His light reaches out to all people.
3. By dying on the cross, he shed his Blood and saved us all from our sins.
4. God is generous and gave us all a wonderful world, with plenty of food and resources. We should not be greedy, and must try to always share what we can with others. This is very appropriate to remember at Christmas.

ACTIVITY
Complete the Advent wreath by 'lighting' the final white candle. You can then help each child to make a christingle. Much of the preparation can be done in advance (they can be lit at home!) Afterwards sing carols with the children.

If plenty of notice is given, the children can bring non-perishable foodstuffs in to make up a hamper to be given to a worthy cause.

CREED

CLOSING PRAYER
Dear Lord Jesus,
on this Christmas morning,
fill us with the joy and wonder
which the shepherds shared with Mary and Joseph.
May our hearts and our homes
be filled with the peace and love
you shared with the world.

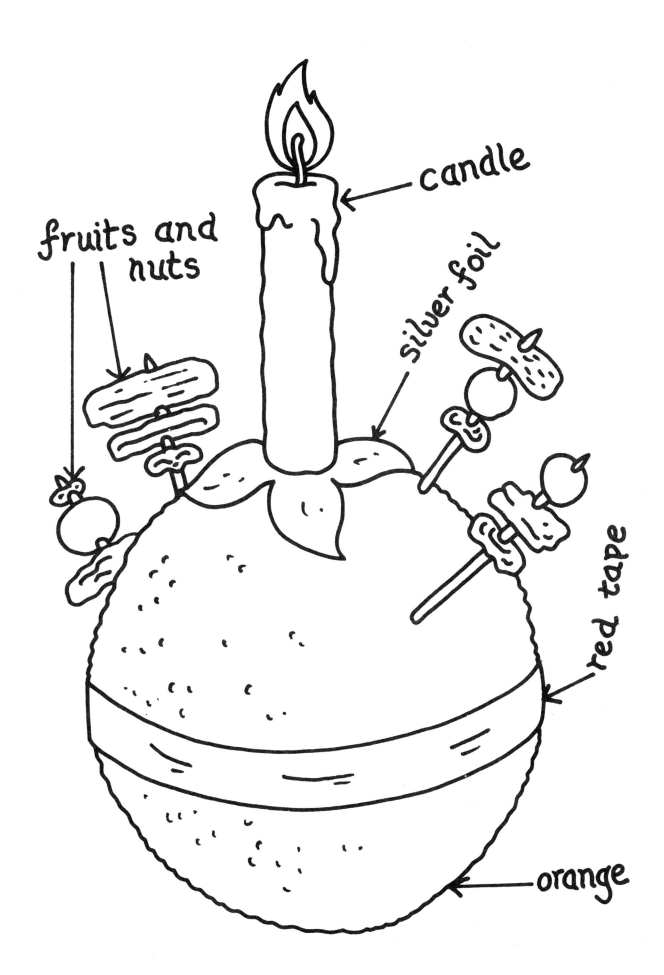

candle

fruits and nuts

silver foil

red tape

orange

The Feast of the Holy Family

INTRODUCTION
Today we celebrate a day set aside to think about the Holy family – Jesus, Mary and Joseph.

SIGN OF THE CROSS

LIGHT THE CANDLES
Light the candles and say Candle Prayer 3: *The light of God.*

SORRY
Close your eyes and listen carefully to the words of this prayer:
God our Father,
you sent us Jesus
to show how loving and kind you are.
Whenever we do something
that makes you sad with us,
we will remember your love for us
and will try harder to be good.

GLORIA

GOSPEL ACCLAMATION
To welcome the Gospel today sing Acclamation 5: *We have come to hear you, Lord.*

GOSPEL (*cf Matthew 2:13-15, 19-21, 23*).
An angel sent by God appeared to Joseph in a dream and said, 'Joseph, your family is in great danger! You must take Mary and Jesus to Egypt now, this very night, and stay there until I tell you that it is safe to return. King Herod wants to find Jesus and kill him.' So Joseph got up and they set off for Egypt that same night. When King Herod was dead, the angel returned just as he had said, and told Joseph that they could return to Israel. So the family went to live in Galilee, in a town called Nazareth.

DISCUSSION
Joseph had to save his family from terrible danger. What was that danger? – King Herod wanted to find Jesus and kill him, because he believed that Jesus could be a King who might overthrow Herod.

Our families protect us from harm too, but what other things are families for?
– for loving us (in what ways?)
– for caring for us (how?)
– for sharing (what things?)
Do the people in your family have different jobs to do?

– going to work,
– cooking,
– gardening,
– walking the dog!
Sometimes we have to share these jobs – if someone is ill, or busy.

Families are all about sharing. They share the good times and the bad times. Our families make us feel loved and safe.

There is one very big family, bigger than any of ours – it is God's family.

God is our Heavenly Father and we are all his children. We are brothers and sisters who share his love.

ACTIVITY
Draw your family and write on each person's name. Pin all the pictures on a board with the caption – 'God's Family'.

CREED

CLOSING PRAYER
(The children can hold hands in a circle for the prayer)

Jesus,
we thank you for our families
and the love we share.
We pray for our family the Church
and our brothers and sisters all over the world.
As we begin a New Year,
we ask you to guide and protect our families,
just as you did the Holy Family.

Mary, Mother of God

INTRODUCTION
Mary is a very special person. She was chosen by God to be the mother of his son. Her life was not easy and there were many sad times, but she believed that God loved her, and would do what was best for her in the end.

SIGN OF THE CROSS

LIGHT THE CANDLES
Light the candles and say Candle Prayer 3: *The Light of God.*

SORRY
Mary, you are the Mother of God. We ask you to pray with us, so that he will know that we are truly sorry for anything we have done wrong.
Read the following prayer:
Do not be afraid, God will always love you.
Whatever you have done,
God will always love you.
As a father loves his child,
he will always love you.
Come back to him and know,
God's love lasts forever.

GLORIA

GOSPEL ACCLAMATION
To welcome today's Gospel sing Acclamation 1: *Share your word with us O Lord.*

GOSPEL (*cf Luke 2:16-21*)
The shepherds hurried to Bethlehem and found Mary and Joseph, and the baby lying in the manger. When they told them what they had seen and heard that night, Mary and Joseph shared their amazement. The mother of Jesus listened carefully and cherished all these things in her heart.

The shepherds went back to their sheep on the hillside, singing God's praises, for everything had been as the angel had said.

When their baby was eight days old, Mary and Joseph named him Jesus, which was the name the angel had given to him when he first told Mary that she was going to have a child.

DISCUSSION
Ask the children to think of some of the things that a mother has to do
  – cooking,
  – cleaning,
  – going to work,
  – shopping.
The list is almost endless! Did Mary do such things?

Mothers are much more than people who look after us and do all this work!
  – They fill our lives with love, even when we are naughty.
  – They make us laugh and smile.
  – They listen to us and answer our questions.
  – They have time for us, and make us feel wanted.
Mary did all of these things for her little boy, Jesus.

We often have pictures or statues of Mary in our homes or Church, do you have one?

Why is Mary so special that we sing about her and pray to her?

There are several important reasons:
1. She said 'yes' to God and agreed to be the mother of his son. Jesus, who is God, was born and saved us from our sins.
2. She knew Jesus all his life, better than anyone else. She can help us to know him too.
3. Mary always did what God asked. With her help we can try to do what God asks of us.
4. Mary is our heavenly mother.

We call Mary our 'mother' because Jesus shared her with us. Just before he died on the cross, he turned to his mother and said: 'My friends are your children now and you are their mother.' (*cf John 19:26-27.*)

ACTIVITY
Ask each child to draw and colour a picture of themselves. These can be arranged around a central picture of Mary – 'The Mother of God.'

CREED

CLOSING PRAYER
Mary,
help us to say 'yes' to God as you did,
even when it is not easy.
Together say the 'Hail, Mary'.
The words of the first part of this prayer come from a part of the Christmas story.
The second part is a prayer for the Church.

Second Sunday After Christmas
God sends his son, Jesus

INTRODUCTION
God created the world, and out of love made people to live in it. His plan for us was destroyed when Adam and Eve disobeyed him by eating the forbidden fruit. He sent someone special to rescue us from our wrongdoings. His name was Jesus.

SIGN OF THE CROSS

LIGHT THE CANDLES
As we light our candles today, we thank God our Father for sending Jesus, the light of the world, to chase away darkness forever.
Together sing the Candle Song.

SORRY
Think about the time since we last met together, have we always been as kind and thoughtful as we should have been?

The words of St Paul remind us of the way we should try to act towards other people:
You are God's chosen people. Always be ready to care for others, and to be kind and gentle. Be patient and calm, and never boast or be proud of your goodness. Just as God always forgives you, so you must always be forgiving towards others. Fill your hearts with love, and whatever you do, do it for God. *(cf St Pauls Letter to the Colossians 3:12-14, 23.)*

GLORIA

GOSPEL ACCLAMATION
To welcome today's Gospel sing Acclamation 1: *Share your word with us.*

GOSPEL *(cf John 1:1-7, 14)*
God has no beginning or end, he is forever the same. God made all things, for he is the provider of life. He sent his only son Jesus who became a human being, to share his everlasting life with us. First, God sent a man called John to tell us about the light of the world, the bringer of life, so that we might prepare for his coming. Jesus lived among us and was full of goodness and honesty. Through his words and actions, he shared the glory of his heavenly Father with us all.

DISCUSSION
It is very difficult for us to understand all about God. What do we mean when we say that he has no beginning or end? (Use the analogy of a circle or a wedding ring to illustrate the idea of no beginning or end. Remind the children of the circular advent wreath.)

Before the beginning of time, before the planets and the stars, before the earth and everything we know was created, there was nothing except God. He created us so that he could make us happy by sharing his life and love.

Two people spoiled his plans for us by disobeying God. Who were they? – Adam and Eve spoiled their friendship with God and had to leave behind the Garden of Eden and the everlasting life they had enjoyed there. God planned to save his people from their disobedience so that they could share his everlasting life again.

Who did he send? Who exactly was Jesus, and why was he so special?

We know how difficult it is to imagine what God is like, but we can get a very good idea by learning about his son, Jesus, and listening to what he said and did.

ACTIVITY
Use the shapes given here to assemble a mobile from thin card as illustrated.

CREED

CLOSING PRAYER
Father you loved us so much
that you sent your only son Jesus
so that we could share your everlasting life.
We thank you for this love
and ask you to help us
to try not to spoil your plans again.

Feast of the Epiphany
Three kings visit Jesus

INTRODUCTION
The three wise men were not Jews. They came from lands far to the East, and were astrologers who used the stars to guide them on their journeys. They also knew of the prophecies of an infant king to be born, a Saviour. Through them, his arrival was announced to the world. Jesus the saving Lord has come not just for the Jews but for *all* people.

SIGN OF THE CROSS

LIGHT THE CANDLES
As the candles are being lit, the children listen to this reading from Isaiah *(cf Isaiah 60:1-3):*
The glory of God is shining on you! All other people will live in the shadows, but you will always have God's light to chase away the darkness. Other people will look at you and see the light of God's love shining out.

SORRY
If we have done anything to make God sad or disappointed with us, we can make a fresh start by singing our sorry song together and trying again.
Sing Sorry Song 4: *When we say that we are sorry.*

GLORIA

GOSPEL ACCLAMATION
To welcome today's Gospel sing the Advent Song.

GOSPEL *(cf Matthew 2:1-12)*
Jesus was born in Bethlehem, a small town in Judaea when King Herod ruled the land. Three wise men from the east had been following a bright star. They went to Jerusalem and asked King Herod where they could find the new-born King of the Jews that they had come to adore. Herod was greatly troubled because he didn't want anyone else to be King, so he sent for his advisors.

'Tell me where this child, the so called King will be born,' he asked.

'It has been foretold by the prophets that he will be born in Bethlehem,' they answered.

King Herod sent for the wise men and said to them, 'I will allow you to search for this child, but you must come back and tell me where to find him. Then I too can go and honour him.'

The wise men set off again on their journey. They followed the bright star until it appeared to stop over a stable. There they found Mary and Joseph with the baby Jesus. They were filled with wonder and joy, and fell to their knees to worship him. They gave him gifts fit for a king, of gold, frankincense and myrrh. An angel warned them in a dream not to return to Herod's palace, so they went back to their own countries a different way.

DISCUSSION
What did the wise men follow to lead them to Jesus? – Years ago, before people had maps and signposts, they used the stars and the position of the sun in the sky to tell them where they were.

Who were the three wise men and where did they come from? – They were believed to be three kings called Melchior, Caspar and Balthazar. They came from countries to the east, although no-one knows exactly where, and are supposed to represent all the peoples of the world.

What gifts did they bring to Jesus?
1. Gold – This was brought by Melchior. Gold is a precious and expensive metal, often worn by kings. This was a sign of Christ's royalty.
2. Frankincense – This was brought by Caspar. Frankincense is a type of incense, which when burned gives off a perfumed, pleasant smelling smoke. This was a sign of Christ's holinesss.
3. Myrrh – This was brought by Balthazar. Myrrh is a perfumed ointment which was used to prepare the dead for their burial. This was a sign of Christ's humanity and his suffering and death.

What warning did the angel give to the wise men?

ACTIVITY
Photocopy this cut-out model preferably onto thin card. The children can then cut out and decorate the three kings and their crowns and gifts. Assemble the kings and mount them on the stand up camels.

CREED

CLOSING PRAYER
Like the three wise men,
we are here today to worship you, Jesus.
We have no gold,
but we give you our love.
We have no frankincense,
we give you our prayers.
We have no myrrh,
so we give you ourselves.

The Baptism of the Lord

INTRODUCTION

Today we hear how Jesus was baptised by John the Baptist in the River Jordan. This was part of God's plan. The story reminds us of our own baptism, when God's spirit became a living spring in each one of us.

SIGN OF THE CROSS

LIGHT THE CANDLES

As we light the candles today, we remember that at our baptism we were given the light of Christ, which burns in our hearts and lights up our lives each day.

SORRY

Lord, as we sing this song together, help us to feel truly sorry if we have not always been good.
Sing Sorry Song 2: *We come to say we are sorry.*

GLORIA

GOSPEL ACCLAMATION

To welcome today's Gospel sing Acclamation 3: *Alleluia, Alleluia.*

GOSPEL (cf Matthew 3:13-17)

Jesus came from Galilee to the banks of the River Jordan to be baptised by John the Baptist. John was surprised by this and said to him, 'Surely this is wrong and it should be you baptising me!' Jesus answered, 'We will do things this way for it is right to follow my Father's plan.' Reluctantly John agreed, and Jesus was baptised in the river. As he stood up in the water, the clouds parted and the Holy Spirit appeared as a dove and settled on Jesus. Then a voice from Heaven said, 'This is my Son, whom I love very much.'

DISCUSSION

Where was Jesus baptised?

What sign appeared so that John and all the people knew that Jesus was the son of God?

Why did the people come to the river Jordan to be baptised? – Being baptised was a sign that they wanted to 'wash away their sins'. To start afresh and make a new beginning before the promised one came.

Why did Jesus come to be baptised when he was God's son and could not have sinned? – Jesus came to be baptised in order to receive the Holy Spirit for his work of teaching and healing, which was about to begin, and so that everyone would know that he was the son of God. By his baptism, Jesus showed the people a way to begin afresh so that they could grow in goodness.

Jesus and many of the people baptised were grown-ups. When are we usually baptised?

Using a doll and suitable props such as a bowl of water, point out the most important features of a baptismal ceremony.

1. Promises are made on behalf of the child by the godparents to obey God's rules and to lead a Christian life.
2. Water is poured over the baby's head three times to represent the rebirth of the child by water and the Holy Spirit, and the washing away of the original sin of Adam and Eve.
3. The baby is anointed with holy oil called Chrism as a sign that God's spirit is making this person special – a member of God's family who shares his everlasting life.
4. The child is clothed in a white garment as a symbol of its purity as a child of God.
5. The godparents or parents, on behalf of the child, are given a lighted candle for they have received the light of Christ and the flame of faith burns in their heart.

Encourage the children to discuss any baptisms they have attended, and to share what they can remember about the occasion.

ACTIVITY

Make a copy of the illustration for each child. Colour the scene of Christ's baptism, and ask each child to colour a picture of their own baptism in the space provided.

CREED

CLOSING PRAYER

Begin by making the sign of the cross. Each time we make the sign of the cross, it is a prayer without words.

Jesus,
accept our sign of the cross
as our prayer to you.
It reminds us that through our baptism
we belong to you,
and are children of God.
Let all who are baptised
walk together in the light of Christ.

First Sunday of Lent
Adam and Eve disobey God

INTRODUCTION
Today is the first Sunday of Lent. The word 'Lent' comes from a very old word which means springtime. It is the time of year when the days are getting longer as summer gets closer. Lent begins on Ash Wednesday and lasts for forty days. Over the next few weeks the readings we will hear encourage us to say 'yes' to God and 'no' to our own selfishness.

SIGN OF THE CROSS

LIGHT THE CANDLES
Say Candle Prayer 1: *Flicker, flicker little candle.*

SORRY
Lent means springtime, a time of year when new life begins and everything starts to grow. We can make a fresh start too, and try extra hard to be good. Together let us sing Sorry Song 1: *Dear Lord Jesus hear our prayers.*

GOSPEL ACCLAMATION
To welcome todays Gospel sing Acclamation 5: *We have come to hear you, Lord.*

GOSPEL (*cf Genesis 2:8-10, 3:1-14, 22-24*)
Adam and Eve lived very happily together in the Garden of Eden. They could eat the fruit from any tree in the garden except the fruit from the tree of good and evil which grew in the middle of the garden.

Now, the Devil hated God, and loved to spoil the good things that he had made. One day he disguised himself as a snake and slithered up to Eve.

'Why don't you taste the fruit on the tree in the middle of the garden?' he hissed.

'We must not because God asked us not to,' answered Eve.

'Do not listen to God,' said the snake, 'Eat it and you will become as wise and powerful as he is!'

So Eve picked a fruit, ate some, and shared it with Adam. Later, when God called to Adam and Eve, they hid from him because they were ashamed and embarrassed.

'Did you disobey me and eat the fruit from the forbidden tree?' God asked them.

'The snake made us do it!' said Eve.

'No. You chose to disobey me,' said God sadly, 'Now you must leave this beautiful garden, for your disobedience has allowed death to come into the world.' So Adam and Eve left the Garden of Eden.

DISCUSSION
Today's story is all about temptation, when you think about or do something that you know is wrong. In the story, who was tempted and what did they do wrong? Like Adam and Eve, we are all tempted sometimes to do something wrong.

God wants us to choose to do what is right, but this is not always easy. During Lent we make promises – we may give up something nice, or promise to do something good. Whatever we do, we try to keep in touch with God, to be less selfish and more generous.

Prompt the children to discuss any Lenten promises they have decided to try to follow.

The emphasis should be on doing things *for* Jesus, rather than simply on giving things up. If they give up biscuits, sweets etc, there should be a positive motive. For children it is often easier to achieve short term goals rather than to try to make one promise for the whole six weeks. They could have a different 'promise' or 'act' for each day or for each week.

ACTIVITY
Either photocopy and colour in the picture, or compile a large picture with the individual characters from the story, with cut-out leaves etc. which can be coloured and pinned onto the completed scene.

CREED

CLOSING PRAYER
Dear Jesus,
there will be times during Lent
when we might find it difficult
to keep our promises.
But if you are there to help us
then we will keep on trying.

Second Sunday of Lent
God's glory on the mountain

INTRODUCTION

When Jesus wanted to pray, he would often find a quiet, peaceful place away from the crowds, where he could be alone with his heavenly Father. One day he took three of his disciples with him. He planned to give them a great surprise by giving them a glimpse of God's glory!

SIGN OF THE CROSS

LIGHT THE CANDLES

As we light our candles today, we think about the brightness of their light which reminds us of God's glory.

SORRY

Ask a child to choose a sorry colour. They can then read the corresponding Sorry Prayer, or the group can say the prayer together.

GOSPEL ACCLAMATION

To welcome today's Gospel sing Acclamation 2: *Light up our hearts*

GOSPEL *(cf Matthew 17:1-10)*

One day Jesus asked Peter, James and John to come and pray with him. He led them to the top of a steep mountain, where it was peaceful and quiet, and they could be alone. Jesus began to pray to his heavenly Father when suddenly he appeared to change! His face and clothes shone with a brilliant light, as dazzling as the rays of the sun. Then the disciples saw Moses and Elijah on either side of Jesus, talking to him. Peter jumped up with excitement and said, 'Lord, this is wonderful! I could make three shelters – one for each of you!' At that moment a cloud streaming with light appeared above them, and a voice said, 'This is my Son, whom I love very much. Listen to what he says.' The disciples were so terrified that they threw themselves to the ground and hid their faces. Then Jesus said gently, 'Get up my friends, do not be afraid.' When they looked up, Jesus was standing alone. As they came down the mountain together, Jesus told them firmly, 'You must not tell anyone about what you have seen today, until the Son of God has risen from the dead.'

DISCUSSION

Jesus led his friends to a mountain top. In the Old Testament, mountains were often the place where God appeared to people.

When Jesus began to pray, what happened, how did he change?

Two people appeared beside Jesus – can you remember their names?

Moses was the man chosen by God to lead his people out of slavery in Egypt, to the Promised Land. He had taken them through the Red Sea and across the desert for forty long years. He collected the Ten Commandments on Mount Sinai. Elijah was a 'prophet', a man who spoke for God. He had warned people not to disobey God and to follow his rules. Like Moses he always trusted God and did whatever he asked.

The disciples were amazed at this sight, but what happened next to make them fall to the ground in fear?

God wanted the three friends to know that Jesus was his son. In days to come, when Jesus would suffer and die, they would remember the glory of God that they had seen on the mountain that day. He was showing himself as they would know him in heaven.

ACTIVITY

Cut out and colour in these figures to create a 'Transfiguration scene'.

CREED

CLOSING PRAYER

Dear God,
Peter, James and John
saw the light of your glory
shining from Jesus
on the mountain that day.
Jesus shares that light
and his love with all of us.
May the light in our hearts
help us to 'change'
so that we will be more like Jesus;
filled with his joy,
happiness and goodness.

Third Sunday of Lent
The woman at the well

INTRODUCTION
Today we will hear about a meeting between Jesus and a Samaritan woman. The Samaritans came from a place called Samaria. The Jews from Galilee and Judaea hated them because the Samaritans had built a temple for God on Mount Gerizim, in their own country, and refused to worship at the temple in Jerusalem.

SIGN OF THE CROSS

LIGHT THE CANDLES
Together sing the Candle Song.

SORRY
Listen to this reading written by a wise man called Micah (cf Micah 6:8-9):
God our Father has told us what we must do: be fair and honest in all that we do and say, be loving and caring towards others. If we do this, then our friendship with God will last forever.

Then encourage the children to close their eyes and make the words of this next prayer their own:
Lord, sometimes we make mistakes,
and forget the things you tell us.
If we have not always been kind towards others,
we are sorry.
If we have not always been honest or fair,
we are sorry.
Send your Spirit to fill us with your love
and to help us to be good.

GOSPEL ACCLAMATION
To welcome today's Gospel sing Acclamation 1:
Share your word with us.

GOSPEL (cf John 4:6-11, 13-19, 28-29, 39-42)
Jesus had been walking all morning and was tired and thirsty. He stopped to rest beside a well called Jacob's Well when a Samaritan woman came to fill her water jug at the well. Jesus asked her, 'Will you give me a drink?' The woman was very surprised because the Jews and Samaritans hated one another and rarely spoke. 'Surely Sir, you are a Jew, why should I share my water with you?' Jesus said, 'If you knew me, it would be you asking me for a drink, for I would give you the water of life.'

The woman was puzzled, 'The well is deep and you have no bucket, so how could you reach this "living water"?' Jesus said, 'When you drink the water from this well, your thirst always returns.

Anyone who drinks the water that I can give will never be thirsty again. This water will become a spring inside them, and fill them with eternal life.'

The woman said to him, 'Sir, share this water with me.' Then Jesus told the woman many things about herself that no other person knew, and she believed that he was truly the Son of God. When she told the people of the town what had happened by the well, they too came to believe that this man was the Son of God.

DISCUSSION
Why was the woman surprised that Jesus had spoken to her? – The woman was a Samaritan and Jesus a Jew, but Jesus had come to share his message with everyone, not just the Jewish people.

When Jesus lived there were no taps or water pipelines, so where did the people get their water from?

Help the children to imagine what a difference it would make to our lives today, if we had to collect water from a well. For example when
  – washing our clothes
  – having a bath
  – filling a swimming pool!
  – watering the garden.

Water is a symbol or sign of life, without it everything would die.

Jesus called the 'water' that he could give, the 'water of life'. What do you think he meant? – The water he was describing was the life which God gives. This life, or grace is poured into our hearts by the Holy Spirit. He fills us with his love and goodness so that we never have to 'thirst' for God. He is the well of God's life in us, from which the living water flows.

ACTIVITY
Photocopy the story of 'The Woman at the Well'. The pages can be coloured and stapled together to make an individual storybook for each child.

CREED

CLOSING PRAYER
We thank you Jesus, for the blessing of water;
for being able to turn on a tap
and know that it will flow;
for the rain and the rivers and the mighty oceans.
We thank you for the 'water of life',
poured out and shared with us at our baptism,
and throughout our lives,
so that we can have everlasting life.

The Woman at The Well

Jesus was tired and thirsty so he stopped at the well.

He asked a Samaritan woman for a drink.

Jesus said "I can give you living water."

"Will you share this living water with me?" she asked.

The woman and her friends believed that Jesus was the Son of God.

Fourth Sunday of Lent

Help us to see!

INTRODUCTION

Can you imagine what it would be like to be blind? Close your eyes tightly or cover them with your hands. Think about the things you have already done this morning – getting out of bed, having breakfast, brushing your teeth, putting on your clothes and shoes. Would you have found them harder to do if you were blind and could not see? In today's Gospel, we hear how Jesus helps a blind man to see with his eyes and his heart!

SIGN OF THE CROSS

LIGHT THE CANDLES

We say together: Fill our hearts with the light of Jesus.

SORRY

If we do something wrong, our hearts are filled with darkness. As we sing 'sorry' together, God's Spirit will fill our hearts with his light and chase the darkness away. Together sing Sorry song 2: *We come to say we are sorry.*

GOSPEL ACCLAMATION

To welcome today's Gospel we sing Acclamation 2: *Light up our hearts.*

GOSPEL (cf John 9:1, 5, 6-11, 32-33, 35-38)

One day Jesus saw a blind man begging by the roadside. The man had never been able to see. Jesus turned to his disciples and said, 'I am the light of the world.' Then he bent down and made a paste with some spittle and a little mud. He put this on the man's eyes and said to him, 'Go to the Pool of Siloam, and wash your eyes.' The man did this, and to his amazement, found that he could see! The people of the town could not believe it. 'Is this really the blind beggar?' they asked. 'It is me!' he answered, and he explained what Jesus had done. 'But who is this man?' the crowd asked. 'I do not know where he came from, or who he is, but I know that he made me see. Unless this man was sent by God he could not have done such a marvellous thing.' The crowd grew angry with the man and chased him away. Later, Jesus found him sitting alone. 'Do you believe in the Son of God?' he asked. 'Yes sir, I believe in him, but I do not know him', he answered. Jesus said, 'You can see him for he is speaking to you.' At once, the man fell to his knees and said, 'Lord, I believe in you!'

DISCUSSION

What did Jesus do to make the blind man see?

How do you imagine he felt when he opened his eyes after washing them?

Who did he think the man was? – The blind man knew that a man called Jesus had cured him. He realised that no ordinary man had done this wonderful thing. Jesus told his disciples that he was the 'light of the world'. He touched this man's eyes and his heart with the light of his love, so that he could 'see' that Jesus was the Son of God.

How can we make sure that we are filled with God's 'light' so that we do not become 'blind' to God's goodness?

One way is to pray every day. When we pray to God we are talking to him and so we 'get to know' him better, and it is easier for him to help us to 'see' the way we should live our lives.

ACTIVITY

Get the children to imagine all the 'new' things that the blind man saw for the very first time when he opened his eyes after washing them. Then either get them to draw the things they have imagined, or colour the examples given here, and mount them around a smiling picture of the man who had been blind.

CREED

CLOSING PRAYER

Dear Jesus,
I give you my eyes
to see others the way you do,
I give you my heart
to fill with the light of your love,
Let your goodness shine out from me
so others may 'see'
that you are the 'light of the world'.

Fifth Sunday of Lent
Lazarus comes back to life

INTRODUCTION

God is the giver of life, and for him, nothing is impossible. In today's Gospel we hear how a good friend of Jesus falls ill and dies. But death is not the end of life, and Jesus uses this event to show people that he is truly the Son of God.

SIGN OF THE CROSS

LIGHT THE CANDLES

As we light the candles we listen to the words of the prophet Isaiah. *(cf Isaiah 9:2-3, 6-7)*

The world was full of darkness and shadows, but now it is filled with light so everyone can see. God sent us his only Son, Jesus, to fill our world with peace and love.

SORRY

God is our loving Father and will always forgive us if we are truly sorry. Remember the story Jesus told about a loving father . . .

There was once a loving father whose son left home and lived a wicked and selfish life. This made his father very sad. One day the son came back and was truly sorry for all his mistakes. His father hugged him and forgave him for everything.

God is our loving Father and he will always forgive us if we are truly sorry.

GOSPEL ACCLAMATION

To welcome today's Gospel sing Acclamation 4: *Praise the Lord.*

GOSPEL *(cf John 11:1, 3-5, 17-29, 33-34, 39-44.)*

Lazarus and his two sisters Martha and Mary, were very good friends of Jesus. They lived in a town called Bethany, not far from Jerusalem, and Jesus often went to visit them. One day, the sisters sent an urgent message to Jesus, because Lazarus was very ill and close to death. Two days later Jesus and his disciples set off for Bethany, but when they arrived they found that Lazarus was dead, and had already been buried for four days. Martha ran to meet Jesus and said to him, 'Lord, if you had been here, you could have saved our brother.' Jesus said, 'Your brother will live again.' 'I know that on the last day he will come back to life,' she answered. Jesus turned to her and said, 'Anyone who believes in me will have eternal life, and he will never die. Do you believe this?' Martha answered him, 'Yes, Lord, because I know that you are the Son of God.'

When Jesus saw the great sadness of Martha and Mary and their friends, he was filled with love. 'Show me where he is buried,' he said. So they took him to the tomb, where Jesus said to them, 'Roll away the stone, and you will see God's glory.' They did as he said, and Jesus looked up to Heaven and prayed. 'Father, I thank you, for I know that you always listen to me. Let these people see and believe.' Then he called out in a loud voice, 'Lazarus, get up and come out!' To everyone's amazement Lazarus appeared, still wrapped in burial cloths, and walked from the tomb. Many people saw what happened that day, and they believed in Jesus.

DISCUSSION

How do you think Martha and Mary felt when their brother Lazarus died?

Have you known anyone that has died, and did you feel sad?

Martha believed in Jesus with all her heart. She knew that through the power of God he could do anything, even have power over death.

Where was Lazarus buried?

What did Jesus do before he told Lazarus to 'come out' of the tomb?

Do you think the people were frightened by what they saw?

If you had been standing in the crowd watching all this happen, do you think you would believe in Jesus more after you had seen Lazarus come back to life?

When did Jesus prove his power over death again?

The spirit of God raised Lazarus from the dead. He lives within each one of us, and through his power, we are raised up after death to join God in everlasting glory.

ACTIVITY

Using a pinboard fix the main Gospel characters in place to depict the scene at the tomb. Strips of tissue paper stuck onto 'Lazarus' can be used to represent the burial cloths.

CREED

CLOSING PRAYER

Lord,
help us to be like Martha,
to see clearly that you are the Son of God
and the life of the world.
Make our belief,
and your life in us,
grow a little stronger each day of our lives.

Palm (Passion) Sunday

(Two alternative liturgies are given, one for Palm Sunday and a longer version which includes the story of Christ's Passion. The reading of the Passion for the adult congregation takes some considerable time, therefore you must check in advance with your priest and then choose the version appropriate for your age group and the time available to you.)

INTRODUCTION
The Jews were waiting for a king to lead them against the Romans and make them free again. When Jesus rode into Jerusalem on Palm Sunday, he was welcomed as this king, but he came as a king of peace and not to bring war.

SIGN OF THE CROSS

LIGHT THE CANDLES
The words of the prophet Isaiah remind us that Jesus, the Prince of Peace, shared the light of his love with us all. *(cf Isaiah 9:2-3, 6-7)*
The world was full of darkness and shadows, but now it is filled with light so everyone can see. God sent his only son, Jesus, to fill our world with peace and love.

SORRY
In this reading from St. Luke, Jesus reminds us that God will forgive us as easily as we forgive others. *(cf Luke 6:37-38)*
Do not always believe that you are right and others are wrong, but treat people the way you would want to be treated. If you are full of forgiveness for others, then God will be full of forgiveness for you.

GOSPEL ACCLAMATION
To welcome today's Gospel sing Acclamation 1: *Share your word with us.*

GOSPEL *(cf Matthew 21:1-11)*
Jesus and his disciples arrived at the Mount of Olives just outside Jerusalem. He sent two of the disciples to the next village to collect a donkey and her foal. 'If anyone stops you, tell them that they are for me,' he said. They brought the animals to Jesus, and put cloaks on their backs so that Jesus could ride on them. When the people heard that Jesus was coming they laid their cloaks on the road before him, and pulled branches off the palm trees to wave in the air. The crowds grew more and more excited and shouted at the top of their voices, 'Hosanna, Hosanna! Blessed is the one sent by the Lord.' Excitement filled the whole city, and some people asked, 'Who is this man?' The people answered them, 'It is Jesus from Nazareth in Galilee.'

DISCUSSION
What did Jesus ask his friends to fetch from the village?

Would you expect a king to ride on a little donkey or a grand horse?

Why did Jesus choose a donkey? – By his actions Jesus was showing the crowds that he was no soldier, but instead he came as a king of peace, riding on a meek and gentle donkey.

What did the crowds wave in their hands and what words did they use to cheer as he passed? – They waved branches from the palm trees they found along the roadside to welcome this king, just was we might wave flags in a procession today. They shouted 'Hosanna, Hosanna!' – which is a word used to praise God.

Do you know why Jerusalem was so crowded at this time? – Many people had come to celebrate the Passover. This was a feast the Jews shared together each year to remember how God had saved them from slavery in Egypt.

ACTIVITY
Because of the length of the adults' Liturgy of the Word today, there is often sufficient time to complete several activities. The suggestions made should be adapted to suit the age group and numbers of children in your particular group.

1. If you are able, enlarge the figure of Jesus on a donkey and photocopy onto thin card. The children can then make the decoration of the figure and donkey colourful and imaginative! Then fix another piece of card to make the figures free-standing. Other children can be involved in making newspaper 'palms' to lay before the finished figure.

2. Make a large frieze of Jesus' entry into Jerusalem. Make the picture detailed and interesting and using it, allow the children to retell the story in their own words.

CREED

CLOSING PRAYER
Lord Jesus,
Prince of Peace and King of the World,
we pray that
and that your peace will spread
throughout our world today
and touch the lives of everyone.

1.

2.

3.

4.

5.

6.

The Passion of Christ
(Alternative version)

INTRODUCTION
On Palm Sunday Jesus rode into Jerusalem and was welcomed as a king by the crowds. Yet only days later, their cries of 'Hosanna!' would change to 'Crucify him!', and Jesus would be put to death. Using today's readings we will follow his journey to the cross, so that we will be ready to share in the glory of his resurrection on Easter Sunday.

SIGN OF THE CROSS

LIGHT THE CANDLES
Light the candles and read Candle Prayer 1: *Flicker, flicker little candle.*

SORRY
Encourage the children to close their eyes and to listen carefully to the words of this prayer:
Father, we must be ready to forgive others,
just as you forgave us.
Even as Jesus was hanging on the cross,
he forgave the soldiers that crucified him.
Help us to forgive anyone who has hurt us,
and never to harm anyone by our words or actions.

GOSPEL ACCLAMATION
To welcome today's Gospel sing Acclamation 1: *Share your word with us*

THE PASSION
The activity and the readings are closely interlinked for the telling of the Passion. Using a large copy of a map of Jerusalem and surroundings briefly outline the events of Holy Week, encouraging the children to give as many details as they can. Place numbers on the map to correspond to a reading and to the illustrated scenes. As a suggestion, complete the first three readings and then distribute the pictures for colouring. When complete, assemble the pictures in order and read the final three readings. With the pictures and the map displayed, encourage the children to recount the events leading up to Easter Sunday themselves.

1. The Passover. *(cf 26:19-30)*
The disciples went to a house in Jerusalem and prepared a room to celebrate the Passover meal. As Jesus shared the meal with his twelve closest friends he said to them, 'One of you will make me very sad tonight.' The disciples were dismayed at his words, 'Surely you are mistaken Lord,' but he answered: 'No. One of you sharing this very meal will hand me over to my enemies.'

As they were eating, Jesus took some bread and said a prayer of blessing. He broke the bread into pieces and shared it with them saying, 'Take this and eat it, this is my body.' Then he took a cup of wine and said a prayer of thanks. He passed the cup to each of them and said, 'Take this and drink it, for this is my blood. Just as my Father promised, it will be poured out to save you from your sins.'

Then they sang some hymns together before setting off for the Mount of Olives.

DISCUSSION
What was the Passover meal?
   It was a meal celebrated every year by the Jews to remind them of how God had saved his people from slavery in Egypt.
   What was the name of the disciple who would let Jesus down?
   What did Jesus share with his friends at this last supper together?
   What was so special about this bread and wine?
   When and where do we share a meal and use the same words that Jesus used?

2. The Agony in the Garden. *(cf Matthew 26:36-50)*
After the Last Supper Jesus took Peter, James and John and went to a garden called Gethsemane. It was quiet and peaceful there and Jesus wanted to pray, for he was filled with great sadness and fear. He said to his disciples: 'Stay awake because I need you with me tonight.' Then he began to pray, 'Father, I am afraid of what lies ahead but I will always do whatever you ask.'

When he returned to the three disciples he found them asleep. 'Wake up!' he said. 'Could you not stay awake with me for such a short time.' Then Jesus went away and prayed as before but returned to find them all asleep again. 'Get up, the time has come.' Judas, one of the twelve disciples, appeared with a crowd of people and walked up to Jesus and kissed him. Then they arrested him and led him away.

DISCUSSION
Where did Jesus go to pray?
Which disciple did he take with him?
Why was Jesus so sad and afraid?
How did Judas betray Jesus?

3. Jesus is condemned to death *(cf Matthew 26:57, 65; 27:1-2, 23-24, 27-29)*
Jesus was taken before Caiaphas the High Priest and the elders. They decided that Jesus should be put to death, and they sent him to the Roman Governor, Pontius Pilate, to be sentenced. Pilate was frightened that the crowds would cause trouble, so he agreed to crucify Jesus even though he knew that he had done nothing wrong. The Roman soldiers made fun of Jesus and made a crown of thorns for the 'King of the Jews'.

DISCUSSION
Why did Caiaphas and the other Jews hate Jesus?

He did not fit in with their ideas because he followed his father's plan. He stood up for truth and what was right and would often disobey or ignore the Jewish priests. They were jealous of his popularity and wanted the people to do what they said, instead of following Jesus.

Pontius Pilate knew that Jesus had done nothing wrong so why did he agree to condemn him to death?

He was afraid that the crowds would riot and cause a great deal of trouble so he gave in to the demands of the Jewish elders.

The soldiers teased Jesus about being 'King of the Jews'. What did they make to put on his head?

4. Jesus carries the Cross. *(cf Matthew 27:31-32)*
The soldiers beat Jesus and then made him carry his own cross. After stumbling and falling several times, the soldiers told a man called Simon to help Jesus.

DISCUSSION
Why did the soldiers make a man in the crowd help Jesus to carry his cross?
What was his name?

5. Jesus is crucified. *(cf Matthew 27:33, 35-38)*
When they got to Golgotha, a name which means 'The Place of the Skull', they put Jesus on the cross. Above him they wrote, 'This is Jesus, King of the Jews'. They crucified a thief on either side of Jesus. One of them said to him, 'Jesus, remember me in your kingdom,' and Jesus answered, 'Today you will be with me in Heaven'. After hanging on the cross for many hours, Jesus called out loudly, 'Father do not forget me,' and then he died.

DISCUSSION
Where was Jesus crucified?

Who else was crucified that day and what had they done wrong?

In Roman times, people were often crucified if they had broken the law.

6. Jesus is placed in the tomb. *(cf Matthew 27:57-60)*
Later on that day, a man called Joseph, who had been a follower of Jesus, went to Pontius Pilate and asked if he could bury Jesus. Pontius Pilate agreed and so Jesus was taken away and laid in the tomb.

DISCUSSION
What was the name of the man who asked to take Jesus' body away for burial?

Where did they put Jesus?

They laid Jesus in the tomb and rolled a large stone across the entrance. This was late on Friday evening and Saturday was the Jewish Sabbath when no-one was allowed to do any work. When a person died the Jews used spices and ointments such as myrrh to prepare the body for burial. They could not do this on the Sabbath, so at first light on the Sunday morning the women would return to the tomb to prepare the Lord's body.

CREED

CLOSING PRAYER
Lord Jesus,
this week as we remember
your suffering and death,
help us to remember those in our world
who are suffering and dying every day.
Your death on the cross has allowed each one of us
to share in the glory of your resurrection
and life everlasting.

Easter Sunday
Jesus is alive. Alleluia! Alleluia!

INTRODUCTION
On Easter Sunday we celebrate the fact that Jesus has risen from the dead and is alive! As you walk into the church you realise that something wonderful has happened. A large bright candle shines out for all to see and the church is decorated with beautiful flowers, a sign of new life. Today we will sing joyfully 'Alleluia, alleluia' as we thank God for Easter morning.

SIGN OF THE CROSS

LIGHT THE CANDLES
Light the candles and then read the following prayer:
Lord, as we light our candles,
we pray that the light of that first Easter morning
will shine on us here today,
and on all people throughout the world
as they celebrate with us.
Alleluia.

SORRY
Jesus died on the cross to save us from our foolish ways so that we could share his everlasting life. If we have done anything to spoil our friendship with God, help us to be truly sorry and to make a fresh start.

Sing Sorry Song 1: *Dear Lord Jesus hear our prayers.*

GLORIA

GOSPEL ACCLAMATION
To welcome today's Gospel sing Acclamation 3: *Alleluia, Alleluia.*

GOSPEL (*cf John 20: 1-9*)
Before sunrise on the Sunday morning, Mary of Magdala went to the tomb. As she got to the entrance, she saw that the stone had been rolled away and that the tomb was empty. She ran to the disciples saying, 'They have taken the Lord from the tomb and we don't know where they have put him!' Peter and another disciple, John, ran to the tomb and found it just as Mary had described, with the linen burial cloths lying on the ground. Peter went into the tomb first, followed by John. Until this moment they had not understood the Scriptures which had said, 'He must rise from the dead.' But now they saw, and they believed.

DISCUSSION
Why did Mary return to the tomb on Sunday morning? – Jesus had died late on Friday afternoon and the women had begun to embalm his body with spices and ointments in preparation for burial, as was their custom. The Jewish Sabbath began at sunset on the Friday evening and work was not allowed on the Sabbath, so they had to wait until the Sunday to complete their task.

What did Mary find when she arrived at the tomb?

Whom did she tell?

As the disciples ran to the tomb, can you imagine what they must have been thinking?
  – had someone taken the Lord's body away?
  – where had they put him?
  – could the unimaginable really have happened?

Peter and John had raced to the tomb and found it empty. They could hardly believe that Jesus might be alive, but at that moment they began to hope that something as wonderful as this really could happen.

On Easter day, and throughout the season of Easter a special candle called the Paschal candle is lit. What does it remind us of? – It reminds us that Jesus, the 'light of the world', has destroyed death and is alive. It is a symbol of new life.

What do we give to each other on Easter Sunday as symbols of new life? – Easter eggs! Just as the chick in an egg must break free from its shell to begin a new life, so too, Jesus had to break free from death in the tomb. He had the new life which God has promised to us all!

ACTIVITY
Help the children to make several Easter banners to decorate the church, or alternatively help them to make this Easter greeting card.

CREED

CLOSING PRAYER
Jesus,
we thank you for the joy of the resurrection,
when you rose from the dead
and were filled with new life.
Help us to remember that you suffered
and died on the cross for us
so that one day we too will share with you
the joy of everlasting life.

Second Sunday of Easter
Doubting Thomas

INTRODUCTION
When Jesus appeared to his disciples for the first time after his death, one disciple was not with them. He became known as 'Doubting Thomas' because he did not believe that Jesus had risen from the dead. He told the other disciples that his disbelief would only end if he could see Jesus with his own eyes.

SIGN OF THE CROSS

LIGHT THE CANDLES
On Easter Day and on every Sunday during the season of Easter, the Paschal candle is lit to remind us that Jesus, 'the light of the world' is alive and will be with us forever. Help us to remember this as we light our candles today.

SORRY
Encourage the children to listen carefully to the words of today's prayer. Choose a 'sorry colour' Prayer.

GLORIA

GOSPEL ACCLAMATION
To welcome today's Gospel sing Acclamation 4: *Praise the Lord.*

Sometimes it is very hard to believe what someone else tells us. Try this light-hearted way of helping the children to understand how Thomas might have felt. Send several children out of the room for a few moments and bring out an unexpected object or objects, for example, a toy lion. Let the children have a good look so that they can describe it to the absent group. When the others return you can tell them that you have all seen a lion and then watch their reaction!

GOSPEL (cf John 20:19-20, 24-29)
Late in the evening the disciples sat huddled together feeling sad and afraid. The doors of the room were locked, to stop the Jews finding them. Suddenly Jesus appeared in the room with them and said, 'Peace be with you'. They were amazed when they saw him and could hardly believe their eyes. But Jesus showed them the wounds in his hands and where his side had been pierced by the sword. They were filled with joy and wonder.

The disciple called Thomas was not with the others when Jesus appeared to them. When they told him that they had seen Jesus, he scoffed at them and said, 'Unless I see for myself the wounds in his hands and his side, then I will not believe you.'

Several days later when Thomas was with the other disciples, Jesus appeared to them again. He turned to Thomas and said, 'See the wounds in my hands and feel the wound in my side and doubt no more.' Thomas fell to the ground and said, 'My Lord and my God.' Jesus said to him, 'Because you have seen you now believe, but blessed are those who have not seen and yet believe.'

DISCUSSION
Why do you think the disciples were feeling sad and afraid?

When Jesus appeared what did he say to them? Why do you think he said this?

Imagine what a shock the disciples must have had when they suddenly saw Jesus appear in the room with them. They probably thought that they were seeing a ghost. Jesus said these words to calm and reassure them.

Thomas did not believe the others when they told him that Jesus had risen from the dead. What proof did he want?

What did Thomas say when Jesus appeared before him?

We believe in what Jesus did and said even though we have not seen these things for ourselves. We also believe that at the Mass the bread and wine are changed into the body and blood of Christ just as happened at the Last Supper.

ACTIVITY
Make a banner as shown opposite with a picture of Jesus and the words WE BELIEVE JESUS IS ALIVE.

CREED

CLOSING PRAYER
Lord Jesus,
help us to remember the words of Thomas,
'My Lord and my God',
and to make them our own prayer.
Help us to 'see' you in
the actions and words of the people we meet
so that day by day
our belief in you will grow stronger.

Third Sunday of Easter
The road to Emmaus

INTRODUCTION
After the death of Jesus, his disciples were filled with despair and disbelief. Only days before, Jesus had been greeted by the crowds as he entered Jerusalem, and now he lay dead in a tomb. Sometimes when you feel sad or upset about something, it stops you from seeing things clearly. This is how it was for two disciples as they made their way to Emmaus early one morning.

SIGN OF THE CROSS

LIGHT THE CANDLES
Light the candles and then read:
Jesus said, 'Let your goodness shine out like a light in the darkness, so that through you, the love of our heavenly Father will touch the lives of others.' (cf Matthew 5:16-17)

SORRY
Ask one of the children to choose a sorry colour and read the corresponding prayer aloud together.

GLORIA

GOSPEL ACCLAMATION
To welcome today's Gospel read the following acclamation, with the children joining in with the alleluias.

As we listen to your word, help us to shut out other thoughts and think only of you. Then as we receive the word of God may our hearts be filled with your love. Alleluia, alleluia!

GOSPEL (cf Luke 24:13-35)
Early one morning two disciples of Jesus were walking sadly towards a village called Emmaus. They felt totally miserable as they talked about the events of the past days, and the death of Jesus. As they walked, Jesus himself joined them, but they did not recognise him. Jesus asked them, 'What are you talking about together?' One of them answered, 'Surely you must have heard about what happened to Jesus of Nazareth! He was handed over to the chief priests and the Roman Governor who had him crucified. We believed that he was the Saviour sent by God. We have heard that his body is missing from the tomb where they laid him, but we do not know what has happened.'

Jesus said to them, 'Do you not believe what the prophets have foretold?' and he began to explain to them the prophecies about himself in the Old Testament. When they arrived at Emmaus, the disciples asked Jesus to stay and share a meal with them. When they were at supper Jesus took some bread, blessed it, broke it and gave it to them. At that moment they saw clearly that the stranger was in fact Jesus, but he had already disappeared from their sight. 'Of course it was the Lord,' they said, 'Remember how our hearts seemed to burn as he shared the scriptures with us. How could we have been so blind!' At once, they returned to Jerusalem to tell the other disciples that Jesus had risen from the dead, and that they had known him in the breaking of the bread.

DISCUSSION
Have you ever felt really disappointed when something has gone wrong?
- you have planned a picnic but at the last moment it rains.
- a friend is coming to play but has to cancel because they are ill.
- your football team almost makes it to the top of the league and then loses all its important matches.

You can imagine then how the disciples of Jesus felt! They were terribly disappointed and depressed about his death. Everything had gone so wrong during the past few days. How could this have happened when they had seen Jesus working so many miracles?

At first, did they believe that Jesus had risen from the dead? – They knew that his body was missing from the tomb, and they did not understand the things that Jesus had said about 'rising from the dead'. They were quite sure that people did not come back to life.

What made them realise who he was? – He blessed the bread and broke it. It was his special way of sharing himself with his friends. Through sharing God's word and the breaking of bread, their eyes were 'opened' and they could 'see' clearly.

How can we know Jesus too? – Through the breaking and sharing of the Eucharist at Mass. At that moment we too recognise that Jesus is present with us.

ACTIVITY
Either give each child a copy of the illustration to colour, or make a larger picture, and after colouring add cut-out loaves etc. to the scene.

CREED

CLOSING PRAYER
Lord Jesus,
each time we come together
to share in the breaking of bread,
help us to recognise you
and to feel our hearts burn with your love.

Fourth Sunday of Easter
The Good Shepherd

INTRODUCTION
A shepherd's lonely job was to find food for his sheep and to protect them from wild animals. In summer there was very little grass to eat, and often he had to travel long distances with his flock, searching for pasture. At night he would gather his sheep into a fold, and then lie across the entrance to make a 'gate'. Today we hear how Jesus calls himself 'the Good Shepherd'.

SIGN OF THE CROSS

LIGHT THE CANDLES
Light the candles and then sing the Candle Song together.

SORRY
Close your eyes and think about all the things which have happened over the past week. Have we always been as kind and thoughtful as we should have been? Have we done anything to make God feel sad or disappointed with us? If we are truly sorry in our hearts then God our Father will always forgive us. Listen carefully to the words of this reading. (cf Psalm 25:11-16)

God is full of kindness and love, and wants to show us all the path we must follow. He leads us with patience and understanding, and forgives us when we stray and lose our way. When we look to him for help, he rescues us from harm and helps us to try again, for he is full of love and forgiveness.

GLORIA

GOSPEL ACCLAMATION
To welcome today's Gospel sing Acclamation 5: *We have come to hear you, Lord.*

GOSPEL (cf John 10:2-5, 9-11)
One day, Jesus said to the crowds, 'A shepherd knows his sheep, and his sheep know him. When he calls their names, they know his voice and they follow him, one by one, through the gate of the sheepfold. The shepherd walks ahead of them showing them the way. He guides and protects them from danger and harm. The flock will not follow a stranger, instead they scatter and run away because they do not know his voice.'

Then Jesus said, 'I am the Good Shepherd, I know my own and my own know me. If anyone follows me I will lead them safely on their journey to the fullness of everlasting life.'

DISCUSSION
How did the sheep recognise their shepherd? – They knew the sound of his voice, and he was able to call each one of them by their name.

If you were a shepherd in charge of a flock what would you have to do to take care of it?
- make sure that the sheep have plenty to eat.
- make sure that none of them wander or get lost.
- protect them from thieves and wild animals.
- find them shelter from snow and bad weather.

In this country where do farmers keep their sheep? – In fields surrounded by hedges or fences to stop them from straying.

In the land where Jesus lived, do the shepherds have green fields with fences as we do in this country? – Because of the hot dry climate there is very little grass and the shepherd must lead his sheep from place to place to find enough food to eat. Often it is steep and hilly and the sheep must carefully follow their shepherd along the path that he shows them. They rely on him to find food and water for them, and to protect them from wild animals. (Show any pictures you can find of such terrain.)

Why did Jesus call himself the Good Shepherd?

Like the shepherd, Jesus will stay with us always. He knows all of us by name and calls us to follow him. He will lead us along the right path to heaven and will protect us from harm along the way. With him before us we can feel safe and secure because we can trust him to take care of all our needs.

ACTIVITY
Make a large picture of Jesus, the Good Shepherd, leading his flock along a path. Each child can write their name on a cut-out sheep, stick on a cotton wool fleece and add their sheep to the scene. Alternatively use this colouring picture with the children sticking cotton wool onto the sheep.

CREED

CLOSING PRAYER (cf Psalm 23:1-4, 6)
The Lord is my shepherd,
he gives me everything I need.
He leads me to lie down in green meadows
and to drink beside cool, deep pools.
He is my strength and protection
and guides me along the right path.
Even in times of darkness and trouble
I will not be afraid,
for he is always beside me
and will protect me from harm.
I know that his goodness and love
will stay with me all the days of my life.

Fifth Sunday of Easter
I am the Way

INTRODUCTION
Few of us would set off on a journey to a place we had not been to before, without a map or some guide to take with us. Nobody would set off with no idea of how to get there, for then we would certainly get lost! Today Jesus tells his disciples that they already know the way to the place he is going, even though they have never been there before. We will see how confused they became, and how Jesus explained all that they needed to know!

SIGN OF THE CROSS

LIGHT THE CANDLES
Light the candles and say Candle Prayer 3: *The light of God.*

SORRY
While he was in prison, Saint Paul wrote a letter to the people of Colossae, to remind them how they should live if they want to follow in the footsteps of Jesus. *(cf St Pauls Letter to the Colossians 3:12-14, 23):*
You are God's chosen people. Always be ready to care for others, and to be kind and gentle. Be patient and calm and never boast about or be proud of your goodness. Just as God always forgives you, so you must always be forgiving towards others. Fill your hearts with love, and whatever you do, do it for God.

As the children close their eyes, read this prayer slowly:
Father, forgive us
if we have hurt anyone by our thoughts or actions, and help us to forgive those who have hurt us.
We ask this through Jesus our Lord.

GLORIA

GOSPEL ACCLAMATION
To welcome today's Gospel sing Acclamation 2: *Light up our hearts.*

GOSPEL *(cf John 14:1-6)*
Jesus said to his disciples, 'Do not be afraid or worried, trust in me as you trust in God. In my Father's house there are many rooms, and I am going there to prepare a place for you. Then I shall come back to take you with me, and we will be together again. You already know the way to the place I am going.' Thomas felt unsure and asked Jesus, 'Lord how can we know the way, if we do not know where you are going?' Jesus answered 'I am the way, the truth and the life. Through me you will know how to find my Father's house'

DISCUSSION
Why did the disciples feel anxious and afraid? – Because Jesus had told them that soon he would be leaving them.

When Jesus talked about going to his Father's house, where do you think he meant? – He was talking about Heaven.

Which disciple felt uncertain about what Jesus had told them?

Jesus said that he is 'the way'. Do you know what he meant? – The word 'way' can have several different meanings. Ask one of the children to demonstrate 'the way' to brush their hair or wash their hands, – they show us *how to do* something. Then ask another child to explain 'the way' to their house, – they tell us *how to find* somewhere. Jesus is 'the way' because he shows us what we must *do* so that we can *find* Heaven.

When we are born we begin our journey through life, following Jesus who shows us the way towards heaven. Our signposts which guide us as we travel are God's commandments and all the things Jesus taught us. If we follow these signposts and *do* what pleases God then we will *find* the right path which leads us to everlasting happiness.

ACTIVITY
Depending on the age range of the group, either get the children to draw around their feet and then cut out the 'footprints', or give out small foot cut-outs to be coloured. These can be used to follow the 'way to Heaven,' with signposts which help to show the way. Alternatively the children can draw or print onto the photocopied picture.

CREED

CLOSING PRAYER
Before Jesus was born, the people of God used to sing and say prayers and poems called psalms. In this psalm they ask God to 'show them the way'. *(cf Psalm 25:4-5,8-9)*

Teach me your ways Lord,
make them known to me.
Teach me to walk in your truth,
for you are my Saviour
and I can always place my trust in you.
The Lord is just and good.
He shows the humble the way
and teaches them his will.
With loyalty and love
he leads all those who obey his commandments.

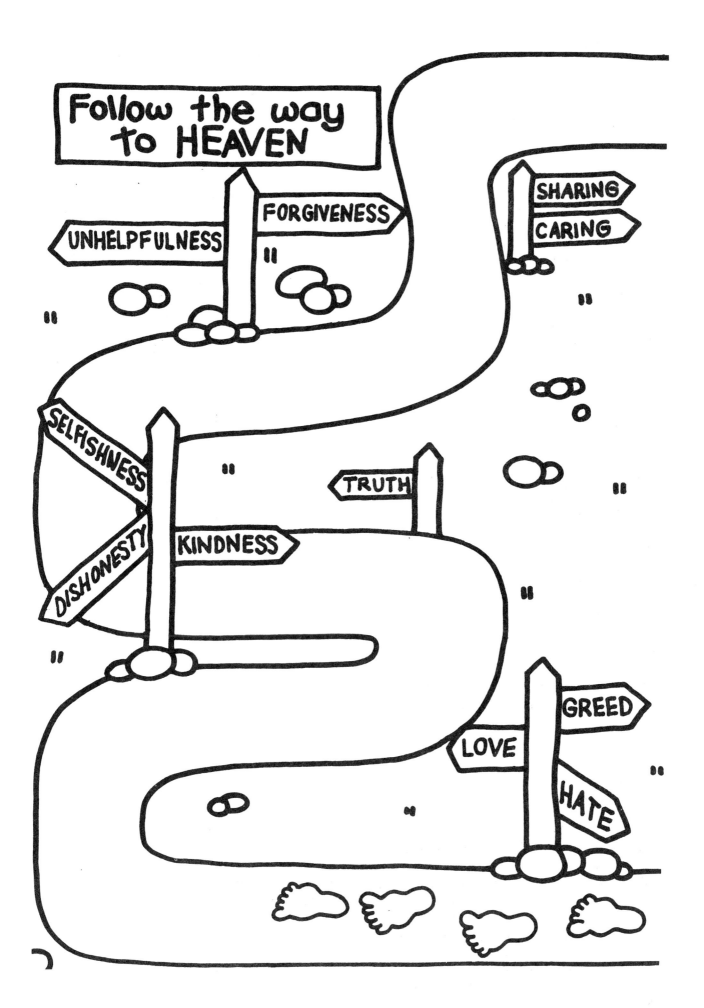

Sixth Sunday of Easter

I will not leave you on your own

INTRODUCTION

As Jesus shared the Last Supper with his apostles, he told them that soon he would be leaving them. They were frightened and upset by his words, but he promised to send someone to help them. He would not leave them on their own.

SIGN OF THE CROSS

LIGHT THE CANDLES

As the candles are lit, the children listen to this reading by the prophet Isaiah (cf Isaiah 60:1-3):
The glory of God is shining on you! All other people will live in the shadows, but you will always have God's light to chase away the darkness. Other people will look at you and see the light of God's love shining out.

SORRY

As we sing the words of the song, help us to be truly sorry if we have done wrong. Sing Sorry Song 1: *Dear Lord Jesus hear our prayers.*

GLORIA

GOSPEL ACCLAMATION

To welcome today's Gospel sing Acclamation 4: *Praise the Lord.*

GOSPEL (cf John 14:16-20)

One day, Jesus said to his disciples, 'I will not leave you on your own, I will ask my Father to send you a helper who will stay with you always. The Spirit of God will be with you and in you, though others will not be able to see him or know that he is there. He will fill you with wisdom and understanding. Soon the world will not see me again, but you will know that I am truly alive.'

DISCUSSION

Jesus was going to leave his disciples and return to his heavenly Father.

Whom did he promise to send? – A special helper – the Holy Spirit.

What would this helper look like? – Jesus told them: 'Others will not be able to see him or know that he is there.' The Holy Spirit is one of the great mysteries of God. He is invisible, and one way of describing him is as being like a wind. St John said this about the Holy Spirit: 'The wind blows wherever it pleases; you hear the sound it makes, but you cannot tell where it comes from or where it is going. So it is with the Spirit of God.' (cf John 3:8)

Why did Jesus send the Holy Spirit? – Through the Holy Spirit, Jesus remained with the apostles, and he remains with us in the same way today. God sent his Spirit to the apostles to begin the teaching of the Gospel throughout the world. The apostles knew that all the power and strength of their work lay in Jesus. They were useless without him and could not carry on with his work. Through the Holy Spirit he remained with them and his work could continue.

When do we receive the Holy Spirit in a special way? – At our baptism and confirmation. The spirit is God's gift to us, when he pours his love into our hearts.

The word 'Spiritus' means breath or wind and that is how we often describe God's Spirit.

If someone asked you to describe the wind, what would you tell them?
- it cannot be seen, but we can see what it does, by making things move, trees bending and leaves blowing around.
- we can feel it as it blows against our skin.
- it can be very gentle or very powerful.

We cannot see the Spirit himself but we can see what he does through the lives of people around us who allow him to guide their words and actions.

If you blew all of the air out of your body and did not breathe any more in, what would happen?

Without breathing you cannot live. The Spirit is the breath of God, who fills us with life and makes us strong.

ACTIVITY

Help each child to make a windmill to remind them that wind is one of the forms which the Spirit can take.

CREED

CLOSING PRAYER

Come Holy Spirit,
and breathe your life into us,
so that we can bring Christ into the world
and touch the lives of others with his love.

WINDMILL.

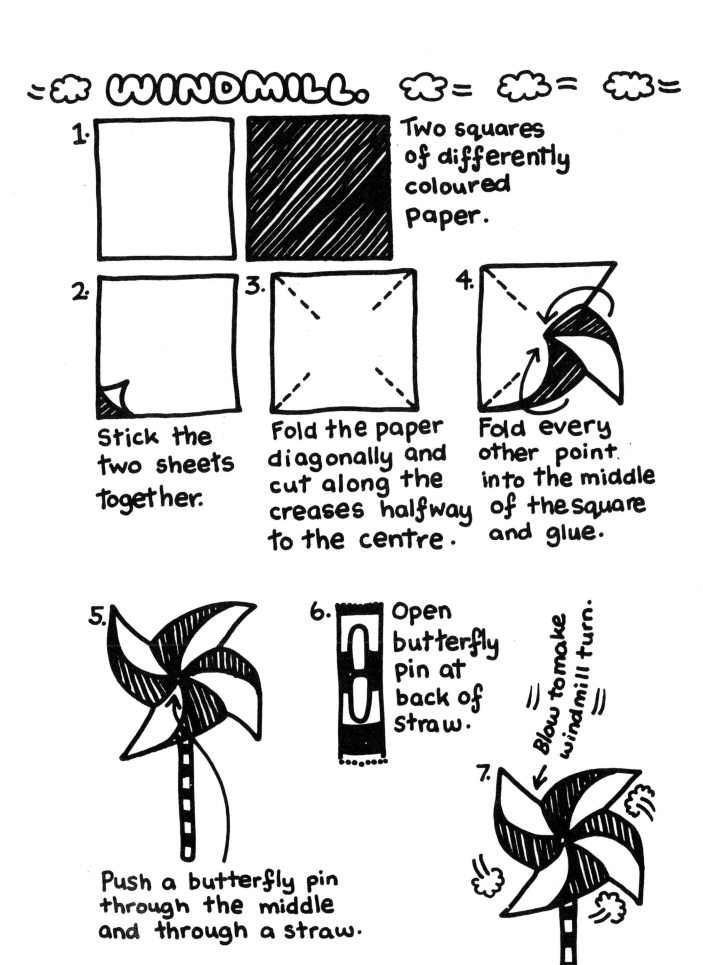

1. Two squares of differently coloured paper.

2. Stick the two sheets together.

3. Fold the paper diagonally and cut along the creases halfway to the centre.

4. Fold every other point into the middle of the square and glue.

5. Push a butterfly pin through the middle and through a straw.

6. Open butterfly pin at back of straw.

7. Blow to make windmill turn.

Seventh Sunday of Easter
Keep in touch

INTRODUCTION
Before Jesus left his friends and returned to his Father in Heaven, he prayed that God would stay close to them and watch over them always. In their prayers, they would keep in touch with Jesus through the power of the Holy Spirit.

SIGN OF THE CROSS

LIGHT THE CANDLES
Light the candles and say Candle Prayer 1: *Flicker, flicker little candle.*

SORRY
Allow the children a short period of contemplation, to think about the events of the past week. Encourage them to examine their consciences. Choose a 'sorry colour' Prayer.

GLORIA

GOSPEL ACCLAMATION
To welcome today's Gospel sing Acclamation 3: *Alleluia, Alleluia.*

GOSPEL (*cf John 17:4-11*)
Jesus looked up to Heaven and said: 'Father, I have finished the work you sent me to do, and have told my friends all about you. They know that you sent me here, and that through your power, I have been able to do many wonderful things. They have listened to me teaching and they truly believe in you. Father, I pray that you will keep them safe and watch over them always. When I have gone, the world will still be able to see the glory of God through their faith and love.'

DISCUSSION
When Jesus needed to feel very close to his Father, what did he do? – He would pray.

Can you remember some of the times when Jesus prayed?
- in the Garden of Gethsemane, before he was betrayed by Judas.
- before he raised Lazarus from the dead.
- during the Last Supper, before he broke the bread.

Jesus spent a great deal of time praying to his Father. Often he would go off to a quiet place where he would not be disturbed. Like us, Jesus needed to share his worries and problems with his heavenly Father; he knew that he was never alone.

Why is it important for us to pray? – Praying is having a conversation with God. We talk to God and he listens, and then while we listen, God can talk to us too. In this way we get to know God better, we keep in touch.

Do you pray? When do you pray?

We don't have to have special times for saying prayers. Often we say them at bedtime, but we can talk to God at any time.

Do you ever feel unsure about what to say to God? – God our Father likes to hear about everything we have to tell him, and he is always ready to listen.

The apostles knew how important it was to pray to God, but like us, they often felt uncertain about what to say. One day they asked Jesus to teach them how to pray. What was the prayer he taught them? – The Lord's Prayer. (*Our Father.*)

When we pray it is important to remember several things
- prayers can be simple thoughts and words coming straight from the heart.
- spend a little time with God each day, it doesn't matter where or when.
- sometimes God doesn't seem to give us what we pray for. Do not give up praying, keep on talking to God and listening, for he knows what is best for you, even if it is not what you expected.
- when we pray, we don't just *ask* God for things we want. Remember to praise and thank him for his goodness, to tell him about ourselves and others and say sorry if we have done wrong.
- share your prayers with other people, at school, at home, at Church. Jesus said, 'When two or three of you gather together in my name, I'll be there with you.' The Holy Spirit helps us to pray, even if we do not know what to say to God. God will understand us without having to use words.

ACTIVITY
Give each child their own copy of the Lord's Prayer to colour and decorate.

CREED

CLOSING PRAYER
Together we say the prayer which Jesus himself taught us.
Say the Lord's Prayer, or 'Our Father'.

Our Father who art in Heaven, hallowed be thy name. Thy kingdom come. Thy will be done on earth as it is in heaven.

Give us this day our daily bread and forgive us our trespasses, as we forgive those who trespass against us. And lead us not into temptation, but deliver us from evil.

Amen.

Feast of the Ascension of the Lord

Jesus ascends into heaven

INTRODUCTION

The time had come for Jesus to say goodbye to his friends and to return to his Father in Heaven. They had work to do when he was gone, but through the Holy Spirit they would never feel afraid or alone.

SIGN OF THE CROSS

LIGHT THE CANDLES

Say together: Fill our hearts with the Light of Jesus.

SORRY

Listen carefully to this reading: (cf Psalm 34:11-14)
Listen to me little ones,
and you will learn to please the Lord.
If you want to live a long life,
full of happiness and joy,
turn away from wickedness and lies.
Surround yourself with goodness,
and try with all your hearts
to share Gods' peace with others.

Now we ask God to forgive us as we pray:
If we have been dishonest or unkind:
    Lord have mercy
If we have been thoughtless or selfish:
    Christ have mercy
If we have not shared your goodness and peace
with others:
    Lord have mercy

GLORIA

GOSPEL ACCLAMATION

To welcome today's Gospel sing Acclamation 1:
Share your word with us.

GOSPEL (cf Matthew 28:16-20)

Jesus told the eleven disciples to go to a hill in Galilee where he would meet them. When they arrived there, Jesus appeared to them and said, 'I want you to go to all peoples living far and wide, and make them disciples of mine; baptise them in the name of the Father, the Son, and of the Holy Spirit; and teach them to keep the commandments I have given to you. Whatever you do, and wherever you go, I will always be with you, until the end of time.' Then Jesus was taken up into Heaven and the disciples returned to Jerusalem to wait for the Holy Spirit to come.

DISCUSSION

Where did Jesus go? – He returned to his Father in Heaven.

Why did Jesus leave the disciples? – It was time for Jesus to be with his Father again. He had done everything that his Father had wanted him to do.

How do we feel when someone we love very much has to leave and go away?

How do you think the disciples felt? – They were filled with great sadness because they knew that they would not see Jesus again in this world, and they felt alone and afraid.

Jesus knew how sad and afraid his friends would feel, but he told them he would be with them always.

How would he be with them?
– through the power of the Holy Spirit
– through the sharing of bread and wine at the Eucharistic meal.

Jesus promised to be with his disciples always, and in the same way he shares himself with us through the Holy Spirit and our sharing in the Eucharist.

What was the job Jesus gave to the disciples? – To go out to the peoples of the world and to baptise them in the name of the Father, Son and Holy Spirit. To share his love and teaching with everyone so that they would become Christ's followers.

Who does this job today? – Sometimes people called missionaries travel to far off countries to share God's word and faith with others, but each one of us in our own way can do the same with those around us, because we all have the Holy Spirit living within us and God's goodness working through us.

ACTIVITY

Cut out and paste this picture of the Ascension scene, with Jesus disappearing from sight behind a cloud.

CREED

CLOSING PRAYER

Lord Jesus,
help us to remember
that you are with us always
and we need never be afraid.
Help us to go out
and do your work in this world
until we see you again,
when you come back to us at the end of time.

Feast of Pentecost
The Holy Spirit comes

INTRODUCTION
Today is the Feast of Pentecost, which the Jews celebrated fifty days after the Passover. Today we celebrate the birthday of the Church, and hear how Jesus sent his Holy Spirit to the disciples, just as he had promised to do.

SIGN OF THE CROSS

LIGHT THE CANDLES
Light the candles and then read:
Jesus said, 'Let your goodness shine out like a light in the darkness, so that through you, the love of our heavenly Father will touch the lives of others.' (cf Matthew 5:16-17)

SORRY
Think about the words of this song, and remember that God our Father will always forgive us if we are truly sorry. Sing Sorry Song 4: *When we say that we are sorry.*

GLORIA

ACCLAMATION
May the love of God's spirit burn in our hearts.

READING (cf Acts 2:1-42)
The disciples had gathered together in Jerusalem to celebrate the Feast of Pentecost and to wait for the Holy Spirit that Jesus had promised to send. One day as they were praying together, the room was suddenly filled with the sound of a powerful wind which roared through the house. Then, what looked like small tongues of fire appeared and spread out to touch each one of them. So it was that they were filled with the Holy Spirit.

At once, in their excitement, they rushed outside to tell everyone what had happened to them. As they began to speak, they were amazed to find that they could talk in foreign languages that they had never spoken before. People from lands far and wide gathered in a crowd to listen to these men from Galilee. They were amazed, and came to believe in Jesus.

So it was, from that day onwards, the disciples went around telling everyone about Jesus, and sharing all that he had taught them. They were no longer afraid, for wherever they went, Jesus went with them. Now his Spirit lived inside them, and they would never feel alone again.

DISCUSSION
Ask the children to imagine they are the disciples, sitting quietly together in a room, and imagine the sounds and feelings the disciples must have felt.

What did they hear? – A sudden furious wind, gusting through the room.

How do they think the disciples felt when they heard and felt this mysterious wind? – They probably felt surprised by its suddenness and frightened when they realised it came from *inside* the house, when everything outside was calm.

How else did the Spirit appear? – As small flickering flames which rested above their heads.

If you saw flames above your head, what would you do? – Probably panic and try to put them out! But these were no ordinary flames, they were signs of God's Spirit coming to fill the lives of the disciples with the light and warmth of God.

How did the Spirit change the disciples?
- he made others understand them, even if they did not speak the same language.
- he filled them with courage and power so that they could stand up before the crowds and preach, and work miracles in Gods' name.

What else did the Spirit give to the disciples? – He brought seven gifts: joy, love, patience, kindness, understanding, reverence (respect), courage. All these gifts helped the disciples to be able to go and spread the message of Jesus. The gifts of the Spirit help us to follow the right path on our journey through life towards heaven, they fill us with Gods' goodness.

When do we receive the Holy Spirit in a special way? – He comes to us first at baptism and then his power is refreshed in us at confirmation. Scented oil called Chrism is used to anoint people at baptism and confirmation as a sign that the Spirit has made them special and fills their lives with his 'fragrance'.

ACTIVITY
Pentecost is the Church's Birthday. Make one large birthday card or individual birthday cards to celebrate this special day or wrap seven empty containers with spare wrapping paper and label each with a gift tag to represent the seven gifts of the Holy Spirit.

CREED

CLOSING PRAYER
Come, Holy Spirit,
and fill our hearts with your love.
Work through us to bring Jesus
to those who do not know him,
so that we may share this love with others.

Feast of the Trinity
God the Father, Son and Holy Spirit

INTRODUCTION

God shares himself with us through the three persons of the Trinity. We share the love of God the Father, the goodness of Jesus the Son, and the friendship of the Holy Spirit.

SIGN OF THE CROSS

LIGHT THE CANDLES

As we light our candles today, we thank God the Father for sending Jesus his Son to rescue us from sin, and the Holy Spirit who will always be our friend. Sing the Candle Song.

SORRY

Read this prayer (cf Psalm 14:2-3):
Help us Lord to do what is right.
Make our words and thoughts true and sincere,
So that we harm no one by what we say or do.

We close our eyes and in our hearts we ask God's forgiveness if we have hurt others by what we have said or done.

GLORIA

GOSPEL ACCLAMATION

To welcome today's Gospel sing Acclamation 1: *Share your word with us.*

GOSPEL (cf Matthew 28:16-20)

Jesus appeared to his disciples on a hillside where they had arranged to meet. When they saw him they fell to their knees and he said to them, 'All power in Heaven and on earth has been given to me, and I am sending you out into the world to make disciples of all peoples. Baptise them in the name of the Father and of the Son and of the Holy Spirit, and teach them to obey all the commandments I have given to you. Remember that I will always be with you, to the very end of time.'

DISCUSSION

Does anyone know what Trinity means, and what we are celebrating today? – 'Trinity' means something made up of three, and today we give thanks for the three persons of God.

Who are the three persons who make up the Holy Trinity and what do we know about them?

1. God the Father – He created the world and everything in it. He loves us all dearly and sent his only son, Jesus to rescue us from our sins.

2. God the Son – Jesus was made man. We know many stories which remind us of his kindness and goodness, and his love for *all* people. He taught us how we should live and the path to follow to find our way to Heaven. His love was so great, he died on the cross and rose from the dead to save us from sin.

3. God the Holy Spirit – We have learned that the Spirit takes many forms, wind, fire or a dove. He is invisible but very powerful, and he fills us with God's life and warms our hearts with the 'fire' of God's love and courage.

So there are three persons but only one God. Do you find this difficult to understand? – The Trinity is a *mystery* which we cannot really understand, but because we *know* that God can do *anything*, we *believe* in this mystery. It is part of our faith.

(The Trinity is a very difficult concept for the children to understand, indeed it is very difficult for all of us to understand this essential mystery. It may be helpful however to use the activity below to convey the concept, although naturally even this is a simplification. The Father, Son and Holy Spirit – three different faces of the same God.)

Have ready three hats which will be instantly recognised by the children, for example hats belonging to a fireman, a policeman and a soldier. Ask for a volunteer to come and stand in front of the other children. Get the children to tell you the child's name and then as you place each hat on the child in turn, ask them to say what job the child would do while wearing that hat. 'This is John, the soldier – this is John, the fireman – this is John, the policeman.'

God is rather like the child with the three hats, he is only one God but according to what 'job' he is doing, and what 'hat' he is wearing, he can appear as the Father, Son or Holy Spirit.

ACTIVITY

Photocopy the illustration and ask each child to colour the three 'hats' worn by the one person of God.

CREED

Before saying the Creed together, help the children to think carefully about the words of the prayer, and their belief in God the Father, Jesus his Son, and the Holy Spirit.

CLOSING PRAYER

Say together: 'The Glory Be'

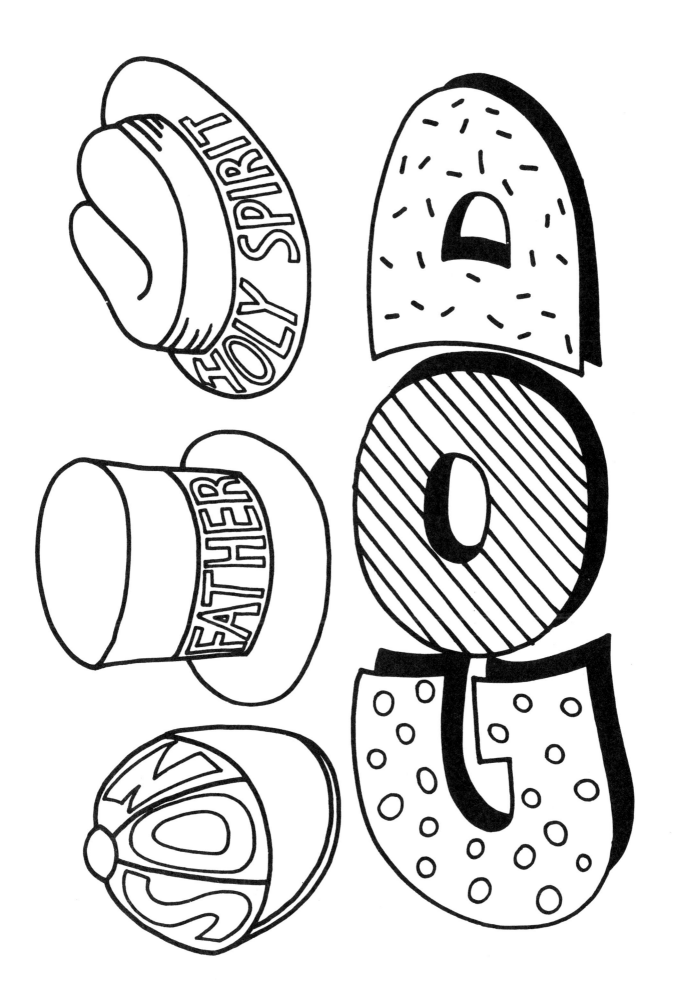

Feast of Corpus Christi
The Body and Blood of Christ

INTRODUCTION
What would happen if we had no food or anything to drink? Together they keep us *alive*, and without their life-giving nourishment we would die. Jesus is the 'bread of life' who shares himself with us in a special way during the Mass.

SIGN OF THE CROSS

LIGHT THE CANDLES
Light the candles and say Candle Prayer 2: *Show me, show me little candle.*

SORRY
Sing Sorry Song 2: *We come to say we are sorry.*

GLORIA

GOSPEL ACCLAMATION
To welcome today's Gospel sing Acclamation 5: *We have come to hear you, Lord.*

GOSPEL (cf Mark 14:22-24)
Jesus and his disciples had gathered to celebrate the Passover meal together. While they were eating, Jesus took some bread, gave thanks to his heavenly Father, broke the bread, and gave a piece to each of his disciples, saying, 'Take this and eat it, this is my body.' Then he took a cup of wine. Again he praised his Father, and passed it to each of his disciples saying, 'Take this and drink it, this is my blood, poured out for you. Do this in memory of me.'

DISCUSSION
At the Last Supper, Jesus and the disciples were sharing a celebration meal in memory of what joyful event? – Every year Jewish families and friends gathered together to share a meal which celebrated the 'Passover' when they remembered how God had freed them from slavery in Egypt.

When do we gather together to celebrate a joyful event with a celebration meal? – When we come to Mass, we come as one large family to celebrate something which happened for all of us – the resurrection of Jesus. We share a meal together just as Jesus did at the Last Supper.

What food and drink did Jesus share with his disciples that night? – Jesus shared a loaf of bread and a cup of wine. He changed the bread and wine into his own body and blood, to nourish them with his life-giving power. Just as our bodies need nourishment to live, so do our spiritual souls.

What happens when we celebrate the Mass together? – At our celebration of the Eucharist, which means 'thanksgiving', we remember the meal which Jesus shared with his friends the night before he died; and we share in his death and resurrection. We believe that through the power of God, the bread and wine become the body and blood of Jesus, who gives himself to each of us in a very special way. Jesus said, 'I am the bread of life', and when we share in the Eucharistic meal, we share life with the Son of God himself.

ACTIVITY
Prepare a simple celebration meal with the children, to help them to imagine the Last Supper, and to understand its relevance to the Eucharistic meal at Mass. If possible sit around a table with a table cloth and re-enact the scene using pitta bread and blackcurrant juice.

Alternatively give the children this colouring in picture.

CREED

CLOSING PRAYER
Lord Jesus,
you are the living bread
which comes to each one of us
in a special way.
Help me to share the joy of your love
with others I meet.

Second Sunday of the Year
Jesus is the chosen one

INTRODUCTION
John the Baptist had been preaching to the crowds and baptising them in the River Jordan. God had told John that he would send him a sign. The Holy Spirit would appear like a dove, and settle on the one he had chosen to send. John would then be ready to show the Son of God to the people.

SIGN OF THE CROSS

LIGHT THE CANDLES
Light the candles and then read: *(cf Matthew 5:16-17)*
Jesus said, 'Let your goodness shine out like a light in the darkness, so that through you, the love of our heavenly Father will touch the lives of others.'

SORRY
Encourage the children to listen carefully to the words of this prayer:
Do not be afraid,
God will always love you.
Whatever you have done,
God will always love you.
As a father loves his child,
He will always love you.
Turn back to him and know,
God's love lasts forever!

GLORIA

GOSPEL ACCLAMATION
To welcome today's Gospel sing Acclamation 4: *Praise the Lord*

GOSPEL *(cf John 1:29-34)*
When John saw Jesus in the distance walking towards him, he said to the crowds, 'Look, there is Jesus, the Lamb of God. He is the special one sent by God whom I have told you about. I saw the Holy Spirit, hovering like a dove, coming down from Heaven and settling on him. He is the one you must follow now, for he will baptise you not just with water, but with the Spirit of God.'

DISCUSSION
What sign did God send so that John would know that Jesus was the chosen one?

John had been preparing the people, but what else did God want him to do?

There are several points worth discussing with the children.
1. John called Jesus the 'Lamb of God' – because he would meekly sacrifice his life for all of us.
2. John's work was coming to an end – he had prepared the people to listen to Jesus and his message.
3. John pointed Jesus out as the chosen one, the Son of God, and told the people to follow him.

Can anyone remember another occasion when the Spirit appeared, not as a dove, but in another way? At Pentecost when the disciples were hidden away in a room after the death of Jesus, the Spirit appeared as flickering flames which came to rest on each of them and the room was filled with the sound of rushing wind.

Certainly he does not always appear as a dove!

ACTIVITY
Give each child a dove to make as shown in the illustration. These can then be hung from a mobile.

CREED

CLOSING PRAYER
When we see these doves,
help us to remember
that your Spirit is with us in all that we do,
helping to guide and protect us always.

1. Fold a sheet of paper like a fan.

2. Cut out dove and cut along dotted line.

3. Push fan through slit, then spread it out and upwards.

4. Join fan in middle above doves middle.

5. Then thread a piece of cotton through top of fan and add to a mobile.

Third Sunday of the Year
Follow me!

INTRODUCTION
It is important to remember that Jesus was a very special person, an extraordinary man. Today we hear him ask some fishermen to leave their boats, nets, homes and families to follow him. The remarkable thing is, that's just what they did!

SIGN OF THE CROSS

LIGHT THE CANDLES
Say together: Fill our hearts with the light of Jesus.

SORRY
We all belong to God's family, and God is our loving Father. We are not always good, and we want to say sorry for the times when we have not loved each other.

All say together: Father forgive us,
Jesus forgive us,
Spirit forgive us.

GLORIA

GOSPEL ACCLAMATION
To welcome today's Gospel sing Acclamation 5: *We have come to hear you, Lord.*

GOSPEL (cf Matthew 4:12-23)
After Jesus had been baptised by John, he went to live in Capernaum, a fishing village beside the Sea of Galilee. One day he saw two brothers called Simon Peter and Andrew, out fishing together. Jesus spoke to them and they were filled with wonder when he said, 'Come and follow me and I will make you fishers of men and women.' The two brothers left their boat and nets at once, and followed him. A little further on Jesus saw James and John, out fishing with their father, Zebedee. Again, Jesus asked them to follow him, and they left their father and went with him. These brothers were the first disciples of Jesus.

DISCUSSION
What were the names of the brothers in the story?
What did they do for a living?
What do you think Zebedee thought when his sons went off with Jesus?
Jesus was obviously a very special person. Something about him was so different, they were prepared to leave everything and to follow him.
What did Jesus mean when he said that he would make them ' fishers of men and women'? –

They would help to spread the 'Good News', the teachings of Jesus. They would gather the people to Jesus like sheep into one flock, or all the fish into one net! These people would learn to know and love Jesus too, and would follow him.
Does Jesus want us to follow him too ?
Sometimes people today give up everything to follow Jesus – for example missionaries.
How can we follow him everyday? – By the way we live and treat others.
– being kind and good.
– following his rules.
– loving God and all his people.
We are all 'fishers' of men and women. In our own way we can encourage others to want to know and follow Jesus, by the lives that we lead.

ACTIVITY
Cut out a fish shape for each child to colour and write their name on. Place each fish in a net (using a vegetable or fruit bag) and then pin this onto a background scene on the board to complete the picture.
Alternatively the children can complete the photocopied picture adding as many varied and colourful fish as they like and finally drawing a net over them all which is attached to the rope.

CREED

CLOSING PRAYER
Jesus, help us to listen
when you ask us to 'follow you'.
Make us strong enough to walk beside you each day.
Help us to share your love
with others that we meet,
so that we too lead people to follow you.

Fourth Sunday of the Year
The secret of happiness

INTRODUCTION
God our father wants us all to be happy, but lasting happiness comes from inside us, when our hearts are filled with love and goodness. Today we hear Jesus explaining the secret of finding such happiness.

SIGN OF THE CROSS

LIGHT THE CANDLES
Sing the Candle Song together.

SORRY
Sing Sorry Song 1: *Dear Lord Jesus hear our prayers.*

GLORIA

GOSPEL ACCLAMATION
To welcome today's Gospel sing Acclamation 1: *Share your word with us.*

GOSPEL (cf Matthew 5:1-12)
One day when Jesus was being followed by a large crowd, he climbed a hillside, sat down,and began to speak:
Happy are gentle people,
for they shall be treated with gentleness.
Happy are people who forgive others,
for they shall be forgiven.
Happy are the poor for they shall see Heaven.
Happy are people who do what is right
and care about others.
Happy are people who make peace
and bring friendship.
Be happy even if people are unkind
and say nasty things to you,
because you believe in me,
for you will have great rewards in Heaven.

DISCUSSION
Imagine if you could have anything you wanted to make you feel happy, what would you choose?
Would such feelings of happiness last forever?
Jesus wanted to give us some 'guidelines' to follow which can make us truly happy. This happiness will stay in our hearts forever. Think of a train rattling along a track. What would happen if the track was broken or suddenly ended? These guidelines keep us on the 'track' to happiness. Without this 'track' our journey would be much harder, and we might lose our way.
Jesus often used stories called parables to explain what he meant. (Choose one parable to talk about in detail, or give a brief outline of each example and discuss what we learn from them).

1. Happy are the poor. *(cf Luke 16:19-25)*
There was once a rich man who lived in a large house and had everything he wanted. On the street outside his house lived a poor man called Lazarus who had nothing. Lazarus died and went to Heaven, and the rich man died and went to Hell. God said to the rich man, 'When you were alive you had everything, but you did not share with poor Lazarus. Now it is the turn of Lazarus to be happy and for you to be miserable.'

2. Happy are those who do what is right. *(cf Luke 10:30-35)*
One day a man was travelling from Jerusalem to Jericho, when a gang of robbers attacked him. They stole everything he had and after beating him,they left him to die. Two men passed by, but neither stopped. Finally, a man from Samaria found the man lying in the road, and was filled with pity. He bandaged his wounds and gave him a drink, before taking him to the nearest inn where he cared for him.

3. Happy are people who forgive. *(cf Matthew 18:22-34)*
Once there was a king who had many servants. One of these servants owed him a lot of money and could not pay him back.The king was ready to punish him, but the servant begged for mercy, and the king forgave him his debt. Later, this servant met another man who owed him a small amount of money. The man could not pay and asked the servant for mercy. The servant was furious and had him thrown into jail. When the king heard of this, he sent for the servant that he had forgiven. 'You asked me for mercy and I forgave you,' the king said. 'Could you not also be forgiving towards this other man?' The king had his servant thrown into jail until he paid back all that he owed.

ACTIVITY
Make a 'Happiness train' with a picture of each child riding on board.

CREED

CLOSING PRAYER
Jesus,
you shared the secret
of everlasting happiness with us,
and showed us how to find and keep it.
Help us to live by your 'guidelines'
and to share this happiness with others.

Fifth Sunday of the Year
Be a light in the darkness

INTRODUCTION
Without light in our world there would be no life. In some parts of the world, like Antarctica, the sun does not shine for six months of the year, when there is complete darkness. Here, when it grows dark each day, we go to bed and sleep until the rising sun makes it light again. Today Jesus reminds us of the importance of light in our lives.

SIGN OF THE CROSS

LIGHT THE CANDLES
Together we will say our our candle prayer as we remember that Jesus wants each of us to shine like a candle in the darkness. Say Candle Prayer 1: *Flicker, flicker little candle.*

SORRY
As we sing our sorry song together help us to remember the words of the prayer that Jesus himself taught us: 'Forgive us our trespasses as we forgive those who trespass against us.'
Sing Sorry Song 4: *When we say that we are sorry.*

GLORIA

GOSPEL ACCLAMATION
To welcome today's Gospel sing Acclamation 2: *Light up our hearts.*

GOSPEL (*cf Matthew 5:14-16*)
One day Jesus said: 'No one lights a lamp and then covers it up, because then they could not see in the darkness. They put the lamp up high so that its rays shine out! You are like lamps, with the brightness of God's love and goodness shining out from you. When you are good you will bring light into the world around you, and others will see you and thank God for sharing his goodness.'

DISCUSSION
If possible, darken the room and turn on a torch before asking one of the children to cover it up.
What difference does it make in the room ?
Shine the torch slowly around the room and pick out objects or people that the children can name. 'Touch' each child with the ray of light and explain that in a similar way, our 'light', or the goodness in each one of us, can shine out and touch the lives of others. Turn the lights back on.
We heard at the beginning how Antarctica experiences darkness for six months of the year. (Use a globe or an atlas to show the children where Antarctica is). What would the weather be like in such place where there is no sunlight? (Use any pictures you can find of the polar regions.)
Would many plants and animals be able to survive ?
Without light it is very difficult for things to live. It is cold and dark, and there is little to eat.
What can we use to 'make' light?– candles, torches, lanterns, electricity . . .
What happens when we have a power-cut and all the lights go out?
Jesus used this story to make it clear that the light that we are given at our baptism, should be shared with others, to help them to 'see' more clearly and make our world a better place to live!

ACTIVITY
Have circles/rectangles of black paper with the shape of a candle and flame cut out. The children can stick squares of tissue paper over the back to make lanterns to hang as mobiles.

CREED

CLOSING PRAYER
At baptism we became children of God, filled with the light of his Spirit.
Help us to always walk as children of the light, touching the lives of others with God's love.

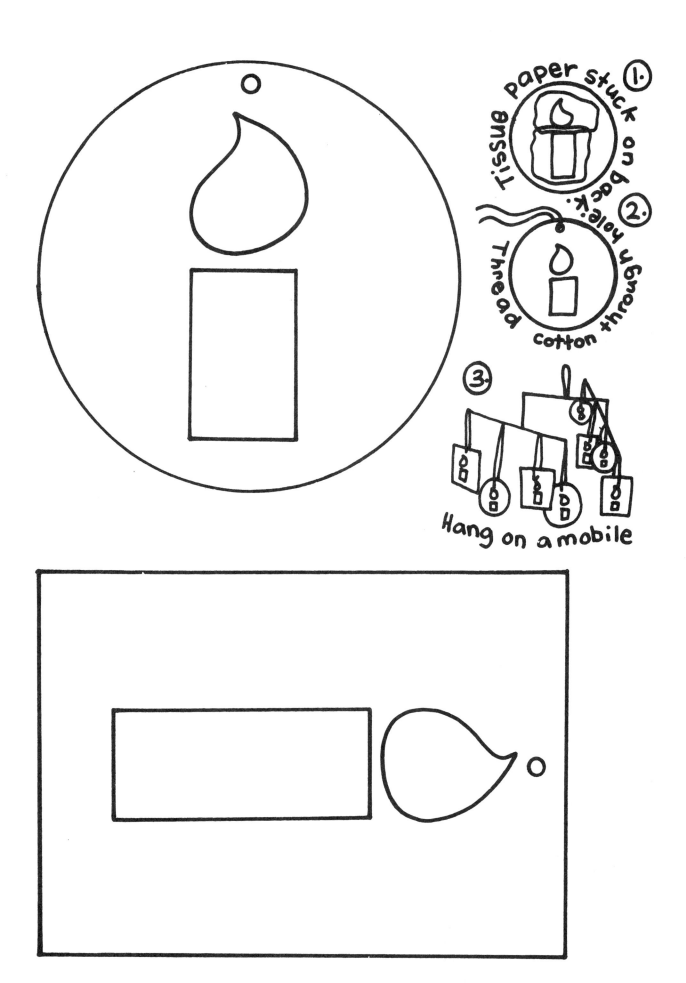

1. Tissue paper stuck on back.

2. Thread cotton through hole.

3. Hang on a mobile

Sixth Sunday of the Year
Rules for life

INTRODUCTION
When Moses was leading God's people through the desert, God gave them ten rules or commandments, to help the people to live in God's way. Today we hear Jesus reminding his followers of these 'rules for life'.

SIGN OF THE CROSS

LIGHT THE CANDLES
Together sing the Candle Song.

SORRY
Encourage the children to close their eyes and make the words of this prayer their own:
Lord, sometimes we make mistakes,
and forget the things you have taught us.
If we have not always been kind towards others,
we are sorry.
If we have not always been honest or fair,
we are sorry.
Send your Spirit to fill us with your love
and to help us to be good.

GLORIA

GOSPEL ACCLAMATION
To welcome today's Gospel sing Acclamation 4: *Praise the Lord.*

GOSPEL (*cf Matthew 5:17-37*)
Jesus spoke to his followers: 'Remember to keep God's rules and always do what is right. My Father's rules do not just tell us what we should *not* do, they also tell us what we *should* do if we truly want to live in God's way.
- Nothing is greater than God so always put him first.
- Do not use God's name unless you mean to.
- Make Sunday God's special day, to share some time with him.
- Love and care for your mother and father.
- Life is precious, so do not harm anyone by your thoughts or actions.
- Always love your friends. When two people marry and promise to always be friends, they should not break that promise and spoil their friendship.
- Always be honest, and do not steal or cheat.
- Tell the truth to others and about others; do not lie.
- Married people give each other the gift of their love. Never be greedy or jealous of others so that you spoil this gift.
- Be happy with what you have and do not be jealous of other people's belongings.

DISCUSSION
Which man did God give the Ten Commandments to?

What are these rules for?

People were confused and uncertain about how to live in a way pleasing to God. So God sent gave them the Ten Commandments to guide them and teach them how to show their love for him and each other. Moses wrote the Ten Commandments down on slabs of stone, but we should keep them 'written' on our hearts. By obeying them we can show God how much we love him and want to please him. These 'rules for life' will guide us and lead us closer to our Father in Heaven.

Ask the children to think of some rules that they know and write them down on a large sheet of paper. They can be divided into DO and DO NOT categories. For example:

- DO have lights on your bike at night.
- DO wear a seat belt.
- DO wear a helmet on a motor bike.

- DO NOT run at the swimming pool.
- DO NOT dive in at the shallow end.
- DO NOT climb electricity pylons.

Why are these rules important? – They keep us from harm and encourage us to do the right thing.

Are rules always easy to obey? – Often they are not, but we should remember that the Ten Commandments are the rules given by God to keep us from harm and to help us do what is right.

ACTIVITY
Give each child a copy of GOD'S RULES to hang up at home. The decorative border can be coloured.

CREED

CLOSING PRAYER
God our Father,
help us to keep
your Commandments 'written' on our hearts
to guide us on our journey through life,
and lead us closer to you each day.

GOD'S RULES

1. Love God and always put Him first.
2. Remember the greatness and mystery of God.
3. Don't use God's name unless you mean to.
4. Make Sunday God's special day.
5. Love and consider your Mother and Father.
6. Never harm others by your thoughts and actions.
7. Learn to be friends with other people so that when you marry someone you will always be their friend.
8. Always be honest; never steal or cheat.
9. Tell the truth to others and about others.
10. Don't be greedy or jealous of other people.

Seventh Sunday of the Year
Love your enemies

INTRODUCTION
Does anyone know what an enemy is? (Someone who hates another person and wants to hurt or harm them). Today we hear Jesus telling us that we must learn to forgive and love our enemies, and never to hate them.

SIGN OF THE CROSS

LIGHT THE CANDLES
Say together: Fill our hearts with the love of Jesus.

SORRY
Jesus told us to be like his heavenly Father, who always forgives; Help us to forgive anyone who has hurt or harmed us. If we have spoiled our friendship with God we ask for his forgiveness as we sing our sorry song.
Sing Sorry Song 4: *When we say that we are sorry.*

GLORIA

GOSPEL ACCLAMATION
To welcome today's Gospel sing Acclamation 3: *Alleluia, alleluia.*

GOSPEL (*cf Matthew 5:38-48*)
One day Jesus said: 'If someone hits you, do not hit them back, instead you must forgive them and try to be their friend. Learn to love your enemies and to pray for anyone who wishes you harm. It is easy to love someone who loves you back, but it is hard to love someone who hurts you. Try to be like God our Father, who always forgives. If you do this, others will see God's goodness in you, and my Father in Heaven will be very pleased.'

DISCUSSION
Jesus tells us to love as God loves – all people, even those we do not like! It is easy to be kind to those who are kind to us, but God wants us to be good to people who hurt us too.

Has anyone ever been hurt by someone else, for example a bully at school?

What happened and how did they react to the incident?

What has Jesus told us to do?

We should not let our anger win. We must try to be generous and kind, and to become friends. This is never easy, but we should try to do what we know is right. If the bully laughs at us and will not listen, do not give up! Tell an adult – a teacher or a parent, and perhaps they can help them to realise that hurting others is wrong and instead they must learn to love.

Do the children know of any countries at war?

All over the world many different nations are enemies and their people are at war. Many people are trying hard to bring peace to these places, to encourage friendship, just as Jesus wanted. In our own small way we too can be peacemakers like them; by offering our friendship to everyone we meet; by trying to end a quarrel between others, and by learning to say sorry and to forgive others who have hurt us.

ACTIVITY
Photocopy the illustrations onto thin card. Cut them out for the children to colour and make into badges which encourage peace throughout the whole world.

CREED

CLOSING PRAYER
Lord Jesus, you once said,
'I leave you my peace, my peace I give you.'
May our hands reach out
to share your peace with others,
and may our hearts always be filled
with forgiveness and love.

Stick a
safety
pin to
the badge's back.

Eighth Sunday of the Year

Do not worry

INTRODUCTION

We are more precious to God than any living creature, and he will always take care of us. He will provide whatever we need, so we should not worry or be afraid, for he is always watching over us.

SIGN OF THE CROSS

LIGHT THE CANDLES

Sing the Candle Song together.

SORRY

We want to be like little candles, sharing God's love with the world around us. If we have done wrong and turned away from God's light and wandered off into the darkness, help us to be sorry and to turn back to the light.

Read the following prayer: *(cf Psalm 14:2-3)*
Those who turn away from you do wrong,
those who are wise worship you.
Lord you see all that we do,
help us to do what is right.

GLORIA

GOSPEL ACCLAMATION

To welcome today's Gospel sing Acclamation 2: *Light up our hearts*

GOSPEL *(cf Matthew 6:25-34)*

One day Jesus said to his friends, 'Do not worry about what you have to eat and to drink, or how to clothe yourselves. Life is more important than food, and the body is more important than the clothes you cover it with.

'Look at the wild birds around you; they do not know where their next meal will come from, yet your heavenly Father feeds them. Surely your lives are more precious than those of the birds.

'See the wild flowers in the field, they do not clothe themselves, and yet they are more beautifully dressed than the richest King! God dresses all these flowers, and yet how unimportant they are compared to you. So do not worry about what tomorrow holds.

'Live a life filled with goodness and do as my Father commands, and he will take care of all your worries, for you are very precious to him.'

DISCUSSION

What sort of things do people worry about?

– their jobs and money.
– what they look like.
– what other people think about them.

Often we worry about small unimportant things. If we worry about ourselves and the things which affect our lives, we can grow into selfish people who always put our own needs first.

Jesus wanted us to realise that God will provide everything we need. What were the two examples he gave us, of Gods' constant care?

– God loves and cares for the little birds, providing food for all their needs.
– Every year without fail, the wild flowers in our gardens and hedgerows are covered with blossoms in all shapes, sizes and colours.
And God makes all this happen.

What did Jesus want us to do?

He wanted us to take our worries to God and share them with him, to realise just how much God our Father loves and cares for us, for we are more precious than all the birds and the flowers. If we have a worry, whether it is large or small, it never seems to be so bad, if we can share it with someone else, and talk it over. The worry or trouble seems to grow smaller and less important.

Jesus wanted us to understand that we should share our trouble with God and trust him to take care of us. Then we can free our hearts and minds of worries so that we will have more time and space for God's love and goodness to work in our lives.

ACTIVITY

Ask each child to draw a picture of themselves on a sheet of paper, then give each child some flowers and birds to be cut out and coloured. (You may find it helpful to do the cutting out yourself beforehand.) They should glue the flowers and birds around the picture of themselves. Add the caption 'Do not worry, God never forgets you.'

CREED

CLOSING PRAYER

Lord, I feel your love around me always.
In times of trouble you are there.
Your love always makes things right again,
because you share your unending goodness with me.

Ninth Sunday of the Year
Build your lives on me

INTRODUCTION
Today Jesus uses a story to warn us about what will become of those people who choose to ignore his words, and instead of listening to what he has to say and acting on it, follow their own foolish ways.

SIGN OF THE CROSS

LIGHT THE CANDLES
Light the candles and say together Candle Prayer 3: *The light of God.*

SORRY
Ask the children to close their eyes and listen carefully to this prayer:
Do not be afraid, God will always love you.
Whatever you have done, God will always love you.
As a Father loves his child, he will always love you.
Come back to him and know,
God's love lasts forever.

GLORIA

GOSPEL ACCLAMATION
To welcome today's Gospel sing Acclamation 5: *We have come to hear you, Lord.*

GOSPEL (cf Matthew 7:24-27)
Jesus told this parable to the crowds, 'Once there was a wise man who built his house on rock, and a foolish man who built his house on sand.

'One day a terrible storm came, and the wind howled and the rain poured down. The river near the two houses flooded over its banks and flowed past the walls of the houses. The house built on rock stood firm, while the other house collapsed and was washed away.

'And so it is, if you listen to me and do as I ask, you will be like the wise man. For those that please my Father will find a place in Heaven. But if you choose to ignore what I tell you, then you will be like the fool whose house was washed away.'

DISCUSSION
Have you ever noticed one of the first things that builders do before they start to build a house? – They dig deep wide trenches in the ground and fill them with concrete. These are the 'foundations' of the house.

What are the foundations for, and why are they so important? – They are the solid base on which the whole house will rest. They are the supports under the bricks which will be used to make the walls of the new house.

Where did the two men build their houses? – The wise man built his on rock, which was probably uneven and very hard to chip away until he had made a level surface on which to build his house. Compared to rock, it was much easier to dig and level the sand for the foolish man's house, and his house was not so strong.

What happened when the rain came and the river rose up and flooded its banks?

(At this point in the discussion some visual props are very useful. Split the group in two, and using wooden building blocks or something similar, ask one group to build a 'house' on top of a brick sitting in a basin or bucket. Ask the other group to make a small sandcastle in the bucket or basin and then build their house on this. Encourage the children to describe what happens next in the story and let each group add a jug of water to the basins and see what happens! It is advisable to practice this in advance!)

Jesus is not teaching us how to build a house in this story, what is he telling us? – Jesus is like the solid rock and our lives are like the houses. If we build our lives on strong foundations and choose to follow Jesus, then we will please our Father in heaven. It may take a lifetime to build our strong foundations, but we will be rewarded with everlasting life. If we ignore Jesus and our lives are built on greed and selfishness then we will be like the fool who built his house on sand, and was left with nothing.

ACTIVITY
Give out these pictures of houses, or ask the children to draw and cut out their own picture. After each child has coloured their 'house', arrange them on a board or as a mobile display.

CREED

CLOSING PRAYER
Thank you, dear Father,
for the many stories which Jesus told us.
Through them he teaches us of love and kindness,
and shows us the way to you.
Help us to remember today's story
as we build our lives,
knowing that Jesus is our rock and our foundation.

Tenth Sunday of the Year
Matthew the tax collector

INTRODUCTION
Have you ever been picked from a crowd to do something special? Perhaps to help a magician to do a trick, to read at school assembly, or as the winner of a competition? One day Jesus chose a man called Matthew to be his friend. This moment changed Matthew's life forever.

SIGN OF THE CROSS

LIGHT THE CANDLES
Say together: May the light of Jesus shine in our lives.

SORRY
God is our loving Father and will always forgive us if we are truly sorry. Remember the story Jesus told about a loving father . . .

There was once a loving father whose son left home and lived a wicked and selfish life. This made the father very sad. One day the son came back and was truly sorry for all his mistakes. His father hugged him and forgave him everything.

In the same way, God our Father will always forgive us when we are truly sorry.

GLORIA

GOSPEL ACCLAMATION
To welcome today's Gospel sing Acclamation 3: *Alleluia, alleluia.*

GOSPEL (cf Matthew 9:9-13)
One day as Jesus was walking along he saw a man called Matthew who was a tax collector. He went over to him and said, 'Follow me.' Matthew did as Jesus told him. They went to Matthew's house where Jesus stayed for supper. Many other tax collectors came and shared the meal with Jesus and his disciples. Jesus overheard a Pharisee asking one of his disciples, 'Why is your master friendly with such dishonest and unkind people?'

Jesus turned to him and said: 'Good people do not need my help, it is people such as these tax collectors who need me; I will forgive them and call them to follow me.'

DISCUSSION
Tax collectors were hated by the Jews, do you know why? – The people had to give a part of any money they earned to the Roman government in taxes. People like Matthew collected the taxes from the people, and often charged them extra money which they kept for themselves. The Jews hated them because they worked for the Romans and were often dishonest.

When Jesus asked Matthew to become a follower, do you think everyone was surprised? – Matthew was greedy and selfish, ready to cheat and take their money. Everyone was amazed that Jesus wanted to befriend this wicked man.

What did the Pharisees say? – Pharisees were Jews who strictly obeyed the Jewish law and were proud of their goodness. They disapproved because Jesus chose to befriend a sinner rather than one of them.

Matthew was not a good man, but are any of us good all the time? – Just because we are not good all the time, Jesus does not stop being our friend. He wanted us to see people like Matthew with God's loving eyes. Not to judge them and to turn away, but to reach out and forgive them.

Do you think that meeting Jesus changed Matthew's life?

Jesus changed the lives of everyone he met. His love and goodness spread to those around him, and they in turn shared it with others. When Matthew followed Jesus that day, his life changed direction as he walked in the footsteps of Jesus, and he realised how selfish and dishonest he had been. Jesus was willing to offer forgiveness and friendship so that Matthew could make a fresh start in life! Matthew had a change of heart.

ACTIVITY
Cut out the figure of Matthew and a set of clothes with which to 'dress' him. These can be coloured and decorated as befits a wealthy man. Stick several bags of gold to a belt on his waist. After colouring, stick the heart shape onto his chest, to show that Matthew had a change of heart.

CREED

CLOSING PRAYER
Dear Jesus,
you were ready to forgive Matthew
and offer him your friendship,
just as your heavenly Father
is always ready to forgive us
and let us make a fresh start.
Help us always to remember this,
so that we are ready to forgive
those we meet on our journey through life.

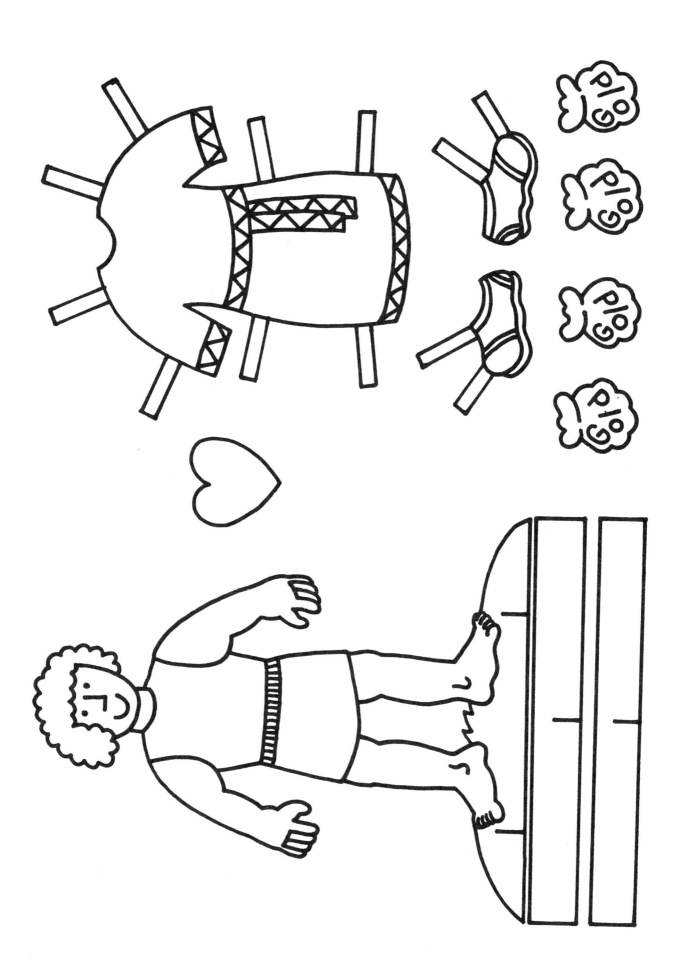

Eleventh Sunday of the Year
The twelve apostles

INTRODUCTION
Jesus chose twelve disciples to become his apostles. They became the foundation stones of the early church, and went out to share all that Jesus had taught them with the nations of the earth.

SIGN OF THE CROSS

LIGHT THE CANDLES
Light the candles and read:
Jesus said, 'I am the light of the world, whoever follows me will have the light of life and will never walk in darkness.' *(cf John 8:12)*

SORRY
It is hard to be good all the time, and God our Father knows and understands this. He is always ready to forgive us when we say that we are sorry. Listen carefully to the words of this reading from the book of Joel, a prophet in the Old Testament: *(cf Joel 2:13)* Turn back to God for he is kind and always ready to forgive. He is full of patience and understanding, and will not punish you for doing wrong if you are sorry.

GLORIA

GOSPEL ACCLAMATION
To welcome today's Gospel sing Acclamation 1:
Share your words with us.

GOSPEL *(cf Matthew 9:35-10:4)*
Jesus had been travelling around the towns and villages, preaching to the people and sharing the Good News about the Kingdom of God. Along the way he had performed many miracles and cured the sick and crippled people that he met. When Jesus saw how many people needed his help, he felt sorry for them, and called together twelve disciples who were his closest friends. Jesus named these twelve as his apostles, and gave them the power to work in his name, before sending them out all over the land to heal the sick and preach to the people. The names of the twelve were: Simon, whom Jesus called Peter, and his brother Andrew; James and his brother John; Philip and Bartholomew; Matthew and Thomas, (another) James and Thaddeus; Simon the zealot; and Judas Iscariot who would later betray Jesus.

DISCUSSION
Jesus called his special team of helpers 'apostles'. Do you know what an apostle is? – The Greek word *'Apostello'* means 'to send'. An apostle is someone who is sent out on a special mission, with a special job to do.

What was the mission God sent them on? – To share the Good News with the people and to perform miracles in the name of Jesus. These twelve became the first bishops of the Church, and their power and leadership has been passed down until the present day.

Which apostle did Jesus choose to be leader of the Church on earth? – Peter. What is the name of our Pope today and where does he live? – St Peter's power and authority has been handed down from pope to pope through the ages. He is the head of the Catholic Church on earth.

Here are some of the things we know about the twelve apostles:

Simon Peter and Andrew – they were brothers and had been fishermen. Peter was the 'rock' on which Jesus chose to build his Church.

James and John – were also fishermen before they became followers of Christ. John was quiet and thoughtful, and Jesus chose him to take care of Mary his mother after his death on the cross.

Matthew – had been a dishonest tax collector who collected money for the Romans. Until he became a follower of Jesus he did not have many friends.

Thomas – was often full of doubt and did not believe what he was told. He became known as 'doubting Thomas'.

Simon (the zealot) – he had belonged to a group who wanted to lead the people in rebellion against the Romans. At the beginning he probably expected Jesus to be the one who would lead the Jews to fight against the Romans.

Judas – was better educated than many of the other apostles. He would be the one to betray Jesus to the high priests.

ACTIVITY
Make paper chains of the twelve apostles and ask the children to pin the names to each one.

CREED

CLOSING PRAYER
Lord Jesus, give wisdom and courage
to our Pope and bishops who are the leaders
of your church on earth.
Help them to carry on with the mission
given to the twelve apostles,
and lead your people to our Father in heaven.

1. 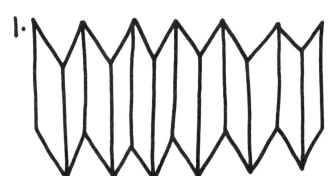 Fold piece of paper into a chain of twelve figures.

2.  Draw one figure on top piece of chain, then cut through all twelve along lines you've just drawn.

3. Colour them all in and add their name.

PETER ANDREW THOMAS

Twelfth Sunday of the Year
Do not be afraid

INTRODUCTION
Imagine how you would feel if your parents wanted to send you to Africa to tell the children there all about Jesus. How would you feel travelling to a strange country all alone? Jesus wanted his disciples to share the Good News with everyone, and they were afraid too.

SIGN OF THE CROSS

LIGHT THE CANDLES
As you light the candles say together Candle Prayer 2: *Show me, show me little candle.*

SORRY
Today we will hear Jesus telling his disciples that they must never feel afraid. We are not afraid to come before Jesus to ask for his forgiveness if we have done wrong.
Listen carefully to the words of this prayer:
Do not be afraid, God will always love you.
Whatever you have done, God will always love you.
As a father loves his child, he will always love you.
Come back to him and know
God's love lasts forever.

In a moment of silence let us ask God's forgiveness for anything we have done to hurt him or other people by our thoughts and actions. After a brief pause, sing together Sorry Song 2: *We come to say we are sorry*

GLORIA

GOSPEL ACCLAMATION
To welcome today's Gospel sing Acclamation 4: *Praise the Lord*

GOSPEL (cf Matthew 10:26-33)
Before Jesus sent the apostles out to bring the Good News to the people, he gathered them together and said: 'Do not be afraid to stand before the crowds and speak, even though there will be many who wish you harm and will not listen. My heavenly Father knows when even one little sparrow falls dead from the sky, and you mean more to him than all the birds in the world. He will watch over you and see how brave you are. If you lose your life for my sake, your reward will be great in heaven and you will share in my Father's glory and have life everlasting.'

DISCUSSION
Why did the apostles need great courage to go and share the gospel with other people? – They had to leave their friends and families and travel to countries where they were strangers. When they got there they had to live as Jesus had taught them, and share his message with the crowds.

Have you ever had to stand up in front of a crowd of people and read to them, or say lines in a school play? Did you feel nervous?

Imagine how frightening it was for the apostles!

Can you remember who came at Pentecost to share his courage and strength with the apostles? – The apostles were transformed by the Holy Spirit. They changed from being frightened men, to being brave enough to stand up before non-believers and tell them that Jesus had risen from the dead.

Do you think they found it easy to convince people that Jesus had done all the wonderful things they spoke of, including coming back to life? – Many did not believe them and treated them as liars, chasing them away from their towns.

Do you know what a martyr is? – A martyr is someone who dies for something they believe in. The first Christian martyr was called Stephen. He was full of God's spirit and preached to the people and worked many miracles in God's name. The authorities did not like what he told the people, and many of the disciples of Jesus spent years in prison or were even killed because of their faith. They were not afraid of dying because they knew that God would raise them up to everlasting life.

How do we share the Gospel message today?– We can *tell* people about Jesus but we must also try to *live* in the way that Jesus taught us. We must share what we believe and the Holy Spirit will give us the same strength and courage that he gave the disciples.

ACTIVITY
Cut out two large hand shapes and a silhouette of a 'person' for each child to complete.

CREED

CLOSING PRAYER
Lord Jesus,
help us to share the good news of the Gospel.
Through the power of your Holy Spirit,
give us the strength and courage of the apostles
to stand up and be witnesses to what we believe.

Do not be afraid: Put yourself in God's hands

Thirteenth Sunday of the Year
Make Jesus welcome

INTRODUCTION
Imagine if you met Jesus today – if he suddenly arrived at your house and rang the doorbell. When you realised who this 'stranger' really was, what would you do and say to welcome him?

Jesus wants us to treat everyone as we would treat him.

SIGN OF THE CROSS

LIGHT THE CANDLES
As the candles are lit, read this passage aloud: *(cf Proverbs 4:18-19)*
The path to our heavenly Father is like the sun rising, getting brighter and brighter as we draw closer to God.
Those who turn away from his love, follow a path as dark as the night, and they stumble and fall as they cannot see the way.

SORRY
Jesus taught us that if we are full of forgiveness for others then our heavenly Father will be full of forgiveness for us. Help us to remember this as we say the prayer of God's family together. (All hold hands for the *Our Father*):
Our Father who art in heaven . . .

GLORIA

GOSPEL ACCLAMATION
To welcome today's Gospel sing Acclamation 2: *Light up our hearts.*

GOSPEL *(cf Matthew 10:40-42)*
Jesus said to his apostles:, 'Anyone who makes you feel welcome in their homes, is welcoming me, for I am with you always. Anyone who treats you kindly and shares their food and drink with you, is sharing their goodness with me and my Father who sent me. However small or great their act of kindness, they will be rewarded for their goodness.'

DISCUSSION
What does it mean to 'welcome' someone? – It means to greet someone with pleasure and friendliness, and to make them feel that you are pleased to see them.

How do you welcome anyone who comes to visit your home? – If it is someone we have just met or do not know very well, we might shake hands and say hello. If it is a relative or a good friend, we might give them a kiss or a hug to welcome them. If they are children, we could also make them welcome by sharing toys or letting them join in a game we are playing.

Would you offer a visitor something to eat or drink? – When we invite someone to share a meal or even just a cup of coffee, we let them know that we want to spend some time with them. Jesus always had 'time' to spend with others, even when he was feeling tired. Remember the story when the disciples tried to stop the little children from coming to see Jesus, but Jesus welcomed them with open arms and spent some time with them.

In today's Gospel, what message did Jesus give us? – Whenever we welcome anyone and treat them kindly, then we are welcoming Jesus. Remember how at baptism we all received the gift of God's Spirit? Because of this gift, each one of us and every person that we meet has the light of Christ burning inside and so we should treat them as we would treat Christ.

St Matthew tells us how Jesus once said: *(cf Matthew 25:35-40)*
I was hungry and you gave me food to eat,
I was thirsty and you gave me a drink,
I was a stranger
and you welcomed me in your home.
My clothes were in tatters
and you gave me your own,
I was ill and you took care of me.
When you did any of these things for others,
you did it for me.

Jesus was trying to tell us that we could not ignore or send anyone away without doing the same to him!

How do you feel when you have acted kindly towards someone? Does it make you feel good inside?

Our reward for being kind and loving towards someone else is a wonderful feeling of happiness glowing inside us. At that very moment the light of the Spirit is truly burning brightly inside us!

ACTIVITY
Make and cut out circles with scenes of people making others feel welcome. Arrange these on a mobile around the central figure of Jesus.

CREED

CLOSING PRAYER
Lord Jesus help us to love and care for everyone, by remembering that each person we meet has the spirit of God living inside them.
Help us to welcome others
knowing that we are really welcoming you.

PICTURES

1. Looking after someone who is ill.
2. Helping someone who has hurt themself.
3. Welcoming a friend and sharing toys.
4. Sharing a meal.
5. Visiting a hospital.
6. Letting someone join your game.
7. Helping someone who is lost.
8. Greeting people with a friendly smile.

Fourteenth Sunday of the Year
Be like children

INTRODUCTION
Sometimes grown ups seem very clever and to know all the answers. Today Jesus tells us that it wasn't always the clever people who first understood him, often it was those who had child-like hearts.

SIGN OF THE CROSS

LIGHT THE CANDLES
As the candles are lit, say together:
May the light of Jesus shine in our lives.

SORRY
If we have made God feel sad or disappointed with us this week, we ask for his forgiveness as we sing our sorry song together. Sing Sorry Song 1: *Dear Lord Jesus hear our prayer, Lord.*

GLORIA

GOSPEL ACCLAMATION
To welcome today's Gospel sing Acclamation 5: *We have come to hear you.*

GOSPEL (cf Matthew 11:25-30)
One day Jesus said, 'Praise be to you, Father, for you have not chosen to reveal yourself to the clever and wise, but to people who see the world through child-like eyes. You have shared your wisdom with those filled with innocence and simplicity.' Then Jesus said, 'Come to me with your worries and troubles and I will take care of you. I am kind and gentle and I will help you to find real peace.'

DISCUSSION
If a creature from outer space came to earth and asked you to describe what a young child or baby was like, what would you tell him?
Among other things young children are:
- dependent on others to look after their needs and take care of them.
- completely trusting. They have total trust in their parents and family to care for them and keep them from harm.
- honest. They do not know how to lie or deceive. When they are happy and content they let you know by laughing and smiling, when they are miserable or upset they let you know by crying loudly!
- loving. They return all the love they receive. They enjoy being hugged and cuddled, and feeling secure in their family's love.
- innocent. They are pure and free from any wickedness. They have no bad thoughts or unkind feelings.
- uncomplicated. Simple things keep them happy and contented: a warm bed, a smiling face, a bottle full of milk!

Jesus once said, 'Do not keep the little children away from me! Only those who are like them will enter the Kingdom of God.' *(cf Matthew 19:13-15)*

Did Jesus expect us to be children forever?

None of us stays a child forever, each of us will grow up to become an adult! Jesus was telling us that he wanted us to keep the 'child-like' qualities of goodness, as we become grown-ups. Remember some of the features of a small child: trust, honesty, love, innocence and simplicity. If we have these qualities as children of God, we will stay close to God's love and never wander from his friendship. With him beside us we can find the path to everlasting happiness in God's kingdom.

What did Jesus tell us to do with our cares and troubles? – Just as a young child has complete faith and trust in its parents, so we can rely on God. We can share our problems and worries and know that we can depend on him to love and take care of us and our needs.

What must we do to find our way to the Kingdom of God? – We must try to live as Jesus did – with honesty and openness and a deep love for God and our neighbour. It is not easy and we will often make mistakes. But God is our Father and we are his children. We can trust him to take care of us and show us the way.

ACTIVITY
Either give each child a colouring-in picture or make one large picture of Jesus embracing the children. Add the caption. 'To enter God's kingdom you must become like a little child.'

CREED

CLOSING PRAYER (cf Psalm 34:11-14)
Listen to me little ones, and you will please God.
If your lives are to be filled
with happiness and joy,
turn away from wickedness and lies;
surround yourselves with goodness
and try with all your hearts
to share the peace of God with others.

To enter God's Kingdom you must become like a child.

Fifteenth Sunday of the Year
The parable of the sower

INTRODUCTION
Jesus often told simple stories called 'parables' to help people to understand something important. Today we hear the parable of the sower.

SIGN OF THE CROSS

LIGHT THE CANDLES
Light the candles and ask the children to listen to these words written by the prophet Isaiah:
(cf Isaiah 60:19)
I, the Lord will be your everlasting light and my glory will shine on you always.

SORRY
God will forgive us just as we forgive others. The number of times he will forgive us cannot be counted because they will never end. In the following reading Jesus reminds Peter of this (cf Matthew 18:21-22, 35):
One day Peter asked Jesus, 'How many times must I forgive someone who wrongs me? Would I have to forgive as many times as seven in a row?' Jesus answered, 'Not just seven times Peter, but more than seventy times seven, for you must forgive from your heart.'

GLORIA

GOSPEL ACCLAMATION
To welcome today's Gospel sing Acclamation 3:
Alleluia, alleluia.

GOSPEL (cf Matthew 13:3-23)
Jesus told the crowds this parable: 'One day a farmer went out to sow some seeds in his field. As he scattered the seeds some fell on the stony path at the edge of the field, where flocks of hungry birds flew down and gobbled them up. Some seeds fell on rocky ground, where although they sprouted, the soil was too shallow for their roots, and the baking hot sun shrivelled them up. Other seeds fell where weeds were growing, and the weeds choked them until they died. Some of the seeds landed on the farmer's richest soil, and grew into strong and healthy plants.'

Jesus explained the meaning of this story to the people:
'The seeds are the things which I teach you, the good news about God. Some people hear God's word but they do not understand; this is the seed which falls on the stony path.
'Some people welcome my words and try hard to follow my ways at first, but then they give up. They are like the seeds which fall on rocky ground; they sprout but then shrivel and die.

'Some people hear my message, but their hearts are filled with other thoughts; the message becomes choked like the seeds choked with weeds, and they cannot produce fruit.

'The seed that falls on rich soil is like those who hear my message and understand it; they grow strong and the harvest is great.'

DISCUSSION
How did the farmer sow his seed?
As he walked up and down the furrow he scattered the seed by hand from a large open basket. (Demonstrate this action to the children as it helps to explain why so much seed fell on poor ground.)
Can you remember where the first handful of seed landed and what happened to it?
It fell on the stony path and was gobbled up by the birds.
Where else did the seed fall and what happened to the them in each of these places?
 – on the rocky soil the seed sprouted at first, but then shrivelled up.
 – amongst the weeds the seed became choked as the weeds grew.
 – on the rich soil the seeds grew tall and healthy producing flowers and fruit.
What did Jesus mean when he talked about the seed in this story? – The seed was God's word which Jesus brought to share with us. Some people do not listen, others listen but give up trying to follow Jesus because it is not always easy. Some people listen and understand; they really try to live as Jesus taught them.
Are we like the stony path, the rocky ground, the patch of weeds or the rich deep soil? – If we listen to God's word and understand it, God's love will grow in our hearts like a strong healthy plant. We will bear much fruit by allowing his love to show in our actions, our thoughts and in our words .

ACTIVITY
Colour the picture of the sower in his field with the different places where the seed can fall.

CREED

CLOSING PRAYER
Jesus help us to listen to
and understand your message,
so that our hearts and lives
will be filled with God's love.

Sixteenth Sunday of the Year
The wheat and the weeds

INTRODUCTION
Today Jesus tells us another parable and warns us about what will happen at the end of time to those people who do not listen to him.

SIGN OF THE CROSS

LIGHT THE CANDLES
Sing the Candle Song together as the candles are being lit.

SORRY
Help the children to reflect over the events of the past week.
- did they hurt or upset anyone by their thoughts or actions?
- were they selfish or unkind?
- did they do something which they should not have done?

As we listen to the words of this reading, help us to ask God for his forgiveness (cf Psalm 25:11-16):
God is full of kindness and love, and wants to show us the path we must follow.
He leads us with patience and understanding, and forgives us when we stray and lose our way.
When we look to him for help he rescues us from harm, and helps us to try again, for he is full of forgiveness.

GLORIA

GOSPEL ACCLAMATION
To welcome today's Gospel sing Acclamation 1: *Share your word with us.*

GOSPEL (cf Matthew 13:24)
Jesus told the people another parable:
'One day a farmer sowed his field with wheat, but that night as he slept, his enemy crept into the field and scattered weed seeds amongst the wheat.

'Days passed and as the wheat sprouted and grew, so did the weeds, and the farmer realised what his enemy had done. One of the farm workers asked him, 'Master, do you want us to pull up the weeds?' But the farmer answered, 'No, let them grow together until harvest time, because if you pull up the weeds now you might pull up the wheat too! When the harvest comes, the harvesters can separate the wheat from the weeds. Then I can store the wheat in my barn, and burn the weeds.'

When the disciples asked Jesus to explain the story he said: 'I am the man who sowed the wheat, and the devil is my enemy who scattered the weeds. The wheat seeds are the people who hear my word and follow me, and the weeds are the wicked people who will not listen to me. The end of the world will be like harvest time, when good and bad people will be separated by angels sent by God. The good people will share God's glory and happiness in heaven, but the wicked people will be punished and will never see God.'

DISCUSSION
Can you remember from last week, how the farmers sowed their seeds?

In today's parable, what happened to the farmer's field of wheat?

Why does no one like weeds? – Weeds stop the other plants from growing tall and strong. They choke them with their roots and block out the sunlight with their leaves.

Why did the farmer not want his workers to pull out the weeds? – He did not want to risk losing any of the good seed. Like the wheat and weeds, God allows good and bad people to live side by side. Goodness and love are strong and God wants to allow wicked people a chance to change their ways before the end of time.

Can you think of any examples of people who changed their way of life after they had met Jesus? Remember Matthew the tax collector, who gave up everything to follow Jesus and Zacchaeus the dishonest tax collector who made a fresh start after Jesus had forgiven him.

What did Jesus promise for good and bad people at the end of the world?

By the life we lead on earth, we can choose to be like the wheat, stored safely in the farmer's barn, and live with God forever in heaven, or we can be like the weeds, burned at harvest time, and never be with God.

ACTIVITY
Colour the bundles of wheat and weeds. Untangle the maze to show what happens to them. Label the barns 'The Kingdom of God'.

CREED

CLOSING PRAYER
Jesus, show us the way to eternal life.
Walk beside us on our journey,
until your angels lead us
to share your everlasting happiness at the end of time.

God's kingdom

God's Kingdom

Seventeenth Sunday of the Year
Priceless treasure

INTRODUCTION
Today Jesus tells us a story to explain that the Kingdom of Heaven is like a priceless treasure that we would swap our most precious possessions for.

SIGN OF THE CROSS

LIGHT THE CANDLES
As we light our candles today, we will say together Candle Prayer 2: *Show me, show me little candle.*

SORRY
When the disciples asked Jesus to teach them how to pray he said the 'Our Father' or the Lord's Prayer. In it he reminds us all that God will 'forgive us our trespasses as we forgive others'. Do you understand what this means? (Allow the children to share their thoughts.) It means that we will be forgiven in the same way that we forgive others who hurt us.

Help us to remember this as we say the 'Our Father' together:
Our Father . . .

GLORIA

GOSPEL ACCLAMATION
To welcome today's Gospel sing Acclamation 4: *Praise the Lord*

GOSPEL (*cf Matthew 13:44-46*)
Jesus said to the crowds, 'One day a man was digging in a field when his spade struck a box which was buried there. When he opened the box he was amazed to find it was full of treasure. He quickly buried the treasure again, went away and sold his house and all that he owned. With the money he made, he bought the field from the farmer, and then ran back and dug up the treasure.

'There was another man who was a merchant who bought and sold pearls to earn a living. One day he happened to find the most perfect, beautiful pearl he had ever seen. He too went away and sold everything so that he would have enough money to buy that pearl for himself.'

Jesus said. 'God's kingdom is the real treasure, as perfect and precious as the pearl; you would give up everything you have for it, because it is worth more than anything else in the whole world.'

DISCUSSION
Do your parents have things which are very precious to them? – A favourite ornament, a piece of jewellery, a car or a picture.

How do they treat these precious things? – People often keep these things safe from harm, and only take them out to be looked at or touched on special occasions.

Do you have something which is very precious to you, which you treasure more than anything else?– It might be a toy, a book, a favourite teddy or some item which is not important to other people but means a great deal to you.

Like the grown ups, do you treat your 'treasure' carefully because it means so much to you? Would you be willing to give it away or swap it?

Jesus wanted us to understand that God's love for us is like priceless treasure. It means more than any possession we have on earth; it is worth giving up everything we own to have it.

What must we do to find the treasure of God's kingdom? – By living as Jesus taught us and following his example we will have God's love which is worth more than all our worldly possessions. Some examples of this way of living:
– sharing
– loving
– forgiveness
– kindness
– generosity
– honesty
– truthfulness.
By living in this way we are sharing in God's Kingdom now on earth, the greatest and most precious treasure.

ACTIVITY
Cut out the large 'treasure chest' and several 'jewels'. Entitle the jewels with some of the words listed above or add your own suggestions (the children may come up with some of their own). Decorate the jewels imaginatively! Label the chest 'God's kingdom' and fill it with the priceless jewels.

CREED

CLOSING PRAYER (*cf Psalm 119:36-37, 43-44*)
Lord, help me
to store up my riches in heaven not on earth,
To know what is important
and not to waste my time on worthless things.
To always speak the truth and do what you ask
because of the love I have for you.

Eighteenth Sunday of the Year
The miracle of the loaves and fish

INTRODUCTION
Through the power of God, Jesus was able to share five loaves and two fish with a crowd of five thousand people. Today he shares himself with us through the Eucharist, the bread of everlasting life.

SIGN OF THE CROSS

LIGHT THE CANDLES
Light the candles and read the following prayer:
Jesus, you told us that you are the light of the world,
shining in the darkness to guide us on our journey.
If we keep our eyes on the light,
we will not wander into dark places
and our journey will lead us to you in heaven.

SORRY
In this reading from St Matthew, Jesus reminds us how important it is for us to forgive and make our peace with others if we want to love God and come to him. (cf Matthew 5:23-26)

If you are about to come before God to pray and then remember that you have quarrelled with someone, first go away, settle your argument, and make your peace with them.

Encourage the children to think of anyone they need to 'make friends' with again, remembering that God will be as forgiving with us as we are with others.

GLORIA

GOSPEL ACCLAMATION
To welcome today's Gospel sing Acclamation 2:
Light up our hearts.

GOSPEL (cf Matthew 14:13-21)
A large crowd had followed Jesus to a hillside beside the Sea of Galilee, to hear him teaching. As it grew late in the day the disciples asked Jesus to send the people away to find some food for themselves. 'They do not need to leave,' said Jesus, 'we can share our food with them.'

'But all we have for ourselves are five loaves and two fish, and there must be five thousand people to feed!' exclaimed the disciples. 'Bring the food to me,' said Jesus and he told the crowds to sit down quietly. Jesus took the loaves and fish and gave thanks to God. He blessed the bread, broke it, and handed it to the disciples to share with the people. There was plenty for everyone to eat, and when they had finished eating, they filled twelve baskets with the scraps. The people were amazed and they went away telling everyone about the miracle they had seen that day.

DISCUSSION
Why were the disciples surprised when Jesus told them to share their food with the crowd? – They only had five loaves and two fish, so how could they possibly feed so many! Jesus shows us that we must be ready to share whatever we have with others.

Have you any idea how big a crowd of five thousand people is? (Compare the size of your Sunday congregation or the local school, something familiar to the children so they appreciate how many people needed to be fed.)

What did Jesus do with the loaves of bread? – He blessed them according to the Jewish custom, broke them and gave them out to the disciples.

Can you remember another occasion when Jesus blessed bread and shared it with other people? – The Last Supper.

How do we remember this meal on Sunday? – When the priest blesses the bread and wine at Mass so that they can become the body and blood of Christ for us to share in the Eucharistic meal. Just as Jesus fed the thousands that day, so he continues to feed millions today with his own body and blood, through the power of God's spirit.

How do you think the disciples felt as they gave out the loaves and the fish? – They had seen Jesus perform many wonderful miracles, and they believed in him. However this did not stop them being amazed by the power of Jesus, as he again proved to them that he was indeed the Son of God.

ACTIVITY
Use small squares of ready gummed paper for the children to stick over the shapes to make a mosaic picture. You may like to show a copy of the famous Byzantine mosaic of the loaves and fishes found at Tabgha where this miracle is said to have taken place.

CREED

CLOSING PRAYER
Jesus,
help us to share whatever we have with others,
and not to be greedy in any way.
As we remember our brothers and sisters
in other countries
who have no food,
We pray that the rest of the world
will learn to share too,
so that the world can be a happier place.

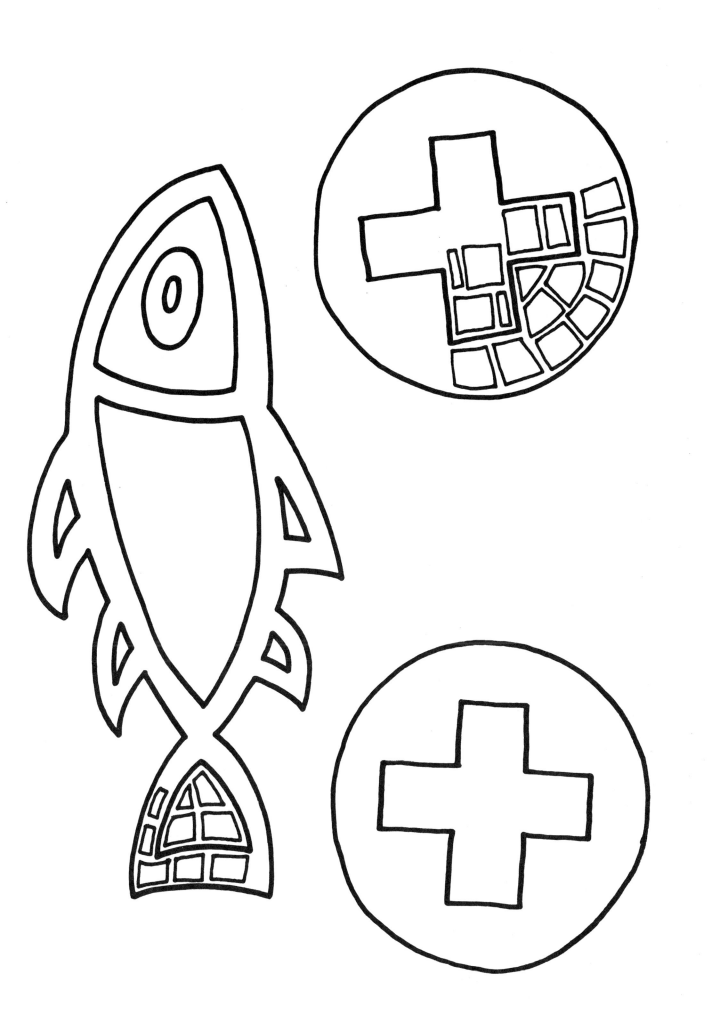

Nineteenth Sunday of the Year
Have faith

INTRODUCTION
Time and time again Jesus shows us that when our faith and belief in him are strong, then anything is possible – even walking on water!

SIGN OF THE CROSS

LIGHT THE CANDLES
Light the candles and say together:
May the light of Jesus warm our hearts and shine in our lives.

SORRY
During a short period of silent contemplation, encourage the children to think about the events of the past week and to examine their consciences. Ask a child to choose a 'sorry colour' Prayer, which can be read aloud by themselves or the group as a whole.

GLORIA

GOSPEL ACCLAMATION
(The children can join in with the alleluias!)
Alleluia, alleluia.
Open our ears, Jesus, to hear your words.
And fill us with your spirit
so that we will understand them.
Alleluia, alleluia.

GOSPEL (cf Matthew 14:22-32)
Before going up to the hills to pray alone, Jesus told his disciples to sail to the other side of the lake. As night fell, the wind grew stronger and the disciples' boat was tossed about by the waves. Suddenly they saw someone coming towards the boat, walking on the water, and they were terrified, because they thought it was a ghost! But Jesus called to them, 'Don't be afraid, it's me!'

Peter shouted to Jesus, 'Lord, if that really is you, tell me to come to you across the water.'

'Come!' said Jesus.

So Peter climbed out of the boat and lowered himself onto the water. Looking straight at Jesus, he began to walk towards him, but as he moved further from the boat and felt the strength of the wind, he grew afraid. Suddenly he began to sink and he cried out, 'Save me, Jesus!' As Jesus reached out his hand and pulled Peter to safety he said, 'Why did you not trust me Peter, is your belief so weak?' When they got back to the boat, the other disciples knelt before Jesus and said, 'You are truly the Son of God.'

DISCUSSION
At first, what did the disciples think they had seen coming across the water towards them? – A ghost.

What did they do? – Imagine how frightened they must have been to suddenly see someone walking on top of the water towards them on a dark stormy night. They probably cried out in fear and tried to hide somewhere on the boat.

What did Jesus do to calm their fears? – He said, 'Do not be afraid.' Jesus said this on several other occasions when the disciples were frightened by some of the amazing things they saw. Remember when he appeared to them in the upper room after his death, and again said, 'Do not be afraid.'

What did Peter do when he heard Jesus calling him to come? – Peter climbed out of the boat and began to walk towards Jesus!

Can an ordinary person normally walk on water? – We can swim in water and we can lie and float in the water, but if we try to stand without anything to make us float we only sink.

What was so special about Peter that allowed him to walk on the water towards Jesus? – Peter was full of courage and faith. Because of this, he was the one chosen by Jesus to be the 'rock', the solid foundation for the Church. He was the first one to realise that Jesus was truly the Son of God.

What happened to Peter when he felt the strength of the wind? – He began to sink beneath the waves, because for just a moment his faith and belief weakened and he felt afraid. Sometimes we are like Peter, full of courage and enthusiasm at first, but often let down by our lack of faith and by fear of the unknown.

What did Jesus do? – Peter was an ordinary person like us, and he would often let Jesus down because his faith was weak. (Remember how he denied Jesus three times after his arrest.) Jesus is always forgiving and ready to reach out his hand to save us just as he reached out that night and saved Peter on the lake.

ACTIVITY
Use squares of coloured paper to make boats with masts and sails.

CREED

CLOSING PRAYER
Lord, give us the courage and faith of Peter,
whose belief was so strong
that he could walk towards Jesus across the lake.
In times of weakness,
reach out your hand to us
and rescue us from our doubts.

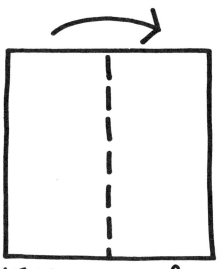

1. Fold square of paper in half.

2. Fold edge of paper back to meet folded edge.

3. Turn paper over and repeat action. Then unfold paper.

4. Fold corners into middle crease.

5. Fold right edge over to folded edge.

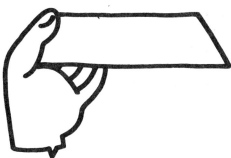

6. Put fingers inside and push corners down with thumbs to make boat 'stand'.

7.

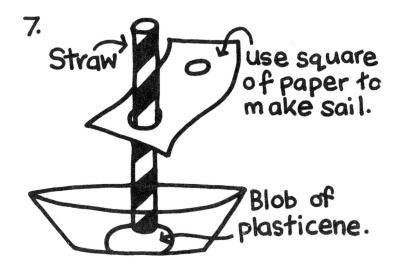

Straw

use square of paper to make sail.

Blob of plasticene.

8.

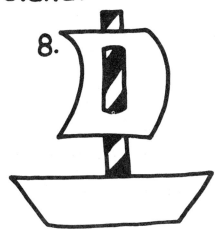

Twentieth Sunday of the Year
The Canaanite woman

INTRODUCTION
Jesus was well known around Jerusalem and in Galilee, so sometimes he made trips to places outside Palestine, where the people did not know him. On one of these trips, Jesus met a Canaanite woman and was struck by the strength of her belief.

SIGN OF THE CROSS

LIGHT THE CANDLES
As we light the candles today, we pray that the light of Jesus will keep shining in our lives and showing us the way. Sing the Candle Song.

SORRY
As we sing our sorry song together let us ask God to help us to make a fresh start. Sing Sorry Song 3: *We want to say that we are sorry.*

GLORIA

GOSPEL ACCLAMATION
To welcome today's Gospel sing Acclamation 3: *Alleluia, alleluia.*

GOSPEL (cf Matthew 15:12-28)
Jesus went to stay near the cities of Tyre and Sidon, where few people knew him. One day a Canaanite woman came to him and cried, 'Help me, Jesus! My daughter's mind is disturbed and she is very ill!' Jesus did not answer the woman, and she carried on crying aloud and begging him to help. The disciples were embarrassed by the shouting and asked Jesus to help her, but Jesus said, 'I have been sent to the Jewish people and not the pagans.' Then turning to the woman he said, 'Surely you would not give the food meant for children to the dog?' The woman threw herself at his feet and answered, 'No sir, but even the dogs get the crumbs that their masters drop from the table!' Then Jesus smiled and said, 'Your belief is strong, and your daughter is well!' From that moment the woman's daughter was cured.

DISCUSSION
Why do you think that Jesus went to stay where no one knew him? – Jesus spent much of his time travelling from place to place, teaching the people and performing miracles as he went. Sometimes he needed a rest, to get away from the crowds and spend some time quietly praying and enjoying some peace.

Do you know what a Canaanite is? – A Canaanite was a person who still practised the old religion which existed in the country before the Jewish religion.

What did the woman want from Jesus?

What did Jesus do?

At first it seemed that Jesus would not help her because he had been sent to bring his message to the Jewish people and not pagans.

What made Jesus help the woman? – Jesus was struck by the strength of her belief in him. She kept asking for his help and would not be put off. She trusted in the generosity and mercy of God, and knew that Jesus could help her.

What can we learn from this story?
- we learn that the message that Jesus brought was for *everyone*, not just the Jewish people.
- that Jesus is ready to help anyone who asks for it, because he loves all of us.
- that when our belief and faith in God is strong enough, our prayers will be answered.

ACTIVITY
Cut out a banner and draw on a cross. Ask one or two of the children to colour or decorate the banner. Divide the individual letters or words of the phrase 'Jesus died to save us all', amongst the other children according to numbers. After colouring these can be stuck onto the banner around the cross.

Altenatively children can cut out and colour the banner opposite.

CREED

CLOSING PRAYER
O God, make our faith in you
as strong as that of the Canaanite woman,
because we believe in you
and know that your word is true.

Twenty-first Sunday of the Year
Who am I?

INTRODUCTION
Everyone knew that Jesus was a very 'special' person! They had seen him cure the sick and blind; feed the crowds with a few loaves and fish, and do many other marvellous things. Yet when Jesus asked his disciples, 'Who do you say I am?' only one person knew the answer.

SIGN OF THE CROSS

LIGHT THE CANDLES
Light the candles and read (cf Matthew 5:16-17):
Jesus said, 'Let your goodness shine like a light in the darkness, so that through you, the love of our heavenly Father will touch the lives of others.'

SORRY
If we have turned away from God, he is always ready to forgive us. Listen to this story:

Zacchaeus was a tax collector who was very rich because he cheated people out of their money. No-one liked him and he had no friends, but Jesus was ready to forgive Zacchaeus and to offer him his friendship. Zacchaeus had a change of heart, and was sorry for his dishonesty and selfishness. He promised Jesus that he would change his ways and try hard to be kind and loving to everyone.

Close your eyes and listen carefully to this prayer as you say 'sorry' quietly in your heart:
Jesus, open our hearts
and make them more loving.
If we have been selfish or unkind
we ask for your forgiveness.
Like Zacchaeus, help us to change our ways
and make a fresh start.

GLORIA

GOSPEL ACCLAMATION
To welcome today's Gospel sing Acclamation 4:
Praise the Lord

GOSPEL (cf Matthew 16:13-18)
One day Jesus asked his disciples, 'Who do people say that I am?' 'Some people say that you are John the Baptist; others say that you are Elijah or Jeremiah or one of the other wise prophets from the past.' Then Jesus said, 'But who do you say that I am?' The disciples were silent until Peter spoke up, 'Master, you are the Son of God.' Jesus smiled at Peter and said, 'My heavenly Father has helped you to understand this. You are the rock on which I will build my church.'

DISCUSSION
Who did the people think that Jesus was? – They thought Jesus was a prophet.

Do you know who the prophets were? – The prophets were wise men who spent their lives telling the people how God wanted them to live. The best known prophets in the Old Testament were Isaiah, Jeremiah and Ezekiel.

Who answered Jesus' question correctly?

How did Jesus know that this was a sign to choose Peter to lead the Church? – It takes a special 'light', given only by God, to let someone 'see' or know in their heart that Jesus is the Son of God. In this way Jesus knew to choose Peter to lead the apostles and the church, after he had returned to heaven.

Does everyone in the world today believe that Jesus is God's son? – Many still believe that he was just another prophet; others simply think that he was a kind and loving man, who helped many people.

What do we believe about Jesus? – We are filled with the Holy Spirit and the light of God so we *know*, like Peter, that Jesus is the Son of God; the one that we must follow to find everlasting life.

ACTIVITY
Give out this outline drawing of St Peter. The children can add the details of his face with felt tip pens and glue on scraps of wool to make hair and/or a beard. Glue on the cut-out 'garments' after they have been coloured, or use scraps of material. Add a staff to represent Peter being the shepherd of God's flock and church on earth.

CREED

CLOSING PRAYER
Lord Jesus, we believe that you are the Son of God.
Your love for us is so great,
that you suffered and died on the cross for us.
May the light of your love always burn brightly
in our hearts and our lives.

Peter knew who Jesus was

Twenty-second Sunday of the Year

God's way

INTRODUCTION

No-one likes to do something difficult when there is an easier way! Sometimes it is hard to do what we know is right, but today Jesus tells us that we should not try to take the easy way out, but follow his way.

SIGN OF THE CROSS

LIGHT THE CANDLES

As we light the candles today, say together:
May the light of Jesus fill our lives.

SORRY

Each one of us is filled with God's spirit. If we have acted selfishly or unkindly towards someone else, we have done the same to God. As we sing our song together, we ask God to forgive us and to fill our hearts and our lives with his love.
Sing Sorry Song 4: *When we say that we are sorry.*

GLORIA

GOSPEL ACCLAMATION

To welcome today's Gospel sing Acclamation 1: *Share your word with us.*

GOSPEL (cf Matthew 16:21-26)

Jesus began to tell his disciples that he would be brought before the high priests, and be put to death before rising to life again.

'Lord, this cannot be allowed to happen!' exclaimed Peter, who was deeply upset by what Jesus had told them.

But Jesus said, 'Peter, your way is not God's way. If you follow me, sometimes things will be difficult, but you must accept them and try not to take the easy way out.'

DISCUSSION

What made Peter feel so upset? – Jesus had told the disciples that he was going to die.

What did Peter want Jesus to do? – Peter knew that if they kept out of harm's way Jesus would be safe, and could not be put to death. He did not want Jesus to go to Jerusalem for the Passover celebration.

Jesus said to Peter, 'Your way is not God's way.' What do you think he meant? – Peter wanted to take the easy way out because he did not want Jesus to suffer and die. Jesus chose to follow God's way; to give up his life so that God could save all of us. Jesus had been sent by God the Father to suffer and die and bring everlasting life to the world. He showed how much he really loved us by following God's way. Like Peter, sometimes we do not fully understand God's way of doing things, but we should trust the Father as Jesus did.

When we find it difficult trying to live as Jesus taught us, should we give up easily?

As Jesus prayed in the Garden of Gethsemane he felt afraid to die. He did not run away and hide, but instead he asked God to give him the courage to do what he knew was right. With the help of Jesus, we too can face up to any difficulties in our lives and choose to show God how much *we* love *him*, by following his way.

ACTIVITY

Photocopy and cut out the bookmark templates to be coloured by the children.

CREED

CLOSING PRAYER

Lord,
we pray for people who are suffering difficulties;
the homeless and unemployed;
the sick and the lonely;
the hungry and the poor.
Share your courage and strength with them
and surround them with your love.

Twenty-third Sunday of the Year
I am with you

INTRODUCTION

Today Jesus reminds us that he will be with us in a very special way, every time we meet together to pray.

SIGN OF THE CROSS

LIGHT THE CANDLES

Light the candles and say Candle Prayer 1: *Flicker, flicker little candle.*

SORRY

St Paul tells us how we should treat other people and reminds us that we should be ready to forgive, just as God forgives us. (*cf St Paul's Letter to the Colossians 3:12-13*)

Always be ready to care for others, and to be kind and gentle. Be patient and calm and never boast, or be proud of your goodness. Just as God always forgives you, so you must always be forgiving towards others.

Close your eyes and speak to God quietly for a few moments.

GLORIA

GOSPEL ACCLAMATION

To welcome today's Gospel sing Acclamation 2: *Light up our hearts.*

GOSPEL (*cf Matthew 18:18-20*)

Jesus said to his disciples, 'Listen to me: whatever you accept on earth, will be accepted in heaven, and whatever you forbid on earth will be forbidden in heaven. When two of you agree to ask for something, then my Father will answer your prayers. Again I tell you that when two or three of you meet together in my name, then I will be there with you.'

DISCUSSION

How many of us have gathered here today?

(Perhaps you could ask one child to stand up and point to each member of the group, as the children count aloud.)

Do you think that the Holy Spirit is here with us now? – Jesus told us that when only a few people meet together in his name, then he promises to be with them. We are here to listen to God's word together and to pray, and we know that the Spirit shares this time with us.

Can you think of other times when two or more people gather together to pray?

Some examples include:
- Church celebrations such as Mass, weddings, baptisms and so on.
- saying prayers as a family, perhaps at bedtime or at mealtimes.
- school assemblies.

(Encourage the children to discuss their experiences of prayer.)

Why is it good for us to come together to pray? – When we meet to pray we come together as one family, and Jesus joins with us in our prayer. Such prayer is very powerful, because we know that God the Father will answer any prayer offered by several people when they pray for the same thing.

What different forms can our prayer together take? – We do not always have to use words. Sometimes we can just sit quietly with a group of people, with each of us sharing our thoughts and feelings with Jesus. We might sing together, or play some beautiful music. All of these are examples of prayer – the important thing is that we *share* them *together*.

ACTIVITY

Cut out several praying figures as given here and have the children colour them. Cut out a larger figure of Jesus and pin him on a board before, arranging the praying figures in a circle around him. Add the caption 'Jesus is with us always.'

CREED

CLOSING PRAYER

Lord Jesus, we know that at this moment
you are here with us.
As brothers and sisters in God's family,
we ask you to listen to and answer
the prayers we bring before you today.

(Either pause for a few moments of silence, or encourage the children to share anything that they might want everyone to pray for.)

JESUS IS WITH US ALWAYS

Twenty-fourth Sunday of the Year

Be forgiving

INTRODUCTION

Jesus taught us that if we wanted God to forgive us, then we must first learn to forgive each other. In today's Gospel, he tells a parable about a forgiving King and his unforgiving servant.

SIGN OF THE CROSS

LIGHT THE CANDLES

Light the candles and sing the Candle Song together.

SORRY

When we forgive someone, or they forgive us, we lose our feelings of anger and hurt; we no longer want to pay them back; we become friends again! Jesus showed us how to forgive others and how he would forgive us. (The children should join in the response to the prayer.)

If I have hurt anyone by what I have said or done.
Jesus I am sorry.
If I have ignored someone or made them feel unloved.
Jesus I am sorry.
If I have been unforgiving and full of anger.
Jesus I am sorry.

GLORIA

GOSPEL ACCLAMATION

To welcome today's Gospel sing Acclamation 3: *Alleluia, alleluia.*

GOSPEL (cf Matthew 18:23-35)

One day Jesus said, 'There was once a king who had many servants. One servant owed the king a great deal of money, but he had nothing to pay him with. 'I will sell you and your family as slaves, and use the money to pay for your debts,' said the King.

The servant fell to his knees and begged for another chance, 'Somehow I will repay everything I owe,' he pleaded. The King was a kind and generous man and, taking pity on the servant, cancelled his debts and let him go.

Later that day, the servant met another man who owed him a small amount of money. When he could not pay what he owed, the servant had him thrown into jail.

When the news reached the king, he sent for the unforgiving servant.

'Could you not forgive someone just as I forgave you?' he asked. Then he had the servant thrown into prison until he could pay back all that he owed the king. Jesus said, 'Just as my Father forgives you, so you must be ready to forgive others with all your heart.'

DISCUSSION

Why was the servant in trouble with the King?

At first what did the King do?

What did he do instead? – Even though the servant owed him a great deal of money, he completely forgave his debt and gave him the chance to make a fresh start.

Did the servant show the same forgiveness towards the man who owed him some money? – He quickly forgot the good example shown by the king and what a difference the king's mercy had made to his life.

What happened to the unforgiving servant? – The angry king had him thrown into jail until he could repay all that he owed.

What message does Jesus give us in this parable? – That we must be ready to forgive others, however large or small their wrongdoing, if we want to be forgiven ourselves.

God will always forgive us but in the same way he expects us to show the same mercy to others.

ACTIVITY

Photocopy the series of pictures telling today's parable. After colouring, pin them on a board for the children to look at and discuss.

CREED

CLOSING PRAYER

Jesus taught us a prayer that mentions how we must forgive others when we ask forgiveness ourselves. Listen closely to the words that speak of forgiveness:
Our Father . . .

Twenty-fifth Sunday of the Year
Workers in the vineyard

INTRODUCTION
Not everyone comes to know Jesus early in their lives, for some it might happen only at the end of a lifetime. But Jesus is loving and generous, and today we learn that those who follow him will receive the same reward at the end of time – everlasting life.

SIGN OF THE CROSS

LIGHT THE CANDLES
As we look at the brightness of the candle flames and prepare to listen to God's word, we remember the words of *Psalm 119:*
Your word Lord is a light for my path, a lamp to guide me closer to you.

SORRY
Listen to this story written by a wise man called Micah *(cf Micah 6:8-9):*

God our Father has told us what we must do: be fair and honest in all we do and say; be loving and caring towards others. If we do this, then our friendship with God will last forever.

Encourage the children to close their eyes and listen to the words of this prayer:
Forgive, us Lord, when we have let you down, when we have forgotten
that whatever we have done to others,
we have done to you.
Fill us with the spirit of your love and goodness,
So that we can change our hearts and try again.

GLORIA

GOSPEL ACCLAMATION
To welcome today's Gospel sing Acclamation 1:
Share your word with us.

GOSPEL *(cf Matthew 20:1-15)*
Jesus said to his disciples, 'Early one morning the owner of a vineyard went to hire some men to work for him. He agreed to pay each of them one pound per day.

Late that afternoon he saw some other men who had not worked all day because no-one had hired them. He sent them to his vineyard too and they set to work for him.

At the end of the day he paid each of the workers one pound as he had promised. Some of them began to grumble. 'Why have you paid these men the same as us, when we have worked all day in the hot sun, and they have only worked for an hour?' they said. The owner of the vineyard answered, 'We agreed that each of you would be paid one pound per day, and I have been fair. I can choose how to spend my money, so don't complain because I have been generous.'

DISCUSSION
Do you know what a vineyard is? – It is land which is used for growing grape vines. Jesus often made up stories about vineyards to help explain about the way he wanted us to live. The vineyard was likened to the world, and the workers in the vineyard are ourselves. We work in the world bringing the Good News to the people.

What sort of work would need to be done in a vineyard? – When the bunches of grapes were ripe, they would have to be picked and washed carefully. Some of the grapes might be used for treading, so that their juices could be turned into wine. Some of the grapes might be dried in the sun to make raisins. For the vines to produce a good crop of grapes they needed careful watering, weeding and pruning – so there was always plenty of work to do.

How much did the owner of the vineyard agree to pay his workers?

At the end of the day's work, why did some of them grumble? – They felt that it was unfair of the owner to pay the same amount to all of them, when some had worked longer and harder than others. They could not understand his generosity.

What do you think the message is in this story? – Jesus is like the vineyard owner, going out looking for us, his workers and giving us the chance to come and join him. Even if we arrive 'late in the day', and take a long time in our lives to come to know him, we will all receive the same reward, everlasting life with him in heaven.

ACTIVITY
Draw a grapevine on a large sheet of paper. Cut out bunches of grapes and leaves write the individual words of the following caption on some of the bunches: 'Jesus is always generous.' After colouring, the bunches of grapes and leaves can then be fixed onto the vine so that they can be read.

CREED

CLOSING PRAYER
Lord, you are always generous and kind,
Fill us with the generosity of your love
and make us more understanding.

Twenty-sixth Sunday of the Year
Making choices

INTRODUCTION
Every day of our lives we have to make choices. Sometimes we make the wrong choice, and do something we shouldn't. Remember that whenever we have had a change of heart, Jesus is always ready to give us another chance to put things right.

SIGN OF THE CROSS

LIGHT THE CANDLES
As we light the candles, listen carefully to the words of this prayer:
Dear Lord Jesus, hear me do,
help me find my way to you.
Help me choose not bad, but good,
as you tell me, Lord, I should.
Help me do no wrong, but right,
shining always with your light.

SORRY
Ask one of the children to choose a sorry colour.

GLORIA

GOSPEL ACCLAMATION
To welcome today's Gospel sing Acclamation 4: *Praise the Lord*

GOSPEL (cf Matthew 21:28-32.)
Jesus told this story to the high priests: 'Once there was a man who had two sons. He said to the older one, 'Go and work in the vineyard today,' but the son answered, 'I will not go because I don't want to.' Later the son changed his mind and went to work after all.

When the man asked his other son to go and work in his vineyard too, he said, 'Of course I will go,' but he did not do what he said he would.

Jesus asked the high priests, 'Which of these sons did what their father wanted?'

'The older one of course,' they replied.

Jesus said to them, 'The people you call sinners will enter God's kingdom before any of you, because they listened and believed what John the Baptist told them. You would not listen and believe, and your hearts have not changed.'

DISCUSSION
Did the older son do what his father wanted straight away? – At first he chose to do what he wanted and not what he knew was right. Later he felt bad about this choice, had a change of heart and went to work in the vineyard.

What did the second son do? – Although at first he agreed to go and work, he chose to ignore what his father had asked, and do what he wanted instead.

Why did Jesus compare the older son with the people the high priests called sinners? – These people had made bad choices in their lives and done the wrong thing. But they listened to John the Baptist's message, and like the older son they realised that they were wrong. They too had a change of heart and tried to do what was right.

Why were the high priests like the second son? – They heard John the Baptist's message but had not listened to it. They were not ready to admit that they had made the wrong choices in their lives, or to ask for God's forgiveness. Their hearts were not ready to change and they were not willing to live as Jesus showed them.

What is the message of this parable? – Even if we get things wrong and make foolish choices, God will always give us a second chance to make things right again, if we have a change of heart. By making the right choices in our lives, we will be welcomed into the kingdom of God.

ACTIVITY
Give each child a copy of the maze so they can find the way to God's kingdom.

CREED

CLOSING PRAYER
Lord, when I choose the way to go,
help me choose the good way.
When I choose the things to say,
help me say what you'd say.
Help me always do what's right;
keep me always in your sight.

Twenty-seventh Sunday of the Year
Listen to God's message

INTRODUCTION
Jesus came to share the Good News and to bring God's message to all people. He wanted them to learn how to live in the love of God and one's neighbour, and to know what mattered most in life. Many people did not listen, and so Jesus told them that he would give his message to others.

SIGN OF THE CROSS

LIGHT THE CANDLES
Listen carefully to the words of this reading from the Book of Proverbs as we light our candles. (cf Proverbs 4:18-19)

The path to our heavenly Father is like the rising sun, getting brighter and brighter as we draw closer to God. Those who turn away from his love, follow a path as dark as the night, and they stumble and fall because they cannot see the way.

SORRY
Sing Sorry Song 4:
When we say that we are sorry.

GLORIA

GOSPEL ACCLAMATION
(The children can join in and say the alleluia's)
Alleluia, Alleluia
Lord, open our ears and hearts, so we will hear and understand the message of your Gospel.
Alleluia, Alleluia.

GOSPEL (cf Matthew 21:33-43)
Jesus told another parable to the people: 'There was once a farmer who owned a vineyard. He had to go away on business, and so he put some farm workers in charge of the vineyard. When it was time to harvest the grapes, the farmer sent some servants to collect his share. But the farm workers beat his servants and chased them away. The farmer did not give up, and sent more servants to collect what belonged to him. Again, they were beaten and chased off. Finally the farmer sent his own son, 'I am sure that they will treat him better,' he said. Instead the farm workers seized the son and killed him.'

Then Jesus asked, 'What will the farmer do when he arrives at the vineyard?'

The people who had been listening answered, 'He will punish the farm workers and put other people in charge of his vineyard.'

DISCUSSION
Imagine if the vineyard was the whole world.

Who would be in charge of it all? God made the world, and everything belongs to him. In the story he is like the farmer. God trusts us to take care of what we have been given, just as the farmer trusted the farm workers.

What happened when the farmer sent his servants with a message? – The farm workers were not willing to listen to the message. They were greedy and selfish and they chased the servants away.

In the Old Testament, God sent many of his servants with messages for the people. What were they called? Do you remember any of their names? – They were called prophets, and they were sent by God to tell the people to turn back to God and lead lives full of God's goodness and love. Some of the greatest prophets were Jeremiah, Isaiah and Ezekiel.

Do you think people treated the prophets as badly as the farm workers treated the servants in the story? – Often the message of a prophet was ignored or the people refused to believe it, and sometimes they too were chased away.

In the parable, the farmer was compared with God the Father. Who do you think we can compare with the farmer's son? – God the Father sent his only son, Jesus, to carry his message, just as the farmer in the story sent his son. Many heard his message and turned back to God, but some refused to listen and believe, some even put Jesus to death. Just as the vineyard would be taken from the farm workers who would not listen to the master's message, so the kingdom of God will be taken from those who do not listen to God's message, and given to others who listen and live according to God's way.

ACTIVITY
Help each child to make a face which reminds us how important it is to use our senses to understand the message Jesus shared.

CREED

CLOSING PRAYER
Jesus, open our ears to hear your message
and help us to understand it.
Help us to share the message
of your saving love with others,
so that they too can share in your kingdom.

MAKE A FACE

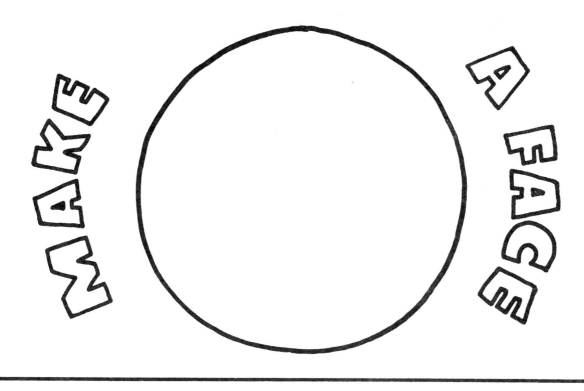

Twenty-eighth Sunday of the Year

The wedding party

INTRODUCTION
God gives each one of us an invitation to join him in his heavenly kingdom and the celebration of everlasting life. We must choose whether to accept the invitation or turn away from his loving offer.

SIGN OF THE CROSS

LIGHT THE CANDLES
As the candles are lit we say together: May the light of God's love shine in our lives.

SORRY
Lord help us to be good, and forgive us if we have failed to do what is right.
Sing Sorry Song 1: *Dear Lord Jesus*

GLORIA

GOSPEL ACCLAMATION
To welcome today's Gospel sing Acclamation 2: *Light up our hearts.*

GOSPEL (cf Matthew 22:1-14)
One day Jesus said, 'The kingdom of heaven is like this:
A king planned a great party for his son's wedding. When everything was ready, he sent his servants to tell all the guests who had been invited to come and join in the celebrations, but each of them had an excuse for not coming. The king was furious and said to his servants, 'These people do not deserve to share in my party, so go out and invite everyone you meet, they can come to the wedding instead!' Soon the hall was filled with people, good and bad alike. The king noticed one man who had not bothered to dress for the occasion. He sent for his servants and the man was thrown out into the dark.'

DISCUSSION
If you want people to come to your birthday party, what do you give or send to them?
What sort of things do you tell them on the invitation?
- the date
- the place
- the time
- what to wear, for example it might be fancy dress or a silly hats party.

Imagine if everything was ready for your party –
the cake, the games, the bouncy castle, but when you went to collect your guests no-one wanted to come. How would you feel?

In the story, what did the king do when no-one who had been invited came to the wedding celebration? – He invited everybody to the party. In the same way God invites all of us into the kingdom of Heaven. If we refuse to accept his invitation we are like the guests who refused to come to the King's celebration.

Why was the man at the end of the story asked to leave? – He had accepted the King's invitation, but he had not bothered to make the effort to dress for the occasion. If we accept God's invitation to join him in the kingdom of Heaven, then we must make the effort to do what is right and follow God's way or we cannot become part of the final celebration at the end of time.

ACTIVITY
Either give each child a copy of an invitation to fill in and complete
OR
ask them to draw a picture of the wedding party.

CREED

CLOSING PRAYER
Lord Jesus,
you invite each one of us
to enter the kingdom of Heaven.
Help us to make the effort
to do things God's way,
so that we can accept your offer
and be ready to share in your glory
at the end of time.

INVITATION

Dear_ _ _ _ _ _ _ _ _

I invite you to follow me
and to share in the
celebration of God's glory
at the end of time

Love from Jesus

REPLY

Dear_ _ _ _ _ _ _ _

Thankyou for inviting me
to follow you so that I
can share in the joy of
your kingdom

Love from_ _ _ _ _

Twenty-ninth Sunday of the Year
Give to God what belongs to God

INTRODUCTION
Everything we have was given to us by God, who pours out his love for us with unending generosity. How often do we remember to say 'Thank you' or to return just a little of what we have been given?

SIGN OF THE CROSS

LIGHT THE CANDLES
As the candles are lit, read this prayer to the children:
If we keep our eyes on the light,
we need never feel afraid,
Jesus will walk before us,
guiding us through life
towards the kingdom of Heaven.

SORRY
Lord Jesus we want to love others,
and to live as you did, but it is not easy
and often we make mistakes.
Help us to choose
to do what pleases God,
and to put things right
if we have done wrong.
(Allow the children a few moments to talk to God quietly themselves).

GLORIA

GOSPEL ACCLAMATION
Alleluia, Alleluia
Lord, help us to listen carefully to your word today. Open our ears and hearts so that we will hear and understand your message.
Alleluia, Alleluia.

GOSPEL (cf Matthew 22:15-21)
The Pharisees wanted to trick Jesus into saying something which would get him into trouble. So they went to him and said, 'We know that you are honest and are not afraid to speak the truth. Tell us then, should we give our money to the Romans or to God?'

Jesus answered, 'Why do you want to trick me? Show me your money.' They gave him a Roman denarius and he asked them, 'Who is the person on this coin?' 'Caesar,' they answered.

Then Jesus said, 'Give back to Caesar what belongs to him, and give to God what is God's.'

DISCUSSION
At the time when Jesus was born, the Romans had ruled over the land of Palestine for about sixty years. The Romans needed many soldiers to keep law and order, because the Jews were very unhappy under Roman rule. The Jews were most upset by the very high taxes which they had to pay to the Romans.

How did the Pharisees try to trick Jesus? – They were jealous of Jesus because he was so popular with the people and he often criticised the Pharisees. They hoped to get Jesus into trouble with the Romans, they were expecting him to tell the people to give their money to God and not to the Romans. Anyone who did not pay their taxes was immediately arrested and punished.

What did Jesus ask them to do? – He asked them to show him a Roman coin, which was called a denarius. Just as we have the leader of our country on our coins, so a picture of the ruling Emperor was depicted on each Roman coin.

Can you remember the name of the Roman Emperor at that time?

Whose head is shown on the coins in this country?

(If you have any foreign coins, allow the children to look at these and compare them with British coins. Show the children any pictures you can find of Roman coins particularly those with a picture of Caesar).

Did Jesus tell the people to stop giving their money in taxes to the Romans?

Jesus answered this trick question wisely. He told the people to give back to Caesar what belonged to him. But at the same time giving back to God what belonged to God.

If not money, what do you think Jesus wanted the people to give to God? – He wanted them to return the love which God gave to them. We too can share everything with our heavenly Father by giving him the gift of ourselves; all that we are and all that we have.

ACTIVITY
Ask the children to think of one everyday thing which they could offer to God as a sign of their love for him. It could be tidying a room, spending time with someone, making someone smile or saying a prayer. Ask them to draw a picture of whatever they choose and pin it on the board with the caption 'We offer our lives to God.'

CREED

CLOSING PRAYER
Father in heaven I give you today,
all that I think, and do, and say.
Fill me with grace and make me strong,
with you at my side I won't go wrong.

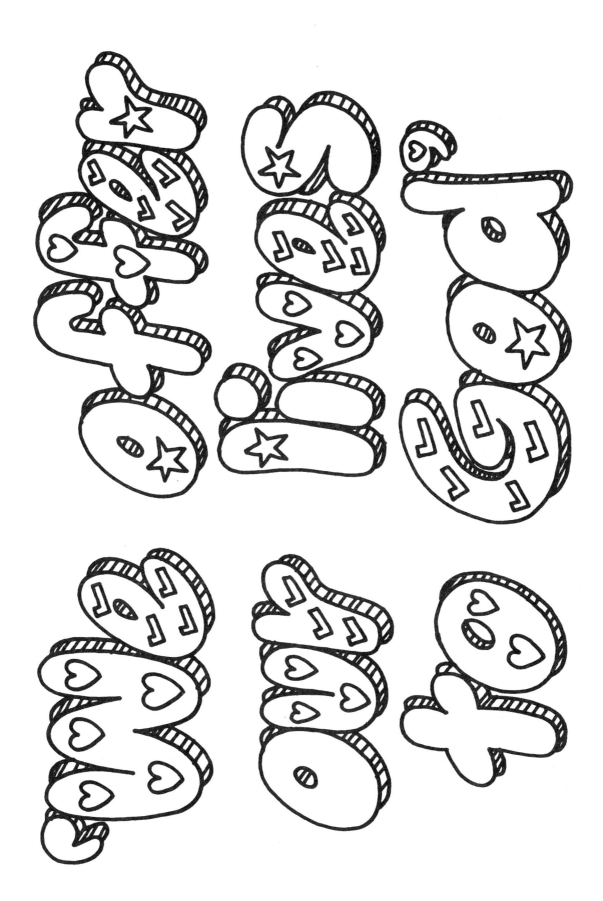

Thirtieth Sunday of the Year
Living love

INTRODUCTION
Jesus taught us to love God and to love each other more than anything else in our lives.

SIGN OF THE CROSS

LIGHT THE CANDLES
Jesus,
help us to listen to your word today.
And let the light of your love
shine out like these candles,
touching the lives of everyone we meet.

SORRY
When we fall, we pick ourselves up again and carry on as before. As we journey through life, sometimes we get things wrong, we make mistakes, we stumble and fall. Jesus is always there to help us up, so we can carry on.
Sing Sorry Song 4: *When we say that we are sorry.*

GLORIA

GOSPEL ACCLAMATION
To welcome today's Gospel sing Acclamation 1: *Share your word with us.*

GOSPEL (*cf Matthew 22:34-40*)
Again the Pharisees asked Jesus a question which was meant to trick him. 'Which of the commandments is the greatest?' they asked.

Jesus answered 'You must love God with all your might; this is the first and most important commandment. The second greatest commandment is also about love – loving your neighbour as yourself. All the other rules are based on these two commandments.'

DISCUSSION
God gave Moses ten commandments to help his people to lead lives pleasing to God. Can you remember any of them?

(See *Sixth Sunday of Year A.*)

Which two commandments did Jesus say are the most important?

When Jesus talked about loving our 'neighbours', did he mean the people living next door to us? – Our neighbours are not only the people we know well, our friends and those that we like. They include the people we meet by chance every day of our lives; each one of these is a neighbour.

Why do you think Jesus chose these two commandments above all the others? – The kingdom of God is the most priceless jewel, and knowing Jesus is the most precious treasure of all. This means putting the love of God and our neighbour before everything else in our lives. By loving God all we can, each of us becomes more loving in turn, and ready to share that love with each other.

Jesus *showed* us how to love God and our neighbour. He put his words of love into *action* every day, and this is what he wants us to do.

Saint Paul wrote a letter to the Christians who lived in the Greek city of Corinth, to remind them of the perfect love which Jesus had shared with everyone (*cf 1. Corinthians 13:4-7*):
Love never hurries, it is always kind.
It is not jealous, and never boasts of its greatness.
Love is not rude or selfish.
It is always ready to forgive
and forget mistakes we make.
Love is no friend of wickedness,
but delights in honesty and truth.
Love is strong and never gives up.
It never loses its trust in God
or its hope for the future.
Love will survive all things because it is everlasting.

If we remember to put these words into action, then we will be putting the two greatest commandments into *action* in our lives.

ACTIVITY
Photocopy the words of St Paul for each child to decorate and take home with them.

CREED

CLOSING PRAYER
Lord,
I have only one life,
and shall not live this day again.
Help me to remember
that everyone is my neighbour.
If I can do something good
or show my kindness,
then help me to do it today,
for unless love is shared it cannot grow.

Love never hurries, it is always kind.
It is not jealous, and never boasts of its greatness.
Love is not rude or selfish.
It is always ready to forgive and forget mistakes we make.
Love is no friend of wickedness, but delights in honesty and truth.
Love is strong and never gives up.
It never loses its trust in God or its hope for the future.
Love will survive all things because it is everlasting.

Thirty-first Sunday of the Year
Practise what you preach

INTRODUCTION
The Pharisees were the leaders of the Jewish people. They studied the scriptures and were very proud that they obeyed the Jewish law. The ordinary people looked to the Pharisees for good example, but Jesus told his followers that they did not 'practise what they preached.'

SIGN OF THE CROSS

LIGHT THE CANDLES
Light the candles and sing the Candle Song together.

SORRY
Close your eyes and listen to this reading (cf Psalm 14:2-3):
Lord those who turn away from you do wrong,
those who are wise worship you,
Lord you see all that we do,
help us to do what is right.

(Allow the children a few moments to think about these words before reading the following slowly:)

If we have chosen the wrong way,
and made a mistake,
(All) Lord have mercy.
If we have forgotten to share your love with others,
(All) Christ have mercy.
If we have spoiled our friendship with you
and made you sad,
(All) Lord have mercy.

GLORIA

GOSPEL ACCLAMATION
To welcome today's Gospel sing Acclamation 5:
We have come to hear you.

GOSPEL (cf Matthew 23:1-12)
Jesus said to the crowds, 'Listen to what the Pharisees tell you and do what they say, but do not copy what they do. They do not put their words into actions or practise what they preach. They are full of self-importance and pride and you must not follow their example. Only God is important and you must be ready to serve him and one another.'

DISCUSSION
Jesus said that the Pharisees did not 'practise what they preached'. What does this mean? – The Pharisees did not match what they said with what they did. They told everyone what the law said they must do, but then they did not do it themselves. They did not put the words that they preached into action.

We still use this saying today, because we are all very good at telling everyone else what they should do, but we aren't very good at actually doing it ourselves.

Can you think of examples in everyday life when people don't 'practise what they preach'?
– when you visit a friends house to play, you might remind them that they should share a precious toy, but you don't share your favourite toys at home.
– if someone else does something wrong you expect them to say sorry straight away, but are you always ready to say sorry when you get it wrong yourself?

If we tell someone else what they should do then we should be ready to do that thing ourselves. Can you think of any examples of putting your words into action and actually 'practising what you preach'?
– before telling your younger sister or brother to keep their toys tidy, make sure your own toys are tidy.
– if we tell our friends to be honest, then when we find some money in the playground, we should hand it to the teacher, and not put it in our own pocket.

Jesus wanted us to understand that if we want to share the message of his love with others, then it is important for us to do what we say, and show our goodness by our actions. By showing others how much we care for each other, our words are not just empty sounds, they are put into loving action.

ACTIVITY
Hand out the photocopied sheet. Talk about the pictures with the children – who is being helpful and kind and who isn't. Can they add a couple of drawings of their own in the space provided?

CREED

CLOSING PRAYER
Jesus,
help us to make our actions
speak louder than our words.
So that others will see
that we belong to Christ
and may believe in you.

Thirty-second Sunday
of the Year
Be ready

INTRODUCTION

It is easy to be ready for something to happen when we know the day and time to expect it. Today Jesus explains that we must always be ready for his return, even though no-one knows when he will be coming.

SIGN OF THE CROSS

LIGHT THE CANDLES

Light the candles and say Candle Prayer 1: *Flicker, flicker little candle.*

SORRY

Close your eyes and listen to this prayer as you say 'sorry' quietly in your heart:

Jesus, open our hearts
and make us more loving.
Help us to change our ways
and make a fresh start.
If we have hurt you or other people
by being unkind or selfish,
we ask for your forgiveness.

GLORIA

GOSPEL ACCLAMATION

To welcome today's Gospel sing Acclamation 2: *Light up our hearts.*

GOSPEL (cf Matthew 25:1-13)

One day Jesus told this parable: 'Ten bridesmaids were getting ready for a wedding, and together they went to greet the bridegroom, although they were not sure when he would come, or how how long they would have to wait. Five of them were sensible girls who brought flasks of oil to refill their lamps; the other girls did not. The bridegroom was late, and after waiting all afternoon and all evening, the bridesmaids finally fell asleep. It was already midnight when somebody cried, 'The bridegroom is coming! Quickly go and greet him!' The wise bridesmaids refilled their lamps and went to meet him, but the lamps of the foolish girls had gone out, and they had to go off to buy more oil. When they returned, the bridegroom and the five bridesmaids had already gone into the wedding hall.'

DISCUSSION

Has anyone ever been a bridesmaid at a wedding?

What did you wear and what did you do?

In the parable, who were the ten bridesmaids waiting for? – They were waiting to greet the bridegroom when he arrived, and to show him the way to the wedding hall. The bridegroom and bride are the ones who are getting married, becoming man and wife, so he is a very special person at the wedding.

Did they know when he would arrive? – They knew that he was coming, but they did not know the exact time he would arrive.

Why were the wise bridesmaids ready for his coming and the foolish bridesmaids not? – The five sensible girls knew that the bridegroom could arrive at any time – day or night! They brought flasks of oil for their lamps, in case the bridegroom was late, and their lamps had burned low. The foolish bridesmaids did not think ahead and brought no extra oil for their lamps. When the bridegroom suddenly arrived, they were not ready to meet him, and by the time they had filled their lamps, the bridegroom had already come and gone.

Jesus uses parables to give us a message. What do you think today's message is? – Jesus uses this story to tell us that we must always *be ready*. Like the bridesmaids, we know that Jesus will come again, but we do not know the exact day or time. The wise bridesmaids kept themselves ready so that they were not taken by surprise when the bridegroom finally arrived.

How can we keep ourselves ready for when Jesus returns? – If we can live each day as well as possible, and make each day our best, then we will always be ready to greet Jesus when he comes. By trying to be good and to live as Jesus taught us, ready to say sorry when we get things wrong and to forgive others, then we will be like the wise bridesmaids who kept their lamps burning, and be ready for Jesus when he comes.

ACTIVITY

Make the moving models of the lamp as shown. You may find it helpful to photocopy onto thin card.

CREED

CLOSING PRAYER

Lord Jesus,
we know that one day you will return
and we will be with you in heaven.
Help us to make each day our best,
so that we will always be ready
to greet you.

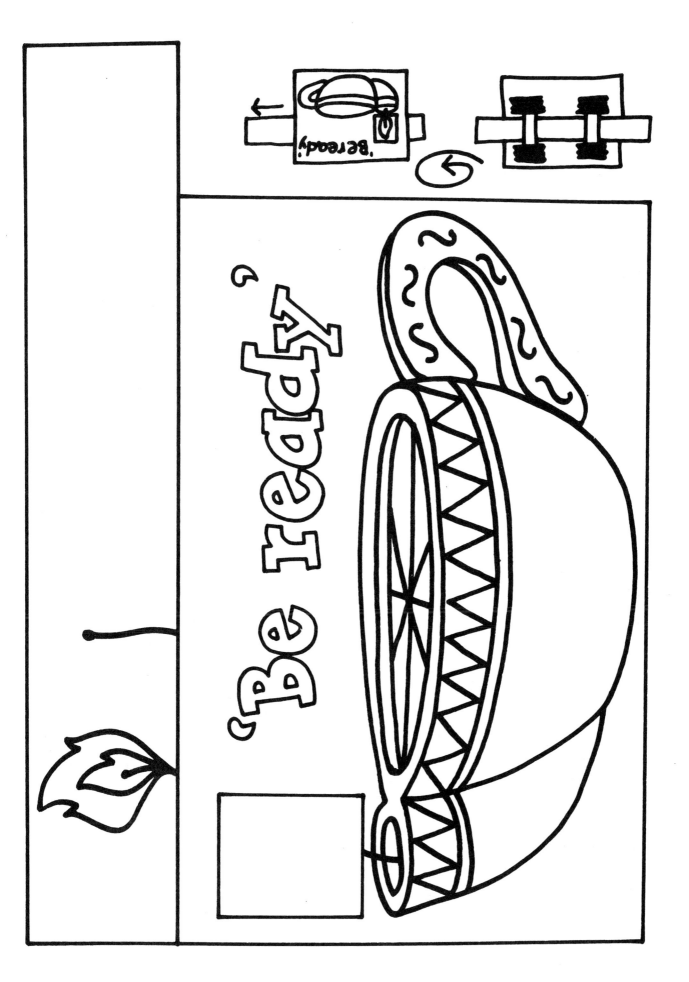

Thirty-third Sunday of the Year
Gifts from God

INTRODUCTION
When we love someone, sometimes we give them a gift, something special for them to use and enjoy. God has given talents to each one of us as a sign of his love; these are gifts from God.

SIGN OF THE CROSS

LIGHT THE CANDLES
Light the candles, and then read (cf Revelation 22:5):
One day there will be no more darkness, no more night. No one will need lamps or the light from the sun. God will light up the darkness with glory and they will see clearly forever.

SORRY
Ask a child to choose a sorry colour. The corresponding Sorry Prayer can be read by them or the group can say the prayer together.

GLORIA

GOSPEL ACCLAMATION
(The talents described in St Matthews Gospel were large units of money used at that time. To avoid confusing the children, the Gospel adaptation refers to the talents given to us by God, using the other sense of the word 'talent' as a skill or gift for doing something. This has been done to help make the Gospel clearer and avoid ambiguity.)
To welcome today's Gospel sing Acclamation 3: *Alleluia, alleluia.*

GOSPEL (cf Matthew 25:14-30)
One day Jesus said: 'Once there were three men who had each been given different numbers of talents. The first man had five, the second man, three and the third, one. They were free to use these talents however they wished. The first man used his talents well and doubled them; the second man also worked hard and used what he had been given wisely, but the third man felt that he had little to offer, so he hid his talent away from everyone and did not use it. The time came to meet the one who had given each of them their talents, and they told him in turn how they had used them. He was very pleased with the first and second men, but not with the third man who had wasted what he had been given.'

DISCUSSION
If we say that someone has a talent, what do we mean? – We mean that they have a special gift or skill for doing something.

In the story Jesus told, each man was given a number of talents. Who gives us our talents? – Any gifts or talents we have, have been given to us by God our Father.

Tell me about some of the talents which God has given to each of you. Encourage the children to talk about one thing which they do well, for example:
– swimming; making people laugh; singing; dancing; being thoughtful; playing a musical instrument; reading.

In the story can you remember what the men did with their talents? – Two of them used their talents well and made them grow and multiply. The other man kept his talent hidden from everyone and did not share it.

What does God want us to do with the talents he has given us? – When someone gives us a present, they love to see us using it and getting pleasure from it. Our talents are gifts from God, given to us because he loves us. They are very precious and must not be wasted, but instead be put to good use.

What will we be asked at the end of time? – Like the men in the parable, God will ask us what we have done with the talents he gave us. Did we use them wisely, sharing them with others for the good of all; or did we hide them away selfishly, without allowing them to grow?

ACTIVITY
Either: cut out a variety of parcel shapes – enough for more than one each, and ask the children to colour them so that they look like wrapped gift boxes. Or: gift wrap some mini packets of sweets (these can be bought loose). Then give each child a label on which to write one of their own talents before attaching it to a box. These can be pinned to a board or carried up in a basket with the caption 'Our gifts from God'.

CREED

CLOSING PRAYER
Heavenly Father, we thank you for the talents which you have given to each of us.
Whatever our gifts may be,
teach us to use them wisely,
and for the good of others.

The Feast of Christ the King
Christ is King

INTRODUCTION
Today is the last Sunday of the Church's year, the Feast of Christ the King. As the year draws to an end, we turn our thoughts to when Christ will return as king at the end of time.

SIGN OF THE CROSS

LIGHT THE CANDLES
Say together:
May the light of Jesus shine in our lives.

SORRY
Listen to this reading (*cf Psalm 34:11-14*):
Listen to me little ones, and you will learn
to please God.
If you want a life filled with happiness and joy,
turn away from wickedness and lies.
Surround yourself with goodness,
and try with all your heart
to share the Peace
of God with others.

We ask God's forgiveness for any mistakes we have made as we pray:
Pick me up Lord,
if I have made a mistake
and fallen again.
Take my hand
and surround me with your goodness
so that I can try again.

GLORIA

GOSPEL ACCLAMATION
To welcome today's Gospel sing this Acclamation (to the tune of *Hickory, Dickory, Dock.*)

Christ is the King of the world,
One day he will come back
And we will see his full glory,
Christ is the King of the world.

GOSPEL (*cf Matthew 25:31-46*)
Jesus told his disciples: 'One day I will return in glory to sort the good people from the bad, and I will turn to you and say:
when I was hungry, you fed me,
when I was thirsty, you gave me a drink,
when you did not know me, you made me welcome,
when I had nothing to wear, you gave me clothes,
when I was ill, you took care of me,
when I was alone, you came to visit me.

And you will ask, 'When did I do all these things for you, Lord?' I tell you, whenever you did any of these things for others you did them for me, and because of your goodness you will share in the glory of my kingdom. Those people who turned others away, and did not care, did the same to me. On Judgement Day they will be sent away, never to share eternal life with me in heaven.

DISCUSSION
Who will return at the end of time? – Jesus will come back at the end of time as 'Christ the King.'

Imagine all the nations of the world standing before Jesus. How will he sort the good people from the bad? – Jesus knows each one of us better than we know ourselves – even down to the number of hairs on our head! He remembers all the times we have been kind and the times when we have been selfish. He will sort out the good people from the bad, according to the lives they have led, and whether they have been loving or unloving people.

What did Christ promise to everyone who lived their lives trying to love others as he had taught them? – If we have lived for Christ, then we will share the joy of everlasting life and happiness with him in the kingdom of Heaven.

What will happen to the people who turned away from Jesus and his love? – At the end of time they will be turned away from the kingdom of Heaven.

How can we make sure that we are sorted with the good people, and not the bad, on judgement day? – No one is good all the time, but we can make our loving actions outweigh the unloving ones. If we fill our lives with love and kindness, seeing Jesus in each person we meet and always treating others with kindness and respect, then our goodness will never be forgotten.

ACTIVITY
Draw some large old-fashioned scales tilting heavily to one side. On squares of paper write some loving and unloving actions. Ask the children to colour these and place them on the relevant side of the scales. Add the caption, 'Christ will weigh up our goodness.'

CREED

CLOSING PRAYER
Lord Jesus Christ, King of the universe,
watch over us and guide us.
Help us to remember that whatever we do to others,
we do to you.

CHRIST WILL WEIGH UP OUR GOODNESS

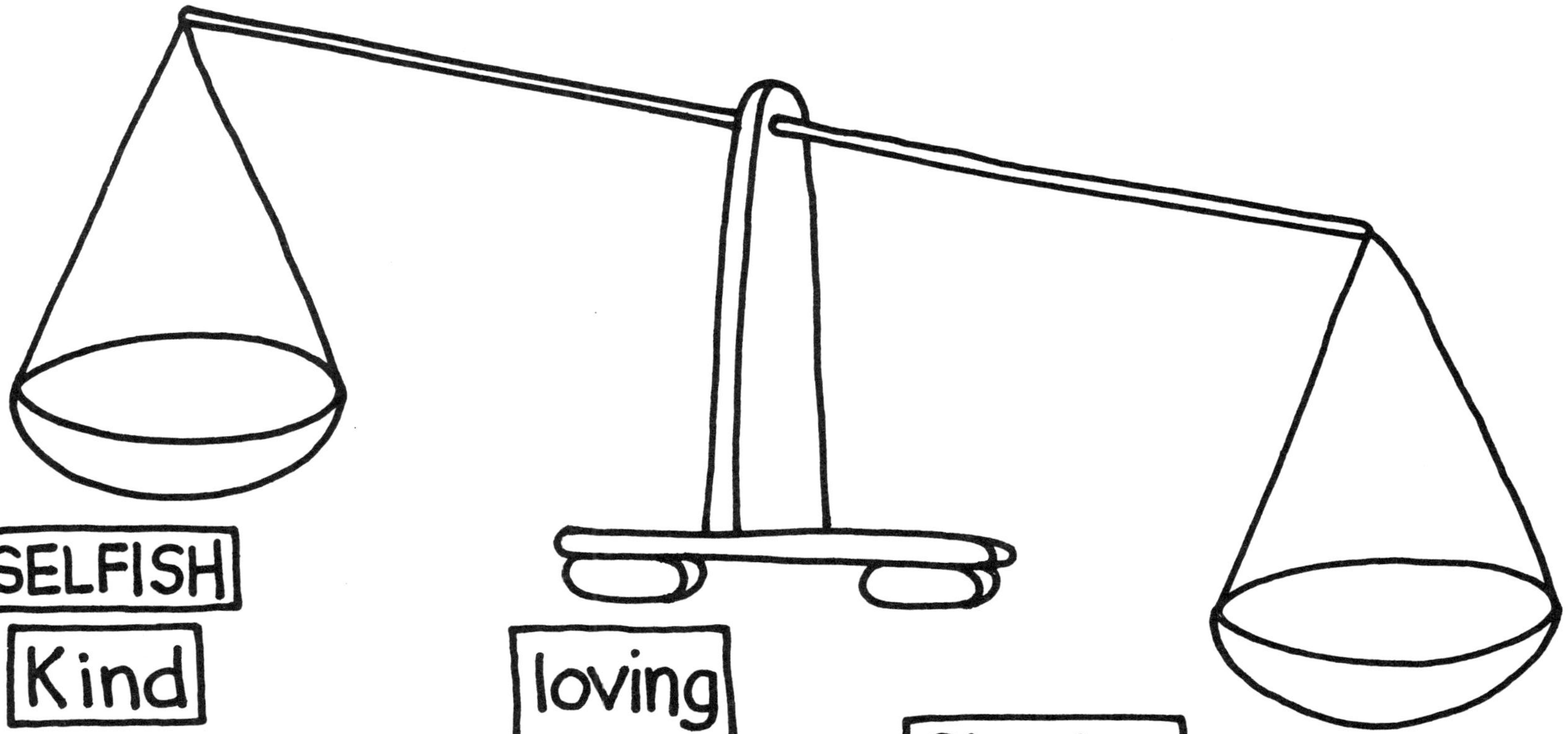

GENEROUS

Sharing

Unkind

loving

greedy

HONEST

SELFISH

Kind

Unforgiving

Forgiving

Solemnity of Saints Peter and Paul

Peter and Paul

INTRODUCTION

Today we celebrate the Feast of Saints Peter and Paul. St Peter was the 'rock' on which Jesus built his Church; his faith was a great source of strength for the early Christians. St Paul was a missionary, whose aim in life was to share the Good News that had transformed his life. Together they were the greatest leaders of the early Church.

SIGN OF THE CROSS

LIGHT THE CANDLES

Light the candles and then read (*cf Matthew 6:16-17*):

Jesus said, 'Let your goodness shine out like a light in the darkness, so that through you, the love of our heavenly Father will touch the lives of others.'

SORRY

Ask the children to close their eyes and make the words of this prayer their own:

Father, forgive us if we have hurt anyone
by our thoughts or actions,
and help us to forgive
those who have hurt us.
We ask this through Jesus our Lord.

GLORIA

GOSPEL ACCLAMATION

To welcome today's Gospel sing Acclamation 2: *Light up our hearts.*

GOSPEL (*cf Matthew 16:13-19*)

One day, Jesus asked his disciples, 'Who do people think I am?'

'Some say you are John the Baptist, others say the Prophet Elijah,' they answered. Jesus turned to his friends and said, 'Who do you think I am?'

Peter answered, 'You are the son of God!' Jesus smiled and said, 'Peter, you are a happy man, because my heavenly Father revealed this to you. You are the rock on which I will build my Church.'

DISCUSSION

What did Peter do for a living before he became a disciple of Jesus? – He was a fisherman, who many believe lived in Capernaum by the Sea of Galilee.

Why was Peter chosen as leader of the early Church? – Peter had been with Jesus since the very beginning of his ministry, and he had witnessed all the marvellous things that Jesus had said and done. He *knew* that Jesus was the son of God, and in this way God chose him to be the shepherd of his flock on earth.

What do we know about St Paul? – Paul was a Jewish Pharisee, and was well educated and very religious. He lived in the city of Tarsus, and never actually met Jesus. He wanted to uphold the Jewish law and traditions and so he had many of the followers of Jesus thrown into prison.

What happened to Paul to make him change? – One day, whilst on his way to a place called Damascus, to arrest some Christians, God appeared to Paul as a brilliant light and asked him to stop hurting the followers of Jesus. Paul changed his ways and instead of being one of the greatest enemies of Jesus, he became one of his greatest friends.

Did Peter and Paul know each other? – They eventually met and became good friends when they realised that they were both working for Jesus. They travelled far and wide preaching the Good News about Jesus and sharing the Christian faith with others.

Why do we have a special day when we remember Peter and Paul? – They are the greatest leaders of the early Church, and they spent their lives working endlessly for Jesus. Both of them suffered for their faith and spent time in prison, but even then they continued their work by writing many letters that we can still read today. We remember their courage and faith, and thank them for sharing Christ's message with the world.

ACTIVITY

Copy and colour the pictures of St Peter 'the Fisherman' and St Paul 'the Missionary'.

CREED

CLOSING PRAYER

Lord, give us the faith
and courage of Peter and Paul,
and help us in our own way
to carry the word of God to others.

Peter the Fisherman

Paul the Missionary

The Feast of the Transfiguration of the Lord

The Lord is glorified

INTRODUCTION

Has anything amazing ever happened to you? Something so wonderful that you can hardly describe it? (Encourage the children to share any experiences.) Today we hear how three of Jesus' disciples were amazed by a vision of God's glory on the top of a mountain.

SIGN OF THE CROSS

LIGHT THE CANDLES

As the candles are lit say together:
May the light of Jesus shine in our hearts.

SORRY

Allow the children a short period of contemplation to think about the events of the past few days and to examine their consciences. Choose a 'sorry colour' Prayer and read it together.

GLORIA

GOSPEL ACCLAMATION

To welcome today's Gospel sing Acclamation 2: *Light up our hearts.*

GOSPEL (cf Matthew 17:1-10)

One day Jesus asked Peter, James and John to come and pray with him. He led them to the top of a steep mountain, where it was peaceful and quiet, and they could be alone. Jesus began to pray to his heavenly Father when suddenly he appeared to change! His face and clothes shone with a brilliant light, as dazzling as the rays of the sun. Then the disciples saw Moses and Elijah on either side of Jesus, talking to him. Peter jumped up with excitement and said, 'Lord, this is wonderful! I could make three shelters – one for each of you!' At that moment a cloud streaming with light appeared above them, and a voice said, 'This is my Son, whom I love very much. Listen to what he says.' The disciples were so terrified that they threw themselves to the ground and hid their faces. Then Jesus said gently, 'Get up my friends, do not be afraid.' When they looked up, Jesus was standing alone.

DISCUSSION

What did Peter, James and John see on the mountain top that day?

Jesus was 'transfigured'! This means his appearance changed as his face and clothes shone like the sun.

What happens if the sun shines in our eyes? – We are dazzled by its brightness and the strength of its light. The light shining from Jesus was as bright as the sun. These rays of light were shafts of God's glory, and a glimpse of his power and might.

Can we see or touch the light from the sun? – We cannot look at the sun's light directly because it's brightness is too powerful for our eyes, we 'see' its light when it reflects off the things around us; things which cannot be seen once darkness falls. We cannot 'touch' sunlight, but we can 'feel' the warmth of its rays. So it is with God! We cannot see or touch him directly, but we see him reflected in everything around us, the whole of creation, and we can 'feel' the warmth of his love in our lives.

How do you think the disciples felt that day? – By what they saw and heard that day, they caught a glimpse of God's glory. They were chosen to share a moment of total happiness and wonder. The memory of that vision would fill them with courage and strength, because they knew that Jesus was indeed the son of God.

ACTIVITY

Give out individual letters of the caption 'Help us to see your Glory', to be coloured brightly. Stick these onto a banner, and get the children to decorate it with things which they feel reflect God's glory in the world. Or instead let the children colour in the picture opposite. Stick it onto card to hang on a wall.

CREED

CLOSING PRAYER

Lord God,
help us to see your glory
in the world around us,
and to feel the warmth of your love
which shines on all living things.

Solemnity of the Assumption

Mary is taken into Heaven

INTRODUCTION
Today we celebrate the Feast of the Assumption, when Mary, the mother of Jesus, was taken up into the glory of Heaven.

SIGN OF THE CROSS

LIGHT THE CANDLES
Light the candles and read:
As we light these candles today, help us to remember that Jesus is *alive* and we share his everlasting life.

SORRY
Mary, the mother of Jesus, is also our mother. She is the mother of the whole world. As we ask for God's forgiveness, we hope that with the help of her prayers she will help us in future to be more thoughtful and kind.

If we have hurt anyone by unkind words,
    Lord have Mercy.
If we have acted selfishly or dishonestly,
    Christ have Mercy.
If we have chosen to do the wrong thing instead of what we know is right,
    Lord have Mercy.

GLORIA

GOSPEL ACCLAMATION
To welcome today's Gospel sing Acclamation 1: *Share your word with us.*

GOSPEL (cf Luke 1:39-56)
After the angel Gabriel appeared to Mary, she set off to visit her cousin Elizabeth who was also expecting a baby. When Elizabeth heard Mary arrive, the baby inside her jumped with joy, and Elizabeth was filled with the Holy Spirit. She said to Mary, 'God has blessed you with a special child and I am so lucky to be visited by the mother of my Lord!' Then Mary answered, 'My heart is full of gladness because God has chosen me, and from this day onwards others will know I have been blessed by God. He has done mighty things for me, and holy is his name. The Lord is forgiving and good; he takes care of the poor and feeds the hungry. He has remembered his promise to our people and will rescue them and lead them back to him.'

DISCUSSION
What did God choose Mary to be? – God chose Mary to be the mother of his son Jesus.

What was so special about Mary that she should be chosen above all others to give birth to Jesus? – We are all born with the stain of original sin, which Adam and Eve earned for us when they disobeyed God. Mary was born without this sin, and was completely pure in body and soul.

She was ready to do whatever God asked of her, and to live a life full of love and goodness.

Because Mary was so special, do you know what happened when the time came for her to go to Heaven to join her son Jesus? – Mary was taken up to be with Jesus in Heaven as she had been on earth, body and soul together. Because of her sinless life and her great love for God, Mary was taken up to be the Queen of Heaven.

Can you think of some of the happiest and saddest moments of Mary's life?
    Suggestions might include:
    – the birth of Jesus
    – the wonderful miracles he performed
    – his resurrection from the dead.
    or:
    – losing Jesus in the Temple.
    – the crucifixion and death of Jesus.

Why is Mary so important to us and the Church?
    Mary said 'yes' to God's plan and so Jesus was made man, died on the cross and was raised from the dead to save us from our sins. Just as she helped Jesus when he was young, she stayed on earth after Jesus ascended into Heaven to help and strengthen the apostles. Just as she was always there for Jesus and the apostles when they needed her, she is always there for us, to pray to God on our behalf, asking him to help us.

ACTIVITY
Have the words of the 'Hail Mary' written out clearly on a large piece of paper. Scenes of Mary's life and flowers can be coloured and glued onto the sheet around the words of the prayer.

CREED

CLOSING PRAYER
Let's say Mary's prayer together:
'Hail Mary, full of grace . . .'

'HAIL MARY'

Solemnity of All Saints
The Saints in Heaven

INTRODUCTION
Today we remember the saints through the ages who have dedicated their lives to Jesus. Their love for Jesus was so great that they were ready to die for his sake.

SIGN OF THE CROSS

LIGHT THE CANDLES
Say together:
May our hearts be filled with the light of God's love.

SORRY
Lord, forgive us our impatience,
or when we've not been true,
for when we did not listen,
or turned away from you.
Give us lots of courage
to make a fresh new start.
Help us to be sorry,
we ask this from the heart.

GLORIA

GOSPEL ACCLAMATION
To welcome today's Gospel sing Acclamation 3:
Alleluia, alleluia.

GOSPEL (cf Matthew 5:1-12)
Seeing Jesus on a hillside, a crowd of people soon gathered and Jesus began to speak to them:
'Happy are people who are forgiving, they shall know forgiveness,
Happy are the poor, for they will have riches in heaven,
Happy are those who do what God wants, for he will answer their prayers.
Happy are the people who share their love and friendship, because it will be returned.
Be happy if people are unkind to you because of me, for you will be rewarded in Heaven.'

DISCUSSION
What feast are we celebrating today? – The Feast of All Saints.

Why do we call some people saints? – A saint is someone who has lived a life of outstanding goodness, and is already with God in Heaven.

Do you know the names of any saints? – Many of us are named after saints, and in some countries the feast day of the saint a child is named after, is more important than the child's birthday!

Some well known saints include:
- Saint Francis of Assisi, who gave up all his wealth for a life of poverty, caring for the poor and the sick. He loved all of God's creatures and treated them as his brothers and sisters.
- Saint Therese, became a nun at the age of fifteen. She lived an ordinary and very simple life, helping with the chores at the convent or praying to God. She offered everything she did, however small, as an act of love for God.

Do ordinary people become saints?

Saint Paul wrote: 'I live an ordinary life and yet I feel that I am not living it, but that Jesus is living it through me. I live by trusting in Jesus, the Son of God.' Saints are people who allow God's spirit to work through them, and to fill them with love so that they can do ordinary things extraordinarily well. Like St Therese we can make everything we do, however small, an act of love for God.

Do you think St Francis and St Therese knew of the happiness that Jesus talked about? – Because they did everything out of love for Jesus, they were filled with the joy and true happiness which comes from being close to him. Their greatest happiness is sharing everlasting life with Jesus in his kingdom.

ACTIVITY
Think of three ordinary things which you could do as an act of love for God, and draw a picture of yourself doing them.
Here are some examples:
Helping at home with the washing up.
Visiting an old person who needs your company.
Praying for someone less fortunate than yourself.
Having a smiley face.
Sharing your toys with someone else.
Being kind to a pet animal.

Pin the resulting pictures on a board and discuss them together.

CREED

CLOSING PRAYER
We ask the saints
to pray for us today.
Give us warm and loving hearts
and help us to do
what Jesus wants us to do.

Harvest Festival

INTRODUCTION
After the harvest has been safely gathered in we come together to give praise and thanks to God for *all* his goodness, and to bring our gifts to share with others just as God shares the gifts of creation with us.

SIGN OF THE CROSS

LIGHT THE CANDLES
Light the candles and say together:
May the light of Jesus burn in our hearts.

SORRY
Listen carefully to the words of this reading from St Luke (*cf Luke 6:44-45*):
Every tree is known by the fruit which grows on it; and a strong and healthy tree will produce good fruit, but a tree which is rotten will have only bad fruit. A person who is good, will have goodness in their heart and will do and say kind things; because what the mouth says, flows from what fills the heart.

Ask the children to close their eyes and make the words of this prayer their own:
Father, help me to be like the good tree
which bears good fruit.
Fill my heart with your love and goodness,
so that my words and actions are only kind ones.
If I have said or done anything unkind,
I ask for your forgiveness.

GLORIA

READING ACCLAMATION
To welcome today's reading sing Acclamation 3:
Alleluia, alleluia.

READING (*cf Leviticus 26:4-5*)
The Lord said, 'I will send the rain you need at the right time, so the land will grow crops and the trees will be heavy with fruit. Your harvests will be plentiful and you will have corn to cut and grapes to pick until it is time to sow again. There will be plenty to eat and everyone will be happy and content.'

DISCUSSION
What happens at harvest time? – At the end of the warm summer months when the crops in the fields and fruit on the trees have finished growing and have ripened, they are 'harvested' or gathered in.

(Children who live in a rural environment should be encouraged to discuss the machinery they have seen at work in the fields, or how other crops such as strawberries are gathered by hand. Other children could discuss any images they have of harvesting from books or television.)

Has harvest time always been important? – Long ago harvest time was the most important time of the year. If the harvest was good then the food was carefully stored, and lasted throughout the year. People celebrated and praised God for his goodness when they knew that they would have enough food to last the winter and would not starve.

In countries like Africa, what happens to the harvest if no rain falls and there is a drought? – Without rain the crops cannot grow and the harvest is poor or might completely fail. With no food to gather, the people go hungry or even starve.

Where do most of us get our food from? – With modern shops and supermarkets most of us can buy what we need without thinking about where it came from. We 'take things for granted' – we expect to have food and homes and clothes without thinking about who provides all these things.

Why do we hold a harvest festival or celebration?
1. We think about the *harvest*.
   Wherever we live in the world and whatever food we eat, *all* of it is a gift from God.
2. We come together to *praise* and *thank* God for all his goodness. By saying 'grace' before meals we can thank God for each meal we enjoy.
3. We gather together to *share* what God has given us by *giving* to people who are in need. Just as God shares his gifts with us, so we want to share these gifts with other people. We remember other people too, and pray for countries where there is famine and starvation, giving whatever aid we can to help them.

ACTIVITY
Photocopy the card and cut round outer edges. Ask each child to add their name and age, and to draw a portrait of themselves. After decorating the cards, these can be delivered with the harvest gifts. Sing together: *All things bright and beautiful.*

CLOSING PRAYER
Father, we thank you
for your goodness and the gifts
which you so freely give to us.
Help us to share what we have
with those around us and those who live far away.

from

FOLD

FOLD

Year B

First Sunday of Advent
Be ready to welcome Jesus

INTRODUCTION
The word 'Advent' means 'coming'; and it is a time of waiting and expectation. Only God knows when the second coming will be, but in today's Gospel we are reminded that we must stay awake and be ready for Jesus when he returns at the end of time.

SIGN OF THE CROSS

LIGHT THE CANDLES
As we light our candles today we begin our preparation to celebrate the birth of Jesus who is the 'light' of the world. Sing the Candle Song together.

SORRY
Close your eyes and speak quietly to God in your heart.

Jesus taught us to pray: 'Forgive us our trespasses as we forgive those who trespass against us.'

We must be ready to forgive anyone who has hurt us by what they have said or done, if we too want to be forgiven. We ask the Holy Spirit to fill us with the strength to do this, as we pray together: 'Our Father . . .'

GOSPEL ACCLAMATION
Sing the Advent Song.

GOSPEL (cf Mark 13:32-37)
Jesus told his disciples: 'Only my Heavenly Father knows when the Son of Man will return, so stay awake and be ready so that you will not be taken by surprise. Like a man who goes on a journey and tells his servants to take care of his home, they must be prepared for his return at any time so that he will always find them ready to greet him.'

DISCUSSION
If someone important is coming to visit you and your family, how do you prepare for their coming?
- tidy your room and the rest of the house.
- dust and clean.
- prepare a meal.
- make up a bed in the guest room.

It is easy to be ready for a visitor when you know the time to expect them, but sometimes they arrive unexpectedly and surprise you! Would you find it more difficult to keep everything just as it should be if you did not know when your visitor was coming?

Does anyone know exactly when Jesus will return to us? – We know that Jesus will return at the end of time, but only God knows exactly when that will be.

What did Jesus tell us to do? – To keep ourselves ready for the time when he will come again.

How can we do this? – Just as we prepare our homes and put them in order for a visitor, so we can prepare our hearts and put our lives in order for Jesus.

Advent is a good time to 'spring clean' our lives! To polish up the good things and make them shine, and to clear out the bad habits so that we can make a fresh start. By living each day as Jesus taught us, filled with goodness and love, we *will* be ready to welcome him when he comes again.

ACTIVITY
Advent is a time when we prepare to celebrate the first coming of Christ and his second coming at the end of time. The activities for this season are intended to help the children to prepare for this in their own way. The events leading up to Christ's birth are the subject of each activity week by week, therefore the theme of the activity may reflect the events leading up to Christmas rather than the theme of the Gospel for the day. When each activity is completed, some time should be spent discussing and explaining the event it illustrates. According to your own particular circumstances the assembled illustrations can be displayed on posters, pinned on a board or attached to stiff card to make a free-standing display.

Cut out the figure of Mary, the window frame, and the individual rays of light. After colouring, arrange them in the scene of the Annunciation, with light from the angel Gabriel appearing to stream through the window. Add the caption: 'Hail Mary, full of grace.'

CREED

CLOSING PRAYER
Lord Jesus,
help us to live as you taught us,
with our lives filled with love and goodness
so that we will be ready to greet you
when you come again in glory.

Second Sunday of Advent
Making a fresh start

INTRODUCTION
God sent John the Baptist to prepare the people for the coming of his son. The message he preached then, is just as important today, as we prepare ourselves for the coming of our Saviour Jesus Christ.

SIGN OF THE CROSS

LIGHT THE CANDLES
As we light our candles today the words of the prophet Isaiah remind us that Jesus is the 'light of the world': *(cf Isaiah 9:2)*
'Those who walked in darkness have seen a wonderful light. The light which shines on them chases the shadows of darkness away from their land.'

SORRY
John the Baptist told the people to ask for God's forgiveness and to change their ways. God is always ready to forgive us and to help us make a fresh start. Sing Sorry Song 4:
When we say that we are sorry

GOSPEL ACCLAMATION
Sing the Advent Song.

GOSPEL *(cf Mark 1:1-8)*
The prophet Isaiah foretold that God would send a messenger, to prepare the people for the Lord's coming. This messenger was John the Baptist, who appeared in the desert telling the people to be sorry for their sins and to make a fresh start in their lives. Many people heard his message and came to be baptised as a sign of their change of heart. John told them, 'Someone is coming who is more powerful than me, and I am not good enough to undo the straps of his sandals. I baptise you with water, but he will baptise you with the Holy Spirit.'

DISCUSSION
What was the name of the prophet who had foretold the coming of John the Baptist?

What is a prophet? – A prophet is someone who speaks in the name of God and has been allowed by God to know and share a part of his plan for mankind.

John was God's messenger; what message was he sent to deliver? – He was sent to tell the people to change their ways and to turn back to God. He told them to make a fresh start by asking forgiveness for their sins and trying to lead lives filled with goodness and love.

John was sent to prepare the people for the coming of Jesus. Do we still need to prepare for Jesus' coming today? – Jesus could return at any time *(recall last week's discussion.)* We can prepare ourselves just as people did in the time of John the Baptist, by putting right what is wrong in our lives and living as Jesus taught us. Advent is a good time to look carefully at ourselves and to make a fresh start if we need to. When can we meet Jesus and ask for his forgiveness? – Through the sacrament of reconciliation we can tell Jesus that we are sorry and receive his forgiveness. Through the priest God allows us to hear that our sins are forgiven, so we can start afresh knowing that God loves us very much.

Can you think of anything you could 'put right' in your life?

ACTIVITY
If the group is small hand out photocopies of the picture and ask the children to colour it. If you have a large group, enlarge on a photocopier and cut out the individual elements of the picture, then reassemble these on a large sheet of paper after they have been coloured. Spend some time with the children discussing the picture and the event it depicts.

CREED

CLOSING PRAYER
Heavenly Father,
help each of us
to make a fresh start this advent;
to put right
what is wrong
and to truly live
as Jesus showed us.

Third Sunday of Advent
Prepare a way to God

INTRODUCTION
News of John the Baptist had spread throughout the land, and crowds of people were flocking to listen to him. The leaders of the Jews decided to send some of their priests and elders to find out who this man really was.

SIGN OF THE CROSS

LIGHT THE CANDLES
Light the candles and read the following prayer:
Jesus is the light of the world.
Help us to live as children of the light,
sharing Jesus with the whole world
by keeping our belief in him
and all that he taught us
alive in our hearts.

SORRY
John the Baptist taught the people that the first step on the way to God was to say sorry if they had done wrong. Help us to remember this as we listen to the words of this prayer:
Lord, help us to choose what is good
and to follow you by living as you taught us.
Forgive us if we have done wrong
and turned away from your love.
Help us to change our hearts and make them new,
knowing that through your love
we can start afresh and try again.

GOSPEL ACCLAMATION
To welcome today's Gospel sing Acclamation 2:
Light up our hearts.

GOSPEL *(cf John 1:19-28)*
The Jews sent some priests to John the Baptist to ask him, 'Who are you?'
    'I am not the promised one,' he answered.
    'Are you Elijah or a prophet?' they asked.
    'No, I am neither of these,' he replied.
    'Well who are you then and why are you baptising these people?'
    John answered using the words of the prophet Isaiah, 'I am a voice crying out in the desert, prepare a way for the Lord! I baptise you with water, but there is one you do not yet know, who stands among you – one who is coming after me. I am not fit even to undo his sandals.'

DISCUSSION
Who did the priests think that John might be? – At first they thought that this extraordinary man might be the Messiah, the saviour promised by God. Then they wondered whether John was Elijah or another prophet.

How did John help the crowds to 'prepare a way for the Lord'? – John explained that true happiness comes from pleasing God and leading lives filled with goodness. Being sorry for the mistakes they had made and the wrongs they had done, and by   changing their lives, they could make a fresh start on the way to God.

Why was John called the 'Baptist'? – When people asked for God's forgiveness and made up their minds to live as God wanted them to, John would baptise them in the river. As they came up out of the water it was as though a new life was just beginning for them.

Is water still used at Baptism today? – Most people are baptised as babies, and some as grown-ups, but water is always used at Baptism. All life needs water and the water used at baptism reminds us that as we are welcomed into the family of God, we share new and everlasting life with him.

Each of us does something wrong sometimes, spoiling our friendship with each other and with God. How can we find our way back to the path which leads to him? – Do just as John the Baptist told the people! Say *sorry* to God for all the things we have done wrong and have a *change* of heart.

ACTIVITY
If the group is small, photocopy the picture and ask the children to colour it. If you have a large group, enlarge and cut out the individual elements of the picture, and reassemble these on a large sheet of paper after they have been coloured. Spend some time with the children discussing the picture and the event it depicts.

CREED

CLOSING PRAYER
Give us the courage to change our hearts
and make us grow strong in love and faith.
We ask this through Jesus Christ our Lord.

Fourth Sunday of Advent
I will do what God asks

INTRODUCTION
Mary loved God so much that she was ready to do whatever he asked of her. Trusting him completely and always ready to please him she agreed to become the mother of his son, Jesus.

SIGN OF THE CROSS

LIGHT THE CANDLES
Light the candles and say Candle Prayer 1: *Flicker, flicker little candle.*

SORRY
Help the children to reflect quietly for a few moments, thinking over the past week and all the things they have done. Have they always done what would please God? Have their words and actions been thoughtful and kind.

Ask one of the children to choose a sorry colour so that they can read the corresponding sorry prayer aloud to the group.

GOSPEL ACCLAMATION
Sing the Advent Song.

GOSPEL *(cf Luke 1:26-38)*
In a town called Nazareth, lived a girl called Mary, who was engaged to marry a man called Joseph. God sent the angel Gabriel to deliver a special message to Mary. The angel appeared to her and said, 'Be happy, Mary, for God is with you.' Mary felt frightened and uncertain about what the angel had said, but he continued, 'Do not be afraid, for you have been blessed by God and are going to have a baby, and you will call him Jesus.' Mary wondered at the angel's words because she was not married to Joseph, but the angel explained, 'The Holy Spirit will come to you, and the power of God will cover you with its shadow. This baby will be holy and called the Son of God.'

Then the angel told her that her cousin Elizabeth was also expecting a baby. Mary said to the angel. 'I am God's servant and will do whatever he asks of me.' Then the angel left her.

DISCUSSION
Ask the children to tell you what they know about angels. What they might look like, and how we might recognise one.

No-one really knows, but often they are depicted as beautiful winged creatures dressed in white and with a halo on their head. When angels appear they are usually as messengers of God.

Can you remember any other occasions in the Bible, when an angel was sent by God to take a message to someone? – In the Old Testament God sent an angel to stop Abraham from sacrificing his son Isaac to prove his love for God. In the New Testament an angel appeared to Joseph in a dream, telling him to marry Mary, and many angels appeared to some shepherds on a hillside to tell them about the newborn saviour. Later an angel appeared in a dream to warn Joseph to take his family to Egypt to escape from King Herod.

How do you think Mary felt when the angel appeared to her? – At first she was frightened and confused by the angel, but he was able to reassure her and calm her fears.

How would you feel if you saw an angel?

What message did the angel have for Mary? – That she would become the mother of God and that her cousin Elizabeth was already expecting a baby.

Why was the news about Elizabeth so amazing? – Elizabeth and her husband Zechariah had never been able to have any children and now they were both old. When Mary went to visit Elizabeth and found that everything was as the angel had told her, she knew that indeed she had been chosen by God.

How did Mary react to Gabriel's message? – She listened carefully to his words and agreed to do God's will. At the moment she agreed to become the mother of God, she also became the mother of us all.

ACTIVITY
If the group is small, photocopy the picture and ask the children to colour it. If you have a large group, enlarge and cut out the individual elements of the picture, and reassemble these on a large sheet of paper after they have been coloured. Spend some time with the children discussing the picture and the event it depicts.

CREED

CLOSING PRAYER
Mary said 'Yes' to God's messenger
and became the mother of God.
Let us ask for her help so that we too
will always say 'yes' to whatever God asks of us:
Hail Mary . . .

Feast of the Holy Family
Joy in the temple

INTRODUCTION
God sent his only Son into the world to be born as a helpless baby. The Holy Family cherished and loved him until the time came for him to share his Good News with the world.

SIGN OF THE CROSS

LIGHT THE CANDLES
As we light the candles today let us remember the words of Jesus who said:
'I am the light of the world, whoever follows me will have the light of life and will never walk in darkness.'

SORRY
Ask the children to close their eyes and listen to this reading, before talking to God in their hearts, and making a fresh start if they need to.
(cf Psalm 119:36-37, 43-44)
Lord, help me to store up my riches in Heaven and not just on earth.
To know what is important so I don't waste my time on worthless things.
To always speak the truth, and to do what you ask because of the love I have for you.

GLORIA

GOSPEL ACCLAMATION
To welcome today's Gospel sing Acclamation 5:
We have come to hear you.

GOSPEL (cf Luke 2:22-40)
Mary and Joseph set off for the temple in Jerusalem to offer thanks to God, as was the custom after the birth of their first child. At the temple they met an old man called Simeon. Simeon was a kind and good man who was filled with the Holy Spirit. When Mary and Joseph brought Jesus to the Temple, Simeon took him in his arms and said, 'Thank you, Lord, for allowing me to see the saviour you promised.' He blessed Mary and Joseph, and they were amazed by everything he said.

An old woman called Anna often prayed at the temple. When she saw Jesus she began to praise God loudly and to tell everyone about the child who had come to save the world. When Mary and Joseph had done everything they were supposed to do, they returned to Nazareth in Galilee. Jesus grew into a strong and wise child, because he had been blessed by God.

DISCUSSION
What makes us a family?
- We often share a family name to show that we belong together – our surname.
- A family can be made up of a mother, father and child or children; several different people all living together. (Be very sensitive to the situations of the children in the group for whom this may not be true.)
- A family shares its experiences and love with the people who belong to it.

Who were the Holy Family and how were they like our families? – In many ways they were probably very similar, sharing a home and belongings; loving and caring for each other; celebrating birthdays together. Having to do everyday things like cleaning, going to work and going to school.

Can you think of any other similarities?

In what ways would their family life have differed from ours?

The daily life of the Holy Family would have been very different because they had no electricity, fridges, washing machines or running water.

(Encourage the children to discuss any differences they can think of.)

Which family do we all belong to?

We all belong to the family of God, and because of this we are all brothers and sisters. We also belong to the Christian family which we joined when we were baptised.

Do you know where the name Christian comes from? – We take our name from Christ. A Christian chooses to follow Jesus by living as he taught us, and by loving God and our neighbours with all our heart. We are all brothers and sisters who are able to call God our Father.

ACTIVITY
Photocopy and cut out the face templates to represent the different peoples of the world. Cut out individual words or letters which together read, 'One world, One family'. Ask some of the children to colour these faces or letters, while others are colouring a central picture of the world. These can be displayed as illustrations on a pinboard or sheet of paper.

CLOSING PRAYER
Dear Jesus, please bless our families
and help us to be loving and forgiving.
Help each of us to remember that
we are all brothers and
sisters in the one family of God.

First Sunday of Lent
God saves Noah

INTRODUCTION
Today we begin the season of Lent, a time to prepare our hearts for the new life which Jesus brings at Easter. Lent lasts for forty days, just as Jesus spent forty days in the desert before going out to share the Good News. It is a season of hope and new life as days lengthen and spring approaches. In today's reading we hear about Noah's faith in God and the promise that God made to mankind.

SIGN OF THE CROSS

LIGHT THE CANDLES
A the candles are lit, say together:
May the light of Jesus burn in our hearts.

SORRY
During Lent we hear the word 'repentance' many times. This means being sorry for things we have done wrong. Lent is a time of thinking about our past mistakes, and looking forward to starting again by turning over a new leaf. During this season we make a special effort to become more like Jesus.
And so let us close our eyes and pray:
Lord Jesus,
give us the courage to admit
when we get things wrong.
Knowing that because you love us,
you are always ready to be forgiving.

ACCLAMATION
To welcome today's Reading sing Acclamation 5:
'We have come to hear you.'

READING (cf Genesis 6:5-9:17)
God looked down on the world he had made and was filled with sadness when he saw the wickedness of his people. God decided to destroy all the wicked people, except for Noah who was a good and just man.

God told Noah, 'Build an ark and fill it with pairs of every sort of animal so that they will multiply again. Take plenty of food for them and your family, because I will send enough rain to flood the world.' Noah did everything God had commanded.

The rain began and carried on night and day until all the land had disappeared under the mighty waters of the flood. Everything was destroyed, except for Noah and and the animals which were safe in the ark.

After many days, Noah sent out a dove and it returned to the ark carrying a shoot from a young olive tree in its beak.

Noah gave thanks and praise to God as the flood waters began to disappear. Then God said, 'I will make a promise never again to send such a flood to destroy the world, and as a sign of this promise I will put a rainbow in the sky.'

DISCUSSION
Why did God destroy the world he had created? – Because of the wickedness of mankind, who had chosen to ignore God and turn away from him.

Why did God choose only to save Noah and the animals? – God is fair and just and he chose to rescue Noah and the other creatures who had done nothing wrong. Noah was ready to listen to God and to do whatever he asked, because he had faith and trust in his love and goodness.

What sort of bird did Noah send out, and what did it bring back to the ark? – It was a dove, which came back with an olive branch in its beak. Even today, the dove and the olive branch are used as symbols of peace and hope.

What promise did God make to Noah and all living creatures? – God loves us and would rather forgive than punish us. He made an everlasting promise to the human race that he would never flood the world again.

What sign did he set in the sky to remind us of this promise?   A rainbow appears when sunlight shines through raindrops and splits the light into all its colours. It appears as the rain stops and the sun begins to shine, and is a symbol of joy and hope.

ACTIVITY
Using card, cut out and colour the ark. Glue on the windows with the animals looking out, and glue the stand made from thick card onto the ark to make it free standing. Fold some pieces of card for the animals, using outlines as shown in the illustration. Ask the children to cut and colour them and arrange them in a line beside the ark. Finally add Noah to the scene.

CREED

CLOSING PRAYER
Lord, when we look at a rainbow
we are reminded of your
promise to the world.
Help us to keep any promises we have made
because of our love for you.

Fold

Fold

Glue

Glue

Back.

Rectangle
of card.

Fold

Fold

Stick
card
onto
ark.

ANIMALS

Fold

Don't cut along
the fold.

Cut out Noah figure
and stick onto ark.

Stand up
animal.

Second Sunday of Lent
Trust me

INTRODUCTION
Abraham was a good man, and like Noah, he had complete faith and trust in God. God put this trust to the test when he asked Abraham to kill his son Isaac.

SIGN OF THE CROSS

LIGHT THE CANDLES
Light the candles and read: (cf Proverbs 4:18-19)
The path to our heavenly Father is like the rising sun, getting brighter and brighter as we draw closer to God. People who turn away from his love follow a path as dark as the night and they stumble and fall because they cannot see the way.

SORRY
Today we will hear about the great trust which Abraham had in God. In the same way we trust in God's goodness and love for us, because we are not afraid to come before him and admit our mistakes. And so we have the courage to say together: Our Father . . .

ACCLAMATION
Open our ears to hear your word, Lord,
And fill our minds and hearts with understanding and love.

READING (cf Genesis 22:1-13)
God put Abraham to the test. 'Abraham,' he said, 'I want you to take your son Isaac to the top of the mountain, and offer him as a sacrifice to me!'

Abraham loved Isaac very much, but he trusted God completely and was ready to obey him. He loaded his donkey with wood and set off to the mountain God had shown him. On the way, Isaac asked his father, 'Where is the lamb you will sacrifice?' Abraham answered him 'God will provide a lamb.'

When they arrived, they built an altar and piled it with wood. Then Abraham tied Isaac's hands and feet and took out a knife ready to kill his only son.

Suddenly a voice from heaven said, 'Abraham, Abraham, do not kill the son you love so much. Your trust and love for me was so great that you were ready to sacrifice your only son for my sake.' Looking up, Abraham noticed a ram whose horns were tangled in a thorn bush. He offered the ram as a sacrifice to God in place of his precious son Isaac.

DISCUSSION
Do you know what the word 'sacrifice' means? – To sacrifice something means to offer something for the sake of someone else. In Old Testament times, people would sacrifice animals by killing them and offering their lives to God. Life is the most precious gift of all, and these offerings showed how much they loved God.

What did God ask Abraham to do? – To sacrifice his only son Isaac. At that time people often sacrificed animals as a sign of their love and respect for God.

How do you think Abraham must have felt? – Abraham and his wife Sarah were already old when Isaac was born, so he was particularly precious to them. Abraham must have felt very sad indeed, but his faith and trust in God was so great that he was ready to do anything God asked.

How was Isaac saved? – God called out to Abraham to stop him harming Isaac. God had seen how much Abraham loved him. He did not want a human sacrifice, only proof of Abraham's trust and obedience.

In the New Testament, who sacrificed his only beloved son for all mankind? – God sent his only son Jesus to be sacrificed by dying on the cross. Jesus had faith and trust in his father and believed that God's power would raise him from the dead.

What should we learn from the story of Abraham and Isaac? – Abraham was ready to trust God completely and put his love for him before everything else. God saw his obedience and faith and made sure that Isaac came to no harm. We should love God and trust him with all our hearts, just as Abraham did.

ACTIVITY
Photocopy and enlarge these pictures. Then cut them out for the children to colour and assemble into a picture telling the story of Abraham and Isaac.

CREED

CLOSING PRAYER
Lord, give us the faith
and courage of Abraham,
to do whatever you might ask of us.
Make our trust and love for you
grow stronger each day.
We ask this through Christ our Lord.

Third Sunday of Lent
Anger in the temple

INTRODUCTION
Jesus said, 'My father's house is a house of prayer.' So when he came to the temple in Jerusalem and saw how people had pushed God to one side and allowed money and business to become more important, he was very angry.

SIGN OF THE CROSS

LIGHT THE CANDLES
Light the candles and sing the Candle Song together.

SORRY
Let us close our eyes and speak quietly to Jesus, asking his forgiveness for any mistakes we have made or things we have done wrong. (Allow a few moments for quiet reflection.)

GOSPEL ACCLAMATION
To welcome today's Gospel sing Acclamation 4: *Praise the Lord*

GOSPEL *(cf John 2:13-22)*
Jesus went to Jerusalem to celebrate the Jewish Passover. He found the temple in Jerusalem full of people selling animals, and amongst them sat the money changers. He was very angry and overturned the tables of the money changers, scattering their coins everywhere.

Angrily he chased the animals and the merchants out of the temple shouting at them, 'Take all of these things away and stop making my father's house into a market place!'

The temple priests tried to stop Jesus and asked, 'What right do you have to act like this?'

Jesus answered, 'Destroy this temple and I will raise it again in three days.'

'This temple took forty six years to build! How could you rebuild it in three days?' they exclaimed.

The temple which Jesus spoke of was his own body, and after his resurrection from the dead, his disciples would understand what Jesus had said that day.

DISCUSSION
Why did the Jewish people go to the temple? – They gathered there to pray and to offer sacrifices in God's honour.

What did Jesus find in the Temple?

Why do you think that the money changers, and the animals were there? – The animals were sold to those who wished to offer them as sacrifices to God. Ordinary money with the picture of Caesar on it could not be used in the temple. Instead special temple coins were used to buy animals, and to pay the temple taxes. The money changers' job was to exchange the Roman coins for the temple coins.

Why was Jesus so angry? – His father's house had become a market place, filled with people buying and selling, instead of being a place of prayer and respect.

What did Jesus say he could do, which made people believe that he was mad? – Jesus told them that if the temple was destroyed, he could rebuild it in three days. They thought that he spoke of the temple itself, which had taken forty six years to build. Jesus meant the 'temple' of his own body, which would be destroyed by death on the cross, but would be raised to life again after three days.

How should we act in the house of God? – The house of God is a place of prayer where we can be close to God in a special way. When we visit someone else's home we are well behaved and remember our manners, so too we should respect God's house when we go to church.

ACTIVITY
On a large sheet of paper, draw a temple background. Photocopy the animal and stall pictures enough times so that they can be cut out to make a busy temple scene. Add the angry figure of Jesus.

CREED

CLOSING PRAYER
Let us pray for the family
which has gathered here today in God's house
to celebrate Christ's death and resurrection.

Thinking ahead. (see discussion points for the Fifth Sunday of Lent)

Either: Sprinkle some cress seeds onto some damp cotton wool or kitchen roll. Put the seeds in a light place and keep them damp. Tiny shoots will soon appear. Keep some of the dry seeds to show the children.

or: Soak some broad beans in water for 24 hours. Put about 2.5cm (1inch) of water in a jam jar and line it with damp kitchen roll. Put the beans between the glass and the paper about half way down the jar. Place in a light place and watch the roots and shoots begin to appear.

Fourth Sunday of Lent
'The light of the world'

INTRODUCTION
While Jesus was in Jerusalem for the Feast of the Passover, one of the Pharisees called Nicodemus came to see him secretly one night. Nicodemus believed in Jesus and wanted to know more about this extraordinary man.

SIGN OF THE CROSS

LIGHT THE CANDLES
Light the candles and say Candle Prayer 3: *The light of God.*

SORRY
As we sing our sorry song let us ask for God's forgiveness, and his help to make us good. Sing Sorry Song 1.

GOSPEL ACCLAMATION
To welcome today's Gospel sing Acclamation 2: *Light up our hearts.*

GOSPEL (*cf John 3:16-21*)
Jesus said to Nicodemus, 'God loved the world so much that he sent his only son to be the light and to save those who believed in him. The light of the world has come, but many turn away from it and prefer the darkness. Anyone who does wrong is afraid of the light, because their badness will be plain for all to see. The good man has nothing to fear from the light, because he is close to God.'

DISCUSSION
Who is the 'light of the world'? – Jesus is the 'light of the world.'

What happens if you switch on the light in a darkened room? – The darkness disappears and suddenly you can see everything clearly. Jesus is the 'light' who makes us see the way to his heavenly Father, and chases away the temptations which could lead us away from God.

When did Nicodemus come to see Jesus? – Nicodemus came secretly at night, hoping that no-one would see him. He was a Pharisee, a very religious man who studied the scriptures and kept all the commandments of the Jewish law. The other Pharisees did not like Jesus or his teachings, but Nicodemus believed in him and was afraid the others would find out.

If we do something wrong or that we know is naughty, do we like everyone else to see what we are doing, or prefer to keep it a secret?

No-one likes to be found out! This is what Jesus meant about people preferring the darkness, and doing things out of sight hoping no-one will see. When we are good and do what is right we have nothing to hide and don't mind being seen.

We are all children of the light. Do you remember when we received the 'light' of Christ? – At our baptism we were given a candle as a symbol of the light we received from Christ. The love of Jesus and the flame of faith have burned in our hearts since that day. As children of the light we have nothing to fear, knowing that Jesus is always close to us on our journey through life.

ACTIVITY
Using brightly coloured rectangles of paper, help each child to make a lantern which they can carry with them into the church.

CREED

CLOSING PRAYER
Jesus, you are the light of the world.
You promised that
if we stay close to you,
we will never be lost in the darkness.
Help us to stay with you always.

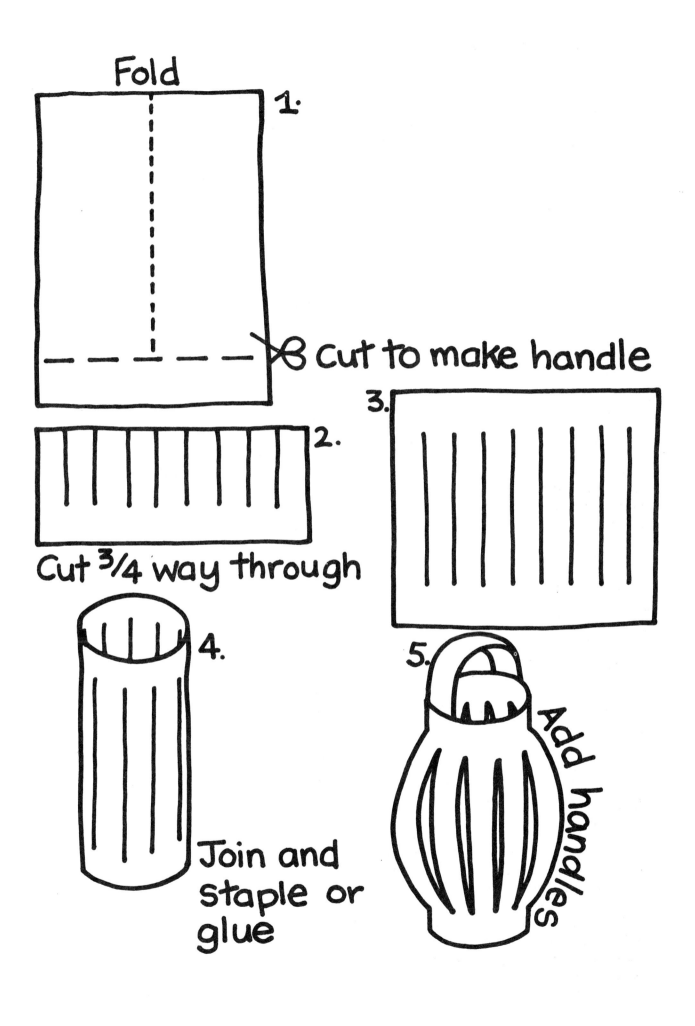

Fold

1.

Cut to make handle

2.

3.

Cut ¾ way through

4.

Join and staple or glue

5.

Add handles

Fifth Sunday of Lent
A grain of wheat

INTRODUCTION
After his triumphant ride into Jerusalem and before celebrating the Passover, Jesus spoke to his disciples about his approaching suffering and death.

SIGN OF THE CROSS

LIGHT THE CANDLES
Light the candles and read *(cf Psalm 16:11)*:
Lord, your light will show me the path that leads to everlasting life, and as you walk beside me on my journey I will be filled with happiness which will last forever.

SORRY
As we listen to the words of this reading, let us ask for God's forgiveness and his help to make a fresh start *(cf Psalm 73:21-26)*:
Sometimes when I feel wronged and hurt by others, I turn my anger towards them; but this is not your way, Lord.
I know that you will never let go of my hand, you will always stand beside me.
Gently you will guide me and with your help I will understand and make your ways my own.

GOSPEL ACCLAMATION
If practical ask one of the children to read the acclamation:
By dying you destroyed death and brought us all to new and everlasting life.

GOSPEL *(cf John 12:23-27)*
Jesus said to his disciples, 'The time has come for me to be glorified. Just as a grain of wheat must die to produce a harvest of many grains, so the Son of God must die so that many can live.'

Jesus was troubled because he knew the time for him to die was fast approaching.

'I could ask my heavenly Father to stop this thing from happening, but it was for this very reason that I have come.'

DISCUSSION
Why did Jesus feel troubled? – He knew that soon he would be betrayed by Judas and would suffer and die on the cross.

Do you think he was afraid? – No one likes to suffer, and Jesus knew what lay ahead of him. He must have felt afraid, but he did not try to avoid what was to happen. Instead he turned to his father and prayed for strength and courage.

What did Jesus say about the grain of wheat? – The wheat plant produces a seed called a 'grain'. A single grain of wheat can produce a plant with many, many grains. To do this the seed itself must die and give up its own life to produce a tall and strong shoot.

Many other familiar plants produce seeds which die so that they can produce new life. Can you think of any examples?

(Encourage the children to discuss vegetable and flower seeds which might be familiar to them. At this point show them the beans growing in a jar or the cress seedlings which were planted earlier. Let them look at the seeds which these plants came from.)

Jesus used the image of the grain of wheat to try to explain what would happen to him. Do you understand what he was trying to tell us?

Jesus wanted us to understand that like a seed his death was necessary, if new life was to be given to many. Jesus gave up his life by dying on the cross so that he could have new and everlasting life which we could share with him.

ACTIVITY
Copy or draw the various stages of the development of a seed from its beginnings to its final harvest. After the pictures have been coloured, help the children to arrange them in sequence and to discuss how the death of one seed can produce a whole new crop. Show the children the cress or bean seeds you prepared a couple of weeks ago. *(See Third Sunday of Lent)*

CREED

CLOSING PRAYER
Lord Jesus,
you willingly gave up your life
so that you could share
your everlasting life
with all of mankind.
Thank you for your courage and love
and for dying to save us all.

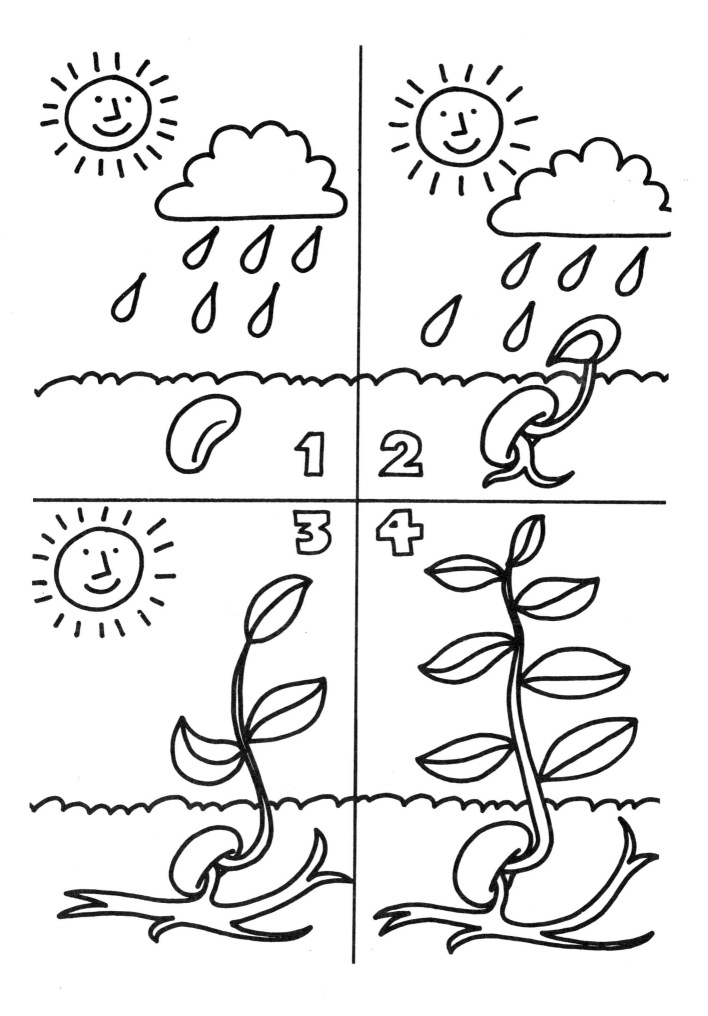

Second Sunday of Easter
Doubting Thomas

INTRODUCTION
Sometimes people use the saying 'seeing is believing', meaning that it is easier to believe something when you have seen it with your own eyes. The disciple called Thomas would not believe that Jesus had risen from the dead without seeing it for himself.

SIGN OF THE CROSS

LIGHT THE CANDLES
Light the candles and then read this prayer:
Lord Jesus,
help us to follow your light,
so that we never lose our way
or walk in darkness.

SORRY
Choose a sorry colour and read the corresponding prayer together.

GLORIA

GOSPEL ACCLAMATION
To welcome today's Gospel sing Acclamation 4:
Praise the Lord

GOSPEL (cf John 20:19-29)
On the Sunday after Jesus had died, his disciples sat huddled together in a locked room, hidden away for fear of being arrested. Suddenly Jesus appeared in the room with them. 'Peace be with you,' he said and he showed them the wounds in his hands and his side. His disciples were overjoyed to see their master again. 'As my father sent me, so I am sending you,' he said. Then breathing on them he said, 'Receive the Holy Spirit, and know that whoever you forgive, I will forgive also!'

The disciple called Thomas was not with the others when Jesus had appeared, and because he had not seen him with his own eyes, he did not believe that Jesus was alive.

A week later Jesus appeared to them again and, greeting them with the words, 'Peace be with you.' He showed his wounds to Thomas and said, 'Doubt no longer, Thomas.' At once Thomas fell to his knees and cried, 'My Lord and my God.'

Jesus said to him, 'You believe because you have seen me with your own eyes. Blessed are those who have not seen and yet believe.'

DISCUSSION
When Jesus first appeared to the disciples in the locked room, which one of them was missing? – Thomas was not with the other disciples, and the Gospel does not explain where he was.

What did Jesus do when he appeared? – He shared the gift of his peace saying the words, 'Peace be with you'. Then he gave them the gift of the Holy Spirit to increase their faith and courage.

When do we offer each other the peace of Christ? – Before sharing the Blessed Eucharist, we offer each other a sign of peace, a peace given to us by Jesus himself.

Did Thomas believe the disciples when they told him that Jesus had risen from the dead? – Thomas could not believe without seeing.

When Jesus appeared again he showed Thomas his wounds. Was he angry because Thomas had doubted? – Because Thomas could see and touch Jesus, he believed that he had risen from the dead. Jesus understood that many like Thomas would hear the story of the resurrection and be filled with doubt.

Can we 'see' the risen Jesus today? – Jesus lives amongst us and we can recognise his presence in the people around us. A kind action or a loving remark are signs of Christ's power working through other people.

What words did Thomas say when he recognised Jesus as the risen Lord? – 'My Lord and my God'. We use these words quietly at the Consecration of the bread and the wine, when we *believe* that they become Christ's body and blood. We cannot see Jesus but we *believe* that he is really there.

ACTIVITY
Cut out the shape of a large cross from a piece of stiff card and either paint it black or cover it with black or dark paper. Prepare small squares of coloured tissue paper, to make 'flowers'. Stick some of these onto the cross, while older children string others together to make a garland to hang on the cross. The 'Resurrection cross' can be attached to a stand or hung as a mobile. Add the caption 'We believe Jesus is risen.'

CREED

CLOSING PRAYER
Today we pray for those like Thomas,
who cannot believe without seeing.
Increase their faith Lord,
and help them to recognise you
in the people they meet everyday.

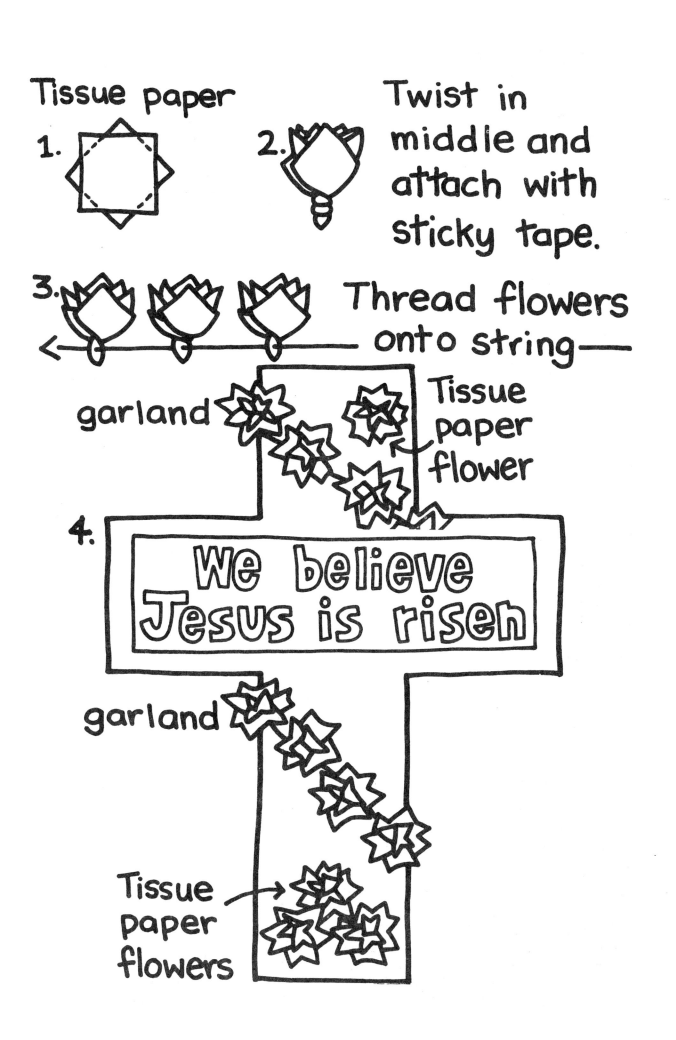

Tissue paper

1.

2. Twist in middle and attach with sticky tape.

3. Thread flowers onto string

garland

Tissue paper flower

4. We believe Jesus is risen

garland

Tissue paper flowers

Third Sunday of Easter
Christ's witnesses

INTRODUCTION
Jesus told his apostles to go out and tell the world that he had died and risen to new life.

SIGN OF THE CROSS

LIGHT THE CANDLES
Read these words (*cf Revelation 22:5*):
The time is coming when there will be no night,
and no-one will need lamps or the light
from the sun,
because the Lord God will be our light for evermore.

SORRY
In a moment of silence let us ask for God's forgiveness for all the times when we have offended others by our words or actions. Sing together Sorry Song 2

GLORIA

GOSPEL ACCLAMATION
To welcome today's Gospel sing Acclamation 1: *Share your word with us.*

GOSPEL (*cf Luke 24:36-48*)
The disciples who had met Jesus on the road to Emmaus, were telling the others what had happened, when suddenly Jesus appeared amongst them. At first they were terrified, because they thought that they had seen a ghost! Then Jesus said to them, 'Peace be with you', and seeing that they were still scared, he added, 'Do not be afraid. Why do you doubt what you can see? Please, look at my wounds and see that I am not a ghost. Touch me, a ghost has no flesh or bones as I have!' They were overjoyed but still filled with disbelief. Then Jesus asked them for something to eat and they watched as he ate some grilled fish.

Then he began to explain the scriptures to them, so that finally, they understood what scripture had said about the Messiah suffering and rising after three days. Jesus said to them 'You are my witnesses because you have seen all these things happen.'

DISCUSSION
How would you feel if you saw a ghost?

How did Jesus calm and reassure his terrified disciples? – He appeared saying the words, 'Peace be with you,' and told them not to be afraid. Then he showed them his wounds to convince them that he really had risen from the dead.

Even after showing the disciples his wounds did they really believe what they were seeing?

Although they were overjoyed to see Jesus again, they were totally dumbfounded to find that he was really alive, so Jesus ate a piece of fish to convince them that he was real and not a ghost!

Jesus told the disciples that they were his *witnesses.* What did he mean? – The disciples had seen and heard for themselves all the marvellous things that Jesus had done. He would send them out to give evidence or proof of this by the way they lived, the miracles they would perform in his name, and the things they would teach.

Can we be witnesses for Christ? – Jesus said, 'Blessed are those who have not seen and yet *believe.*' We may not have seen all these things with our own eyes but we believe. Each of us can be a witness for Christ by living God's way, as Jesus showed us. When we become members of the Christian family we are called to follow Christ and be a witness for him every day of our lives.

ACTIVITY
On a large sheet of paper draw a representative map of the world (it does not need to be accurate!) or if available, use a large map of the world. Photocopy the various modes of transport that the apostles might have used. After colouring, help the children to add them to the map, with large red arrows pointing in various directions. Add the caption, 'Witnesses to the world.'

CREED

CLOSING PRAYER
Lord Jesus,
send us your Spirit
to give us the strength
to live as you taught us.
Help us to bear witness to you
by our actions and our words.

Fourth Sunday of Easter
The Good Shepherd

INTRODUCTION

Jesus takes care of us just as a good shepherd takes care of his sheep. He knows each one of us and we know him, and are glad to follow him wherever he leads.

SIGN OF THE CROSS

LIGHT THE CANDLES

Light the candles and say Candle Prayer 2: *Show me, show me little candle.*

SORRY

Listen carefully to this reading (*cf Psalm 25:11-16*): God is full of kindness and love, and always ready to show us the path to follow. He leads us with patience and understanding, and forgives us if we stray and lose our way. When we look to him for help he rescues us from harm and helps us to try again, because his forgiveness is unending.
(Pause for a few moments of silence.)
Jesus,
you are the Good Shepherd.
Forgive us if we have wandered
away from your path and
guide us back to your love.
We ask this through Christ our Lord.

GLORIA

GOSPEL ACCLAMATION

To welcome today's Gospel sing Acclamation 3: *Alleluia, alleluia.*

GOSPEL (*cf John 10:11-15*)

One day Jesus said, 'I am the Good Shepherd, who is ready to die for his sheep. A man who is hired to look after the flock does not really care about it because he knows that the sheep do not really belong to him. When the hungry wolf appears, the man runs away, and the sheep are worried or scattered. I know each of my sheep by name, and they know the sound of my voice. They will always follow me and I am ready to give up my life for them.'

DISCUSSION

What is a shepherd? – Someone who looks after sheep.

What do you think makes a good shepherd? – A good shepherd cares for all the needs of his sheep – finding them pasture and water, shelter from the weather, and protecting them from wild animals and danger. He watches over them at all times and knows each of them individually.

What did Jesus say about the hired man? – A hired man was paid to look after a flock of sheep. The sheep did not belong to him and he didn't particularly care about them. So when a wolf appeared, the hired man worried more about his own safety and abandoned the flock.

How would you describe a sheep to someone? – White, woolly, bleating. They are timid and gentle animals which like to be kept together with other sheep in a flock. They are not particularly clever and get themselves into all sorts of trouble unless someone is taking care of them.

Do you think Jesus was talking only about sheep? – Jesus is the Good Shepherd and we are his 'flock'. He told this story to make us understand that he cares for us as much as the shepherd cares for his sheep. He watches over us at all times, and knows each of us by name. He goes before us to guide us and keep us from all harm. He takes care of all our needs and we can trust in his goodness.

When Jesus said he would be prepared to give up his life for his flock, what did he mean? – Jesus' love was so strong that he was willing to suffer and die on the cross for our sakes. His sacrifice meant that we can follow him to his heavenly kingdom, where we will share eternal life with him.

ACTIVITY

Using the template given (it will need to be enlarged slightly), cut out some sheep masks from stiff card. Attach these to a stick and help the children to glue cotton wool to the masks.

CREED

CLOSING PRAYER

Jesus,
you are the Good Shepherd
and we are your flock.
Help us to know your voice
and always follow you.

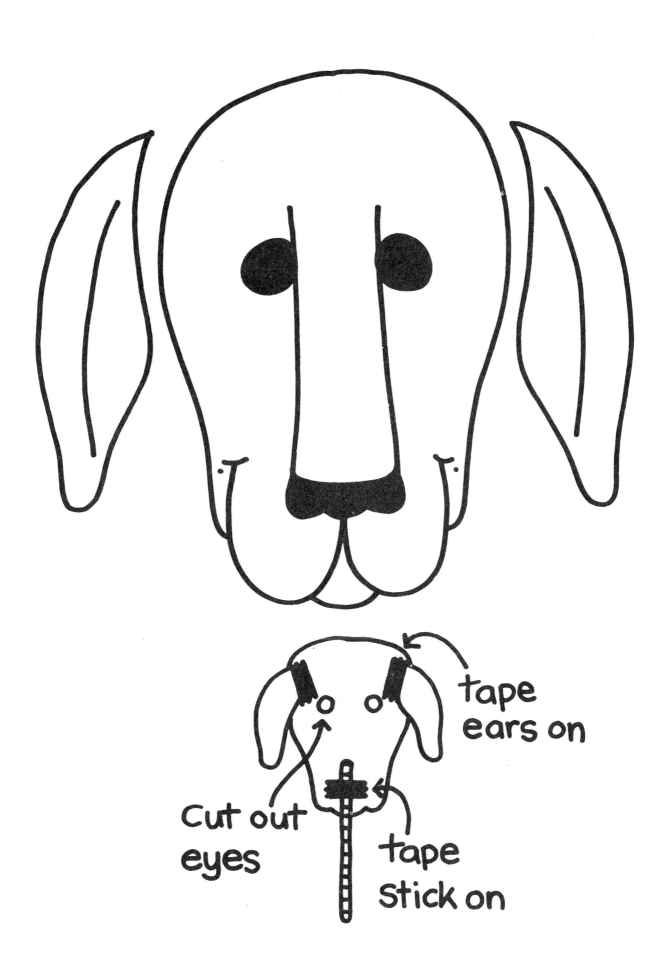

tape
ears on

Cut out
eyes

tape
Stick on

Fifth Sunday of Easter
I am the true vine

INTRODUCTION
A branch cannot live and produce fruit unless it is nourished by the tree or plant to which it is attached. Today Jesus compares himself to a vine, and we are the branches which bear the fruit of his love.

SIGN OF THE CROSS

LIGHT THE CANDLES
Light the candles and sing the Candle Song.

SORRY
If Christ's spirit is living in us then everyone will see the fruits of his presence: love, happiness, forgiveness, generosity and honesty.

Heavenly Father,
the fruits of your Holy Spirit
are not always obvious in our lives.
Prune away the parts of our lives
which stop us from growing strong,
and fill us with your life and your love.

GLORIA

GOSPEL ACCLAMATION
To welcome today's Gospel sing Acclamation 5: *We have come to hear you, Lord.*

GOSPEL (cf John 15:1-8)
Jesus told his disciples: 'I am the true vine and my father is the gardener who tends the vine. Any of my branches which don't bear fruit are cut away, and the branches which carry fruit are pruned by him so that the following year they will produce even more.

Because you have listened to and understood my message, you will bear much fruit. A branch that is cut off the vine will wither and die without producing any fruit. If you stay close to me and carry my words in your heart, then you will bear much fruit and truly be my disciple.'

DISCUSSION
A gardener's job is to make sure that the plants which he or she tends are healthy and strong. One way they can do this is by pruning. Do you know what pruning a plant means? – Pruning means cutting away any dead, damaged or weak stems or branches of a plant or tree. It encourages new growth by making the other buds and shoots grow strong and healthy.

(If possible either demonstrate pruning using some secateurs and a potted shrub or twig, or show the children some pictures of the technique in a gardening book.)

Do you know why it is important to prune fruit trees and vines properly? – Good pruning builds a strong framework of branches, but also encourages good fruit production for many years. By careful pruning, the good gardener keeps his plants strong and healthy, and every year they produce more and more fruit.

(If possible show the children a basket of different fruits – a bunch of grapes, apples, oranges, lemons etc. Talk about the plants on which they grow, and whether they are grown locally or in warmer climates. Explain that vines were a common sight where Jesus lived, and that he used them in the story because they were familiar to everyone.)

In today's Gospel *who* was the vine and *who* was the gardener? – Jesus described himself as being like a vine, with us as the branches. God the Father was the gardener who did the necessary pruning.

In this story what do you think Jesus was trying to explain? – Jesus used the story of the vine and branches to explain that we are all part of him. It is through Jesus that we have life, and through the work of his Father 'the gardener' that we flourish and grow strong. He 'prunes' away the things in our lives that make us weak or stop us from growing strong in faith and love.

What are the fruits that Jesus wants us to bear?

Jesus is living and working in our lives, in our thoughts, our actions and in our words. By being kind and loving, ready to forgive and honest and generous, the fruits of his love are there for all to see.

ACTIVITY
Use enlarged copies of the illustration for this activity or draw a simple outline of a tree trunk on a large sheet of paper. Write 'Jesus is the vine' on the trunk. Ask some of the children to stick on some small twigs into position using sticky tape. Add the caption 'We are the branches.' Ask the other children to colour in large cut-out fruits. Help them to label these with the fruits of God's love, and to attach them to the branches.

CREED

CLOSING PRAYER
Lord,
fill us with your life and love
so that we will produce much fruit
and a rich harvest for your sake.

WE ARE THE BRANCHES

JESUS IS THE VINE

Sixth Sunday of Easter
Love each other

INTRODUCTION

Jesus loves each one of us so much, that he died on the cross so that we could share eternal life with him. He asks us to be generous and to share this love with all of mankind.

SIGN OF THE CROSS

LIGHT THE CANDLES

Light the Candles and read this prayer:
The candle flame is warm and bright
it changes darkness into light.
We feel its warmth and see its glow,
and when we look at it we know,
the light of Christ is burning bright,
for we are children of the light.

SORRY

After a few moments of quiet reflection ask the children to sing Sorry Song 1

GLORIA

GOSPEL ACCLAMATION

To welcome today's Gospel sing Acclamation 4: *Praise the Lord*

GOSPEL (*cf John 15:9-17*)

One day Jesus said to his disciples: 'I love you just as my Father loves me. If you do as I ask then you will always be close to me, and my Father will love you too. I want you to love each other in the same way as I have loved you. I have chosen you to be my friends, and am sending you out to share this love with the rest of the world.'

DISCUSSION

What did Jesus ask his disciples to do? – To love one another as he had loved them. Jesus reminded his disciples many times that the greatest commandments were to love God and to love each other.

What does it mean to love another person? – To love someone else means that you care about another person, about their happiness and the things which happen to them. You want only the best for them, and for them to grow in love and goodness.

Jesus's love for us was so great that he did an extraordinary thing for us. What did he do? – 'Greater love has no man, than to give up his life for others.' Jesus loved us so much that he was ready to die so that we could live and share new life with him in heaven. Sometimes in times of disaster, people behave heroically by saving the lives of others instead of their own. Their love for another person is so great that they put that person's needs before their own.

Jesus asked us to share his love with each other. In what ways can we do this?
We can put our love into action:
– by spending some time with someone who is lonely.
– by offering help to someone who needs it.
– by sharing our happiness with others.
(Encourage the children to make their own suggestions)
We can put our love into words:
– by telling the members of our family how much we love them.
– by praying for the needs of other people.
– by praising and thanking God for all that we have.

Jesus lives inside each one of us so whatever we say or do to each other, we say or do it to him. We can make everything we do a little act of love for God.

ACTIVITY

Make a 'love is . . .' booklet for each child with several blank pages for their own drawings and ideas. Either use the illustration here for the cover, or the children can design their own.

CREED

CLOSING PRAYER

Heavenly Father,
our hearts are brimming over with your love.
Help us to be generous
and always ready to share this love
with everyone we meet.

Seventh Sunday of Easter

Keep us in your eye

INTRODUCTION

On Thursday we remembered the day when Jesus returned to his heavenly Father after saying goodbye to his apostles. Before leaving them, he prayed to his father and asked him to always keep them in his care.

SIGN OF THE CROSS

LIGHT THE CANDLES

Light the candles and say Candle Prayer 3: *The light of God.*

SORRY

Listen to this reading written by a wise man called Micah (*cf Micah 6:8-9*):

God our Father has told us what we must do: Be fair and honest in all that we do and say, be loving and caring towards others. If we do these things, then our friendship with God will last forever.

Close your eyes and offer the words of this prayer to God:

Lord Jesus, often we make mistakes
and forget the things you tell us.
We are sorry if we have been unkind or
if we have not always been honest or fair.
We ask you to forgive us and help us to be good.

GLORIA

GOSPEL ACCLAMATION

To welcome today's Gospel sing Acclamation 2: *Light up our hearts.*

GOSPEL (*cf John 17:11-19*)

Looking up to Heaven Jesus said: 'Father, now I must return to you and leave these friends behind. I have shared your Word with them and watched their faith in you grow, when many others chose to doubt. I have watched over them and kept them safe from danger and those who wish them harm. Now I am sending them out into the world, and I ask you to watch over them always and keep them in your care.'

DISCUSSION

Have you ever had to say goodbye to a close friend or relative, knowing that you would never see them again?

Sometimes our friends move away to live in different parts of the country or even different parts of the world. Some people have relatives who only see them once or twice in a lifetime.

Was it difficult to say goodbye? How did it make you feel?

Saying goodbye is often a time for sadness and tears. Sometimes we are lost for words, and yet have so much we would like to say, but don't know where to begin!

How do you think the apostles felt when they knew that Jesus was finally returning to his father? – They had grown to love him very much, so much that they were prepared to go out and be witnesses for Christ. They probably felt sad and somewhat afraid about what lay ahead of them .

Thinking back to Ascension Thursday, who was the 'helper' that Jesus promised to send? – The Holy Spirit would give the apostles the strength and courage they needed for their mission. They knew that they were not being left alone, but would be watched over always.

Before Jesus finally said farewell, what did he do? – He prayed to his heavenly Father and asked him to take care of his very dear friends, that they would never be alone.

At times when we are feeling worried or afraid, what should we do? – We can pray, just as Jesus did for his friends. We can ask Jesus to watch over and care for us, with complete confidence that he will hear us and answer our prayer because he loves us so much. With Jesus beside us, we have nothing to fear.

ACTIVITY

Ask the children to colour these shapes of our world, sun, moon, stars and clouds. Then take two semicircles of paper, one blue and one black, and place them together to make a circle larger than the globe. Pin the globe to the centre of this background. Help the children to pin the sun, a rainbow, clouds etc. onto the blue side of the paper surround, and add the moon and some self adhesive stars to the black part of the surround. Add the caption 'Keep us in your care – day and night'.

CREED

CLOSING PRAYER

Lord, I do not feel afraid
because you are always with me.
With you beside me there is nothing to fear.
I know that you will protect me from harm
and keep me safe from danger.

Second Sunday of the Year
Lamb of God

INTRODUCTION
Some of the men who would become Christ's apostles had been disciples of John the Baptist. It was while they were with John, on the banks of the river Jordan, that they first saw Jesus, the 'Lamb of God.'

SIGN OF THE CROSS

LIGHT THE CANDLES
Light the candles and read this prayer aloud:
Lord, at our baptism
we became children of the light;
help that light to shine out in our lives,
so that others will be touched
by the love and faith
which you have given to us.

SORRY
In today's Gospel we hear Jesus called the 'Lamb of God'. Each week we ask Jesus to forgive our mistakes and failings as we pray together:

Lamb of God, you take away the sins of the world: have mercy on us.
Lamb of God, you take away the sins of the world: have mercy on us.
Lamb of God, you take away the sins of the world: grant us peace.

GLORIA

GOSPEL ACCLAMATION
To welcome today's Gospel sing Acclamation 5:
We have come to hear you, Lord.

GOSPEL (cf John 1:35-39)
John the Baptist was standing with two of his followers when he saw Jesus walking by. 'There is the Lamb of God,' he said, looking at Jesus. On hearing this, the two men left John and followed Jesus. Seeing that they were following him, Jesus turned and asked, 'What do you want with me?' 'We would like to know where you live,' they answered. 'Come with me and see,' Jesus said. So they followed him to his house and stayed with him for the rest of the day.

DISCUSSION
How did John the Baptist describe Jesus? – As the 'Lamb of God'.

Why did John compare Jesus to a lamb? (To encourage discussion, try to provide a picture of a lamb for the children to look at.)

Lambs are meek and gentle, just as Jesus was. Often they were offered by people as a sacrifice to God to show their love for him. Jesus was sent by his heavenly father to proclaim the Good News and to save us. Like a lamb, he was prepared to be sacrificed, to suffer and to die out of love for us, so that we could share everlasting life in heaven.

When John pointed Jesus out, what did the two men do? – John had often told his followers about the one who was to come after him: the Messiah promised by God. John urged his followers to go with Jesus and to become his disciples, so they followed him.

What did Jesus do when he saw the two men following him? – He invited them to join him and took them to his home. They were completely amazed by this meeting, and marvelled at everything Jesus said.

One of these men became an apostle of Jesus. Do you know his name? – His name was Andrew and he was the brother of Simon Peter. After this first meeting with Jesus he ran to tell his brother Simon Peter all about Jesus because he believed that Jesus really was the saviour of the world.

ACTIVITY
Give each child a cut-out sheep and a square of coloured paper with the caption 'Jesus is the Lamb of God' written on it. Ask them to glue the sheep onto the piece of card and then stick on some cotton wool as its fleece. Attach a piece of thread to each card and suspend these from a mobile display.

CREED

CLOSING PRAYER
Andrew saw the Lamb of God and followed him.
Help us to follow you every day, Lord,
so that others will know that we are Christians
and will follow you too.

Jesus is the° lamb of God

Third Sunday of the Year
Follow me

INTRODUCTION
Jesus called the first disciples to follow him, and they left everything and went with him. Today each of us is called to follow Jesus by sharing God's love with everyone as he taught us to.

SIGN OF THE CROSS

LIGHT THE CANDLES
Light the candles and sing the Candle Song together.

SORRY
Listen carefully to the words of this story told by St Matthew (cf Matthew 18:21-22, 35):

One day Simon Peter asked Jesus, 'Master, how many times must I forgive someone who hurts me? As many as seven times?' Jesus answered, 'Not just seven times, Peter, but seventy times seven! You must always forgive someone from your heart.'

Ask the children to sit quietly and think about what they have just heard before reading this prayer:

Dear Jesus, please help me to be forgiving
and ready to forget the mistakes
made by other people,
just as you are always ready to do for me.

Jesus gave us the gift of his peace to be shared with other people. Later when we share in the Eucharistic meal at Mass today, we will offer a sign of peace. We have asked for God's forgiveness in our prayer and now we offer a sign of peace and friendship by shaking hands with each other.

GLORIA

GOSPEL ACCLAMATION
To welcome today's Gospel sing Acclamation 2:
Light up our hearts.

GOSPEL (cf Mark 1:14-20)
After John the Baptist had been arrested by Herod, Jesus began to preach to the crowds and proclaim the good news. One day while walking beside the sea of Galilee he saw Simon Peter and his brother Andrew casting their nets to catch fish.

Jesus called out to them 'Come, follow me and I will make you fishers of people.' The brothers left their nets and followed him. Further along the shore Jesus saw James and his brother John who were mending nets with their father Zebedee. Jesus called them too, and at once they left their father and followed him.

DISCUSSION
Can you remember the names of the brothers who left their boats and nets to follow Jesus? – Simon Peter and Andrew; James and John.

What did Jesus say to them? – He asked them to follow him and become 'fishers of people'. Jesus needed someone to help him with proclaiming the Good News of God, and to carry on his work when he had returned to his heavenly Father. These men would help him to lead people back to God, and to teach others of God's great love for them.

Many people followed Jesus and became his disciples, but Jesus chose a small number of them to carry on his work. How many did he choose, and can you remember some of their names? – Jesus chose twelve apostles. The name 'apostle' was given to a follower of Jesus who had been specially chosen. They were all close friends of Jesus, who were chosen to preach and perform miracles in his name.

The names of the twelve apostles were:

Simon Peter, Andrew, James, John, Philip, Bartholomew, Matthew, Thomas, (another) James, Thaddeus, Simon and Judas.

Does Jesus call us to follow him too? – When we are baptised into the Christian family we are called to be followers of Christ. But Jesus calls us to follow him every day.

How can we do this?

To follow Jesus we do not usually have to leave home like the first disciples did! By loving God and our neighbour we can follow Jesus every day by living as Jesus taught us to.

ACTIVITY
The children can cut out these invitation cards. They can then fill in the blanks and decorate their cards.

CREED

CLOSING PRAYER
Jesus, help us to follow you each day,
so that in our own small way
we can help to make our world a better place.

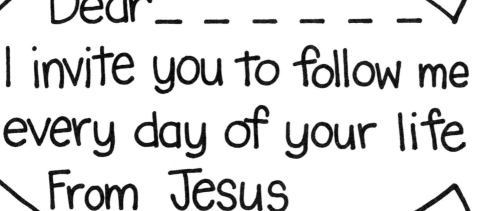

Dear _ _ _ _ _ _ _
I invite you to follow me
every day of your life
From Jesus

Dear Jesus
Thankyou for your invitation
I would love to be one of
your followers
From _ _ _ _ _ _ _

Fourth Sunday of the Year
The power of Jesus

INTRODUCTION
Everyone knew Jesus as an ordinary carpenter, the son of Mary and Joseph; but Jesus was also the Son of God. Today we hear how the people in Capernaum began to realise that there was something very special about Jesus of Galilee.

SIGN OF THE CROSS

LIGHT THE CANDLES
Light the candles and read the words of the Old Testament prophet Isaiah (cf Isaiah 60:19):
'I, the Lord will be your everlasting light and my glory will shine on you always.'

SORRY
God our loving Father is always ready to forgive us and welcome us back to his love.
One day Jesus told a story: 'Once there was a loving father whose son left home and lived a life of selfishness. His father felt sad and lonely, but never stopped loving his son. One day the son returned to ask for his father's forgiveness. His father hugged and kissed him and forgave everything he had done.'

We all make mistakes and do things which are wrong. If we remember this story we will never feel afraid to say sorry to God, because he will always forgive us if we are truly sorry.

GLORIA

GOSPEL ACCLAMATION
(All) Alleluia, alleluia
Your word is a light for my path, a lamp to guide me closer to you.
(All) Alleluia, alleluia.

GOSPEL (cf Mark 1:21-27)
Jesus was staying in a town called Capernaum, and on the Sabbath day, he went to the synagogue to pray. There he began to teach the people, and they were amazed because he spoke to them of God, in a way that no one else had ever done before. Suddenly he was interrupted by a man who was disturbed by an evil spirit. He shouted loudly at Jesus, and everyone was afraid. Jesus said in a firm voice. 'Be quiet, spirit, and leave this man in peace.' The man began to shake, and then with a loud cry, the spirit left him. Everyone was amazed by what had taken place. 'What is happening?' they asked. 'This man Jesus can explain scriptures like no one else, and even the spirits will obey him.'

DISCUSSION
What is a synagogue? – A synagogue is a building where the Jewish people meet to pray and listen to the scriptures.

Where do we meet to listen to God's word? – We meet every week in Church to listen to God's word. But there are many other opportunities to hear God's word – at home with our family or at school assembly.

Each week we gather together as a family to listen to the word of God. Which book are the readings taken from? – The Bible is a very special book which tells of God's great love for his people. It is divided into two main parts – The Old Testament and the New Testament.

What is the difference between the Old and New Testament? – The Old Testament tells us about the history of the Jewish people and of God's love for all creation. The New Testament tells us about the life and teaching of Jesus and his apostles.

Why is it important to listen to these readings? – God speaks to us through the words of the readings. He calls us to follow him and by listening carefully and understanding what we hear, he can work in our lives.

Do you know which day is the Jewish Sabbath? – The Jews celebrate their sabbath on Saturdays, while we celebrate ours on Sunday. Each Sunday we remember and celebrate the Resurrection of Christ.

Which two things made the people realise that there was something special about Jesus?
1. Jesus explained the scripture readings to them in a way that was very different. As God's son, he understood the scriptures as no one else could, and was able to explain their true meaning.
2. The people saw a glimpse of Jesus' power when he cured the man filled with an evil spirit. He revealed something of God's power and might over all living things.

ACTIVITY
Four popular stories from the Old and New Testaments are illustrated. Each picture and story should be discussed and explained to the children. They can be made into individual booklets or enlarged and pinned on a display board after colouring.

CREED

CLOSING PRAYER
Help us to listen carefully to your words, Lord, and to keep them forever in our hearts.

Fifth Sunday of the Year

Jesus cures the sick

INTRODUCTION
Jesus loves *all* people with a love so great that he died for us. Throughout his life he showed this love by curing the sick and making time to share with others.

SIGN OF THE CROSS

LIGHT THE CANDLES
Light the candles and read:
Jesus you are the light of the world; may we see the light of your love and feel its warmth in the lives of the people we meet each day.

SORRY
As we sing our song together, let us ask for God's help to make a fresh start. Sing Sorry Song 2

GLORIA

GOSPEL ACCLAMATION
To welcome today's Gospel sing Acclamation 1:
Share your word with us.

GOSPEL (*cf Mark 1:29-39*)
After preaching in the synagogue, Jesus and his disciples went to Peter's house to share a meal together. When they got there, Peter's wife told them that her mother had been taken ill and was suffering from a high fever. Jesus went to her, took her by the hand and, as he helped her up, the fever disappeared and she felt well again.

That evening, crowds of sick people gathered around Peter's house, and Jesus cured many of them. Early the next morning, Jesus went off to a quiet place to pray.

When his disciples found him, they said, 'Lord, everyone is looking for you. They have heard of the marvellous things you have done.'

Jesus told them, 'I must go and visit other villages too, because I came to tell the Good News to everyone.'

DISCUSSION
In today's Gospel, who became ill? – The mother of Peter's wife. She was suffering from a fever or high temperature.

Have you ever suffered from a fever? How did you feel?

What did Jesus do when he heard of the woman's suffering? – Immediately he went to her to comfort her and make her well again.

Who arrived at Peter's house that evening? – Everyone in Capernaum soon heard about Jesus, from his amazing teaching in the synagogue to his power over illness and evil spirits. A crowd of people suffering from all kinds of diseases gathered outside Peter's house to wait for Jesus.

What did Jesus do? – Even though he was tired, he took pity on the sick and cured many of their diseases. Jesus never turned away from anyone who needed him. Like Peter and his wife, they must have marvelled at the power of Jesus. His compassion and love was so great that he always helped those who needed him. Their love for him must have grown even greater that day.

What did Jesus do early the next morning? – He went off to spend some time alone with God praying and talking to his heavenly Father. Despite the crowds and being so busy healing the people, Jesus remembered to make some time to spend with God.

What does Jesus teach us by his actions? – Jesus helps us to understand that there are many people in the world who need our help, and we too should always be ready to give our time to help them. One way we can help those who are sick and suffering is by praying for them and asking Jesus to make them better.

Often before performing a miracle, Jesus would pray to his heavenly Father. Time after time he reminds us of the importance and power of prayer, and of making time to spend with God. Do each of you remember to spend a little time each day in prayer?

ACTIVITY
Photocopy the illustrated prayers and compile a booklet for each child. Include a few blank pages, and encourage the older children to write and illustrate their own prayers.

CREED

CLOSING PRAYER
Lord Jesus,
you are always ready to make time for others,
especially those who come to you
with worries or troubles.
Thank you for your love and goodness,
and help me remember to make time
to spend alone with you.

OUR WORLD

God our Father, I think it's a pity we spoil Your world with our litter and pollution. Teach us how to look after the world You made for us.

PEOPLE IN NEED

Help us to pray for all those in need. People who are sad or lonely; for those who have no home; for those who are ill, please make them well again. We ask You to show all these people how much You love them.

HAIL MARY

Hail Mary full of Grace, the Lord is with thee. Blessed art thou among women and blessed is the fruit of thy womb, Jesus. Holy Mary, mother of God, pray for us sinners, now and at the hour of our death.

Amen

OUR FATHER

Our Father who art in Heaven, hallowed be Thy name. Thy Kingdom come, Thy Will be done on Earth as it is in Heaven. Give us this day our daily bread and forgive us our trespasses as we forgive those who trespass against us, and lead us not into temptation, but deliver us from evil.

Amen

Sixth Sunday of the Year
Jesus cures the leper

INTRODUCTION
Jesus never judged people by their appearance or paid any attention to what others thought of them. Time and again he made tax-collectors and other outcasts feel welcome and loved. Today we hear how Jesus changed the life of a leper who asked for his help.

SIGN OF THE CROSS

LIGHT THE CANDLES
Light the candles and say Candle Prayer 2: *Show me, show me little candle.*

SORRY
After a few moments of quiet reflection, ask one of the children to choose a sorry colour and say the corresponding prayer together.

GLORIA

GOSPEL ACCLAMATION
To welcome today's Gospel sing Acclamation 3: *Alleluia, alleluia.*

GOSPEL (cf Mark 1:40-45)
One day a leper came to Jesus, and falling on his knees he said to Jesus, 'If you really wanted to, you could help me and cure my leprosy.'

Jesus was filled with compassion, and reaching out to touch him, he said, 'Of course I want to help you!'

At that moment the leprosy disappeared and the man was cured. Jesus sent him away asking him not to tell anyone about what had happened, but the man was so overjoyed he told everyone he met. Soon crowds of people followed Jesus wherever he travelled.

DISCUSSION
Do you know what a 'leper' is? – A leper is the name given to a person suffering from a terrible disease called leprosy.

Do you know anything about leprosy and what can happen to people who suffer from this disease? – Leprosy is an infectious disease which if untreated can deform and cripple people who suffer from it. It is caused by a tiny germ and attacks the hands, feet, and other parts of the body. Lepers cannot feel the infected parts of their bodies and often through injury, lose fingers and toes. Leprosy can also cause blindness. (For leaflets and details about Leprosy contact The British Leprosy Relief Association, Fairfax House, Causton Road, Colchester, Essex CO1 1PU)

What happens if you catch an infection like measles or chickenpox?

Are you allowed to go to school and mix with your friends? – To avoid anyone else catching your illness you are usually kept at home, and away from everyone else.

In Jesus' time, how do you think lepers were treated by other people? – Lepers were sent to live together, far away from the towns and villages. They carried bells or shouted aloud so that people could hear them coming, and could avoid them. Because of their disfigurements people were frightened by their appearance, and they led sad and miserable lives.

How did Jesus treat the leper? – Jesus reached out and touched the leper as a sign of his deep love and willingness to help. Because of this love, Jesus completely transformed the leper's life so that he no longer had to suffer.

Does leprosy still exist today? – Leprosy thrives where there is poverty and it is still common in Asia, Africa and South America. (If possible, show the children where these countries are on a map or globe.) Because it can be cured with modern medicines, lepers are no longer treated as outcasts to be afraid of. People have learned to treat lepers with the same kindness and love as Jesus did.

ACTIVITY
Help the children to make a picture with a sliding figure of the leper, before and after, Jesus cured him.

CREED

CLOSING PRAYER
Jesus,
just as the leper trusted in your love and compassion, we can too.
Help all those who are suffering or ill,
and touch them with your love
so that their lives will be transformed.
Lord hear us.
(All) Lord graciously hear us.

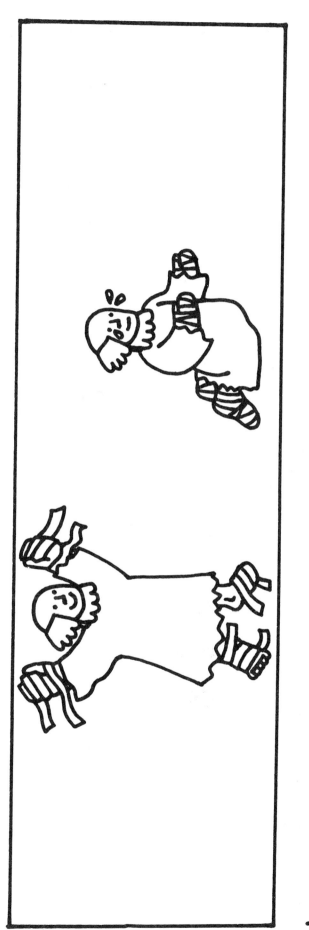

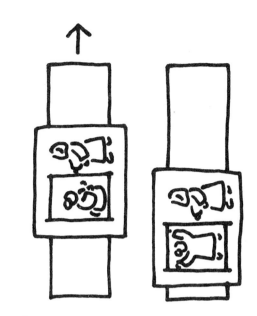

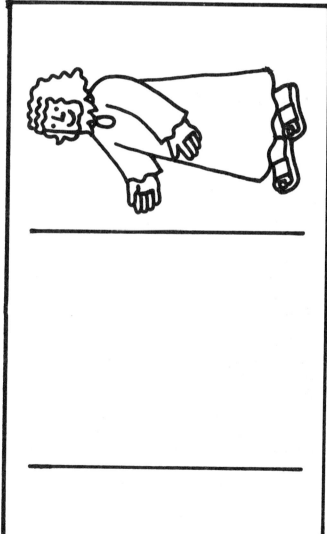

Seventh Sunday of the Year
Don't give up

INTRODUCTION
Have you ever been in a situation where things seemed hopeless or impossible? Did you give up or carry on trying until you succeeded? In today's Gospel we hear how the determination and faith of a cripple's friends finally paid off.

SIGN OF THE CROSS

LIGHT THE CANDLES
As we light the candles today, we pray that the light of Jesus will shine in our lives and show us the path we must follow, to share everlasting life with him.

SORRY
As we journey through life, we will stumble and fall many times, making mistakes and getting things wrong. Jesus is always ready to reach out a forgiving hand, and help us to our feet so we can try again.

Sing Sorry Song 3.

GLORIA

GOSPEL ACCLAMATION
(All) Alleluia, alleluia.
Help us to listen to your word Lord and keep it in our hearts.
(All) Alleluia, alleluia.

GOSPEL (cf Mark 2:1-12)
After Jesus had cured a leper, news of his power spread far and wide. Wherever he stayed, crowds of people gathered outside to hear him preach or hoping that he might cure them.

One day as Jesus was preaching, four men carrying a stretcher arrived. The man on the stretcher was paralysed and could not walk, and his friends hoped that Jesus would cure him. Because the crowds were so great there was not much room, and they could not carry the stretcher close to Jesus. So they climbed onto the roof and made a hole above where Jesus was standing. Then they lowered the stretcher down gently on long ropes. Their faith in Jesus was plain for all to see. Jesus said to the paralysed man, 'Get up, take your stretcher and walk home, my friend.'

Everyone watched in amazement as the man got up, picked up his mat and hurried out to his friends, praising God for all his goodness.

DISCUSSION
Why did crowds of people follow Jesus wherever he went? – Many of these people were crippled or ill, and had heard about the miraculous cures Jesus had performed. They followed him hoping that he would cure them too. Others followed him because they were curious about 'Jesus of Nazareth'! Some believed that Jesus was the promised one sent by God, and came to listen to him and to try to follow his ways.

What was wrong with the man on the stretcher? – The man was paralysed and could not walk. When they found where Jesus was staying, what happened? – They could not get close enough to Jesus to ask for his help, because the crowds were too large.

Have you ever been in a large crowd? Was it difficult for you to push through? Imagine how difficult it was for the four men with their friend on a stretcher!

The men had a sudden brainwave! How did they make sure that they got close enough to Jesus? – They climbed onto the roof of the house and made a hole through which they lowered the stretcher. Poorer homes were simple houses with a roof made from branches which were plastered with mud, with a staircase leading up to the roof.

What did Jesus do when the man was lowered through the roof? – Jesus was impressed by the men's determination and faith. They would not give up even when things seemed impossible, because they believed that Jesus could cure their friend. Jesus rewarded their faith, by making their friend walk again!

What does this story teach us? – When our belief in Jesus is strong enough, nothing is impossible! Against all the odds the friends of the paralysed man were determined to get him close to Jesus. They had complete faith that Jesus would have the power, and the compassion to cure their friend. When faith is so strong, Jesus will never turn us away, but will reach out to help us.

ACTIVITY
Photocopy the bookmarks onto some card and give one to each child. Discuss the crisis illustrated in each picture!

CREED

CLOSING PRAYER
Let us pray
for sick and disabled people everywhere.
May their faith and belief in Jesus be strong,
so that his love will reach out
with its healing touch.

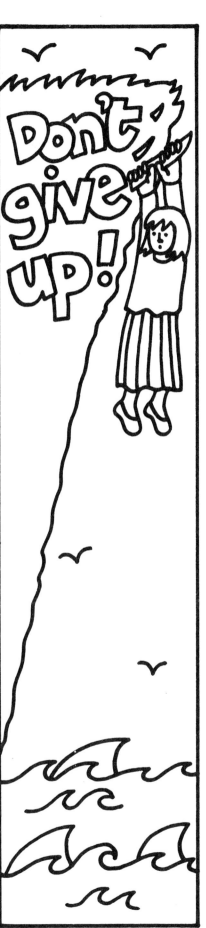

Eighth Sunday of the Year
Pour your love into our lives

INTRODUCTION
Jesus came to bring the Good News that would change peoples lives. Often what he said and did upset many of the Jewish leaders, who would not open their hearts and minds to his message of love.

SIGN OF THE CROSS

LIGHT THE CANDLES
As the candles are lit say together:
May the light of Jesus burn in our hearts.

SORRY
Let us ask God to forgive us if we have spoiled our friendship with him, and to help us make a fresh start today as we pray:
Father in Heaven I give you this day,
all that I think, and do and say.
Fill me with love and make me strong.
With you by my side I won't go wrong.

GLORIA

GOSPEL ACCLAMATION
Say together:
Alleluia, alleluia.
Open our ears and our hearts to your word Lord.
Alleluia, alleluia.

GOSPEL *(cf Mark 2:18-22)*
One day when everyone was supposed to be fasting, the Pharisees and some of the people noticed that Jesus and his disciples were eating as usual. They were annoyed to see that Jewish law was being disobeyed, and they asked Jesus, 'Why are you eating while everyone else is fasting?' Jesus answered, 'The friends of the bridegroom would not fast while he is still with them. There will be plenty of time to fast when he has gone.' Then Jesus said, 'No one would pour new wine into old wineskins, because they would burst and the wine and the skins would be lost forever. New wine must be poured into new wineskins.'

DISCUSSION
What does it mean 'to fast'? – 'To fast' means to go without food for a time. Someone who is fasting, will eat very little food or go without it completely.

Why do people fast? – People fast as a sign of their respect and love for God. Fasting is difficult to do because it is doing something we do not enjoy, but if we do it for God, it is a sign of our love for him.

What did the Jews do on a day of fasting? – On such days the Jews went without food, as a sign of their sorrow for the things they had done wrong. The Pharisees were angry to see Jesus and his disciples apparently ignoring the religious law.

Can you think of any days when we as Christians fast? – During the season of Lent, on Ash Wednesday and Good Friday, we should fast, unless we are very young or very old. Sometimes we hold a 'family fast day', when we go without a meal and send the money we would have spent on food to a charity or aid agency.

Why were the Pharisees angry with Jesus? – Jesus and his disciples were not fasting like everyone else.

What did Jesus say when the people asked him why he was not fasting? – Jesus compared himself to a bridegroom sharing some time with his friends. The bridegroom is not with them for long, and it is important for them to share that time with him before he has to leave them. Jesus also explained how new wine could not be poured into old wineskins. Wine was often stored in animal skins. Old skins could not be used to hold new fermenting wine, because they would burst and all the wine would be lost.

What was the message that Jesus was trying to tell the Pharisees? – Jesus knew that he would not be with his disciples for very long. He wanted them to spend the precious time they had together, listening to his words and everything he taught them. He had come to bring new commandments, about how to love God and each other. These were more important to follow than any other laws. The pharisees were like the old wine skins, set in their ways and unable to hold the new message that Jesus brought to the world.

ACTIVITY
Cut out several large 'wineskins' and a jug shape. Photocopy and cut out the droplet shapes, and write on each of these an example of the love which Jesus pours into our lives. Arrange these on a board, and add the caption 'Jesus pours his love into our lives.'

CREED

CLOSING PRAYER
Lord Jesus,
help us to understand everything you teach us.
Pour your love into our hearts
and fill our lives with your goodness.

Ninth Sunday of the Year
Choose God's way

INTRODUCTION

The Jewish leaders were upset with Jesus and his followers, who often seemed to ignore the Jewish commandments that they followed so strictly. Today we hear how Jesus chose to put God's commandment of love before the rules of the Jewish Sabbath.

SIGN OF THE CROSS

LIGHT THE CANDLES

After the candles are lit, sing the Candle Song together.

SORRY

Read this sorry prayer aloud to the children:
Do not be afraid, God will always love you.
Whatever you have done, God will always love you.
As a father loves his child, He will always love you.
Come back to Him and know, God's love lasts forever.

Allow the children a few moments to reflect on these words and to make their peace with God.

GLORIA

GOSPEL ACCLAMATION

To welcome today's Gospel sing Acclamation 5:
We have come to hear you.

GOSPEL (*cf Mark 3:1-6*)

It was the Jewish Sabbath and Jesus and his disciples went to the synagogue to pray and listen to readings from the scriptures. A man with a paralysed hand was there, and the pharisees watched carefully to see whether Jesus would ignore the rules of the Sabbath and cure him. Jesus knew what they were thinking, so he called the man forward and asked the Pharisees, 'What does the law allow us to do on the Sabbath day? To do a good deed or a bad one; to save someone's life or to end it?'

They did not answer him, and he was annoyed because they were so set in their ways. Jesus turned to the paralysed man and said, 'Hold out your hand.' The man did so, and at once he was cured. The Pharisees went away and began planning how to get rid of Jesus.

DISCUSSION

What is a Sabbath day? – A Sabbath day is a day to rest and worship God. When God created the world he rested on the seventh day, after completing all his work, and he called this day holy. He commanded us to keep one day a week for worshipping God.

On what day does the Jewish Sabbath fall? – The Jewish Sabbath is on a Saturday. It is a strict day of prayer and rest, when work of any kind is against the Jewish law. The Pharisees strictly obeyed the Sabbath commandments and put the importance of obeying these before anything else.

What day of the week is the Christian Sabbath? – Sunday is the Christian Sabbath day, because Jesus rose from the dead on Easter Sunday.

The Pharisees were trying to find fault with Jesus. What did they want to see him do? – They knew of the many miracles Jesus had performed, and his deep love and pity for the crippled and sick. They wanted to see if he would disobey the rules of the Sabbath and cure the man with the paralysed hand.

What question did Jesus ask them? – Jesus asked them if it was more important to choose to do something good for someone even if it meant ignoring the rules of the Sabbath, or to allow someone to suffer.

Did Jesus choose to obey the Sabbath commandments or to help the paralysed man? – Jesus wanted the Pharisees to understand that rules and commandments are there to help people to be good, and not to stop them from acting with kindness and love. The Pharisees had placed too much importance on obeying rules which were stopping them from loving others in the way that God wanted them to.

What are the most important commandments Jesus gave us to follow? – To love God and to love each other as he loves us. Jesus chose to help the paralysed man instead of obeying the Sabbath rules. He showed us that if we choose to put God's rules of love first, then we will make the right decision.

ACTIVITY

Photocopy the picture of Jesus curing the man with the paralysed hand. Ask each child to colour their picture and discuss what they can see in the scene.

CREED

CLOSING PRAYER

Heavenly Father, help us
to make the right decisions in our lives,
so that we always choose to do your will
and lead lives full of love and kindness.

Tenth Sunday of the Year
The family of God

INTRODUCTION
All families everywhere belong to one large family – the family of God. We share one heavenly Father and are all brothers and sisters, as Jesus explains to us today.

SIGN OF THE CROSS

LIGHT THE CANDLES
Light the candles and say Candle Prayer 3: *The light of God.*

SORRY
God is our Father and we are his children. He is slow to get angry and always ready to forgive. Together we ask for his forgiveness with the prayer that Jesus taught us to say: Our Father . . .

GLORIA

GOSPEL ACCLAMATION
To welcome today's Gospel sing Acclamation 3: *Alleluia, alleluia.*

GOSPEL (cf Mark 3:20-21, 31-35)
Crowds of people followed Jesus wherever he went, eager to hear him teaching and to see if all that they had heard about him was true.

One day, such a crowd gathered that it was even impossible for Jesus to have something to eat. When his family heard about this they said, 'Things are getting out of hand! Someone needs to go and take care of Jesus.'

They set off to find him, but there were so many people around him, that they had to send a message to him. Someone came to Jesus and said, 'Your family are outside, and they are waiting to see you.' Jesus said to the people sitting around him, 'Who is my family? All of you are my brothers and sisters! Anyone who does what God wants them to do, will truly belong to my family!'

DISCUSSION
Why were the family of Jesus worried about him? – They knew that Jesus spent much of his time curing the sick and preaching to the crowds. He always put the needs of others before his own, even when he was hungry and exhausted. His family were worried that no-one was taking care of Jesus, and that he would become ill.

What did they decide to do? – Like all families, they cared deeply for each other, and so they set off to take care of him and to make sure that he was eating and resting enough.

When Jesus heard that his family had arrived, what did he ask? – He asked the question 'Who is my family?' He wanted to explain that anyone who did what God wanted them to do, and lived in God's love, belonged to one large family. The members of this family are not related like cousins or aunts or uncles are. They are all related because of the love they share for God and for each other. They share one heavenly Father and are all brothers and sisters of Christ.

What is this one large family called? – The family of God.

When are we called to join this family? – At baptism we were called as Christians to join the family of God, and to follow the teachings of Jesus.

When and where do we meet as one family? – Every Sunday we come to Mass to celebrate the Resurrection of Jesus. We gather to pray and to listen to God's word, which helps us to live as Jesus taught us. Christians throughout the world are united every Sunday, when they gather to worship and praise God for his goodness.

ACTIVITY
Cut out enough circle shapes to allow one for each child, and ask the children to draw a picture of themselves with their family. Draw the number 'one' on a cut out banner as shown, and help the children to write or glue on the words 'We all belong to '1' family of God.' They can then stick their pictures onto the banner.

CREED

CLOSING PRAYER
Loving Father,
as brothers and sisters of Jesus,
we gather together as one family
to worship you and give you praise.
Help us to always treat each other
with love and kindness
just as you taught us to.

Eleventh Sunday of the Year
The kingdom of God

INTRODUCTION
Jesus compares the kingdom of God to a little mustard seed, which grows from a tiny beginning into something great.

SIGN OF THE CROSS

LIGHT THE CANDLES
Light the candles and read this prayer:
At baptism
we are given the light of Christ's love
which burns in our hearts.
As children of the light,
may our goodness shine out for others to see,
so that they too will feel the warmth of God's love
and become part of his kingdom.

SORRY
Let us close our eyes and speak quietly to Jesus in our hearts. (Allow a few moments for quiet reflection.) If we have done anything to make God feel sad or disappointed with us, we ask for his forgiveness as we sing our sorry song together. Sing Sorry song 3.

GLORIA

GOSPEL ACCLAMATION
(All) Alleluia, alleluia.
Reader: Plant your word in our hearts Lord and make it grow.
(All) Alleluia, alleluia.

GOSPEL (cf Mark 4:30-34)
One day Jesus told this parable to the people: 'The kingdom of God is like a tiny mustard seed. Night and day, the little seed sprouts and grows. No-one sees it growing or knows how it happens. Until one day it has become a large and leafy shrub, and the birds of the air find shelter in its many branches.'

Jesus told the people many parables, and later when he was alone with his disciples he helped them to understand their messages.

DISCUSSION
Can you remember what a parable is? – A parable is a short, simple story which Jesus told to explain an important truth or teaching to the people.

In today's parable what did he talk about when explaining about the kingdom of God? – He talked about the tiny mustard seed, and the way that it grows into a large and sturdy plant, to explain how the kingdom of God can grow. The mustard seed plant and its seeds were a common sight in Israel.

Do you know any small seeds which grow into large plants or trees?

(If possible have some familiar seeds displayed and discuss these with the children e.g. apple or orange pips, conkers, acorns, sunflower seeds. Show the children any pictures you can find of what mighty plants these small seeds can become.)

Jesus often talked about the 'kingdom of God', and in today's parable he tries to explain more about this kingdom. What is the kingdom he talks about?

The kingdom of God is the new way of life that Jesus showed us. To live in this kingdom and be a part of it, means that we live as Jesus taught us. We put the love of God and our neighbour before anything else.

How is the kingdom of God like a mustard seed? – The kingdom of God grows from small beginnings like the tiny mustard seed. The word of God is planted in our hearts, and as we grow in kindness, love, understanding and forgiveness we share it with others and in this way God's kingdom grows too.

ACTIVITY
Copy the illustration and ask each child to link each seed with the plant or tree which it becomes.

CREED

CLOSING PRAYER
Jesus taught us to pray, 'Thy kingdom come', and so we pray that the kingdom of God will grow in our daily lives as we say together: Our Father . . .

Link each seed with the tree
or plant it becomes

apple   conker   sycamore

Twelfth Sunday of the Year
Lord of wind and sea

INTRODUCTION
The Sea of Galilee is really a large freshwater lake which at most is approximately 20km (twelve miles) long and 13km (eight miles) wide. Sometimes its calm blue waters are whipped into violent storms by sudden strong winds. One night, as Jesus and his disciples were sailing across the sea, such a storm suddenly began to rage.

SIGN OF THE CROSS

LIGHT THE CANDLES
As we light our candles today, let us remember the words of Jesus who said (cf John 8:12):
'I am the light of the world; whoever follows me will have the light of life and will never walk in darkness.'

SORRY
Ask a child to choose a sorry colour so that the group can read the corresponding Sorry Prayer together.

GLORIA

GOSPEL ACCLAMATION
To welcome today's Gospel sing Acclamation 4: *Praise the Lord.*

GOSPEL (cf Mark 4:35-41)
Jesus and his disciples set off to sail to the other side of the Sea of Galilee. Jesus had been preaching all day, and soon he was lulled to sleep by the rocking of the boat. Suddenly a storm blew up, and great waves began to pound the boat. The disciples were terrified and ran to waken Jesus before they all drowned. Jesus got up, and scolding the sea and wind he said, 'Be at peace!'

At once the wind dropped and the sea grew calm again. Then Jesus asked his disciples, 'Why were you so afraid? Did you not believe in me?' They were filled with wonder because they had seen that even the sea and wind would obey his commands.

DISCUSSION
Have you ever seen the sea when a gale is blowing and there is a storm? – How would you describe it?

High winds can whip up great waves with white, frothy crests. These come crashing into shore with a great roar, sending spray and foam high into the air.

Imagine setting off in a small fishing boat, and suddenly finding yourself caught in a terrible storm. How would you feel?

(Encourage the children to describe any experiences they might have of rough ferry crossings.)

Violent storms can often blow up suddenly on the sea of Galilee, and although some of the disciples had spent much of their time sailing and catching fish, this storm was so bad that even they were afraid that they would all drown.

Today, boats must carry safety equipment to save people from drowning if the boat sinks. Do you think that the disciples had such equipment? – Today people wear life jackets to keep them afloat if they fall in the water. They have radios and flares to call for help and they carry inflatable lifeboats which are ready to use quickly in an emergency. The disciples had none of these things!

In this time of fear and trouble, who did they turn to for help? – They turned to Jesus, and he saw that they were afraid.

What did Jesus do? – He commanded the wind and the waves to be at peace, and to become calm once more. The disciples caught a glimpse of the power of Jesus, the Son of God.

What does this story teach us today? – In times of trouble or fear in our lives, we can always turn to Jesus and ask for his help. We believe that the power of Jesus can overcome all things, because he is the Son of God. Just as Jesus calmed the storm, so he will bring peace and tranquility into our troubled lives.

ACTIVITY
Using the diagram as a guide, either use a sheet of newspaper, or fold a square of coloured paper to make a large model boat. Using modelling clay ask the children to make figures of Jesus and the disciples to go in the boat. Add a large sail, and place the boat on strips of blue tissue paper to represent the stormy sea.

CREED

CLOSING PRAYER (cf Isaiah 41:10)
The Lord says:
Do not be afraid
because I am always with you.
With me by your side
you have nothing to fear.
I will protect you from harm
and save you from danger.

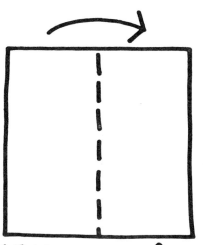

1. Fold square of paper in half.

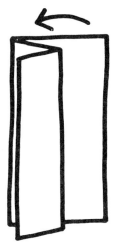

2. Fold edge of paper back to meet folded edge.

3. Turn paper over and repeat action. Then unfold paper.

4. Fold corners into middle crease.

5. Fold right edge over to folded edge.

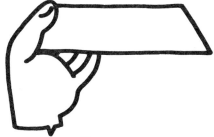

6. Put fingers inside and push corners down with thumbs to make boat 'stand'.

7.

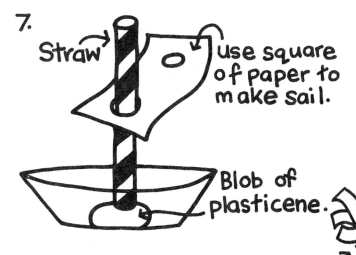

Straw

use square of paper to make sail.

Blob of plasticene.

8.

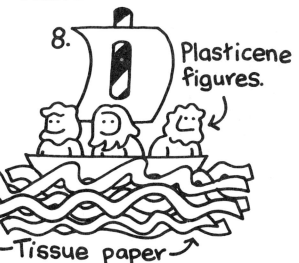

Plasticene figures.

Tissue paper

Thirteenth Sunday of the Year
Jesus gives new life

INTRODUCTION

Jesus knew how precious life is! To be able to enjoy the sun and rain, to be able to love each other and to be part of our world. In today's Gospel, we hear how Jesus used his power to raise a little girl who had died, back to life again!

SIGN OF THE CROSS

LIGHT THE CANDLES

Sing the Candle Song.

SORRY

Before we sing our song together, let us close our eyes and for few moments, tell God how much we love him, and ask for his forgiveness if we have done wrong. Sing Sorry Song 1.

GLORIA

GOSPEL ACCLAMATION

To welcome today's Gospel sing Acclamation 5: *We have come to hear you, Lord.*

GOSPEL (cf Mark 5:21-23, 35-43)

A large crowd had gathered around Jesus, when a man call Jairus came to him and pleaded, 'Master, my little girl is dying! Please come and take her in your arms, so she will be well again.'

Jesus set off with Jairus, but on the way a servant came and told them that the little girl was already dead. Jesus turned to Jairus and said, 'Do not be afraid, just trust me.'

At the house everyone was crying and feeling very sad, but Jesus told them, 'Don't cry, the little girl is not dead, only sleeping.'

They made fun of Jesus! They knew the difference between someone who was sleeping and someone who was dead! Sending everyone else away, Jesus took Jairus and his wife, and the disciples James, John and Peter, up to the room where the little girl lay. Taking her hand gently, Jesus said quietly, 'Little girl, get up!' The little girl got up and walked around the room. They were all so amazed that they didn't know what to say or do next, until Jesus said, 'Give her something to eat, she must be hungry!'

DISCUSSION

Why did Jairus come to ask for Jesus' help? – His little girl was very ill and Jairus believed that Jesus would be able to save her.

What did Jesus do? – When someone asked for help, Jesus never turned them down. He left what he was doing and went off with Jairus at once .

What did Jesus ask Jairus to do when they heard his servants message? – They had been told that they were too late, and the little girl was already dead. Jesus asked Jairus to trust him and to believe in his power. Jesus knew that death was not the end of everything.

Why did the people laugh at Jesus and make fun of him? – They were upset because the little girl was dead: she had stopped breathing and her heart was no longer beating. When Jesus announced that she was only sleeping, they thought he was being foolish and silly.

How do you think Jairus felt, when his little girl opened her eyes and got up? – Jairus had trusted Jesus and believed in him, and yet he was amazed and filled with wonder by the miracle before his eyes. Jesus had brought his daughter back to life when she was already dead. At that moment, Jairus and everyone else in the room had seen the power of God at work – changing death into life!

When do we hope to be raised to life again? – We believe that one day, at the end of time, the dead will be raised up by the power of God to live a new and everlasting life in Heaven.

ACTIVITY

Copy the pictures which tell today's Gospel story for the children to colour. Cut them up and help the children to assemble them in book form.

CREED

CLOSING PRAYER

Dear Jesus,
today we pray for people everywhere
who are sick in mind or body.
In your compassion and love,
reach out and touch them
with your healing power.
(Invite the children to pray for any sick friends or relatives they know.)

We pray that you will heal all our friends and relatives, especially those that we have mentioned in our thoughts and words.

Fourteenth Sunday of the Year
Jesus of Nazareth

INTRODUCTION
In the time of Jesus, Nazareth was a little town in the hill country of Galilee. Jesus spent his childhood there, living with his parents Mary and Joseph. During a visit to Nazareth he found that he was not welcome anymore!

SIGN OF THE CROSS

LIGHT THE CANDLES
Light the candles and read (*cf Matthew 5:16-17*):
Jesus said, 'Let your goodness shine out like a light in the darkness, so that through you, the love of our heavenly Father will touch the lives of others.'

SORRY
The words of St Paul remind us how we should live as brothers and sisters in Christ (*cf Colossians 3:12-14, 23*):
Always be ready to care for others, and to be kind and gentle. Be patient and calm, and never boast or feel proud of your goodness. Just as God always forgives you, so you must always forgive others. Fill your heart with love, and whatever you do, do it for God.

Allow a few moments for quiet reflection.

GLORIA

GOSPEL ACCLAMATION
To welcome today's Gospel sing Acclamation 1: *Share your word with us.*

GOSPEL (*cf Mark 6:1-6*)
Jesus returned to his home town of Nazareth with his disciples, and on the Sabbath day, he went to the synagogue to preach. The people there were amazed by his wisdom and all that he said, and many of them had heard of the miracles that he had worked. But some of the crowd asked, 'Surely this is Joseph the carpenter's son? Isn't his family still living here in Nazareth? How can he know all these things and talk in this way?' They would not listen to Jesus or believe in him. Jesus was saddened and disappointed by their lack of faith and he left Nazareth to go and preach elsewhere.

DISCUSSION
Which town did Jesus come from? – Nazareth. This is why Jesus was called 'Jesus of Nazareth'.

Who did Jesus know, who was still living in Nazareth? – We are told that his family were living there.

Why were the people amazed by Jesus? – Many of them had grown up with Jesus, gone to school together and worshipped with him at the synagogue every week. They knew him as Jesus, the ordinary son of an ordinary couple, Mary and Joseph. Suddenly he had come back and was able to perform miracles and explain the word of God as no-one else could. Jesus of Nazareth was no longer just the carpenter's son!

Was everyone ready to listen to Jesus and to believe in him? – Very few people were willing to listen or believe in Jesus. They doubted his power and his message of love and goodness.

What did Jesus do? – He left Nazareth and travelled from place to place, bringing his message to those who were willing to listen and believe that he was indeed the Son of God.

How can we make Jesus welcome? – By welcoming his word and all that he teaches us. Welcoming him in the people we meet every day, and by opening our hearts to his love and making him a part of our daily lives.

ACTIVITY
Hand out enlarged copies of these pictures. They can be coloured, stuck on card and arranged on a mobile. Discuss the role of Jesus in each illustration, as he reveals himself as the Son of God.

CREED
Each week we tell God and each other all the special things that we believe. Help us to think about this as we say the words of the Creed today.

CLOSING PRAYER
Lord, may our belief in you
help others to find you for themselves
and believe in you too.

Fifteenth Sunday of the Year
Messengers for Jesus

INTRODUCTION
Before returning to his heavenly Father, Jesus prepared his apostles to go out and share the Good News of God's love with the world.

SIGN OF THE CROSS

LIGHT THE CANDLES
Light the candles and say Candle Prayer 2: *Show me, show me little candle.*

SORRY
God is our loving Father and will *always* forgive us if we are truly sorry. Remember the story Jesus told about a loving father . . .

There was once a loving father whose son left home and lived a wicked and selfish life. This made his father very sad. One day the son came back and was truly sorry for all his mistakes. His father hugged him and forgave him for everything.

God is our loving Father and he will always forgive us if we are truly sorry.

GLORIA

GOSPEL ACCLAMATION
To welcome today's Gospel sing Acclamation 2: *Light up our hearts.*

GOSPEL (cf Mark 6:7-13)
Jesus sent his twelve apostles out in pairs, to preach to the people and to cure the sick. He told them to take no money, no spare clothes and no food. 'If someone makes you welcome, then stay with them until your work is finished,' he said. 'But if people are unfriendly and do not want to listen to your message, then walk away and leave them to themselves.'

The apostles set off, and did everything as Jesus had said. Many people turned back to God after hearing their words, and others were cured in Jesus' name.

DISCUSSION
If you were being sent off on a long journey, what sort of things would you want to pack?
- clothes to wear if the weather turned hot or cold.
- food and something to drink.
- several pairs of shoes.
- toothbrush and toothpaste.
- waterproof coat in case it rained.
- money for bus or train fares.

(Encourage the children to add their own ideas to the list.)

What did Jesus tell his apostles to take with them? – They were to go in the clothes they stood in, with nothing extra, except a stick in their hand to help them walk. They had no need of money or food, or any of the extra baggage we would want to take with us on a journey!

Why did Jesus want them to do this? – The most important thing the apostles carried was the message that Jesus had sent them with. This was the Good News that he had brought to share with the world, to lead people back to God's love and everlasting life. To love God and each other, to be forgiving and kind, and to live as Jesus had taught them. God would guide and look after the brave apostles on their mission, taking care of all their needs. Jesus knew that good people would welcome his apostles into their hearts and homes, and take care of them.

How do you think the apostles felt as they set off on their journeys? – They probably felt a mixture of excitement and fear. They did not know what sort of a welcome to expect from the people they preached to, or whether they would succeed in doing everything Jesus had asked them to do. They placed their trust in God to watch over and guide them.

How can we be like the apostles, and share the message of Jesus with the world around us? – We can share Christ's message with the people we meet every day, by making our thoughts, our words and our actions like those of Jesus. By living as he taught us to, and allowing the Holy Spirit to work through us, he can reach out and touch the lives of others, bringing them closer to God.

ACTIVITY
Using the cut-out picture help the children to provide the figure with everything he might need to help him on his journey through life to the kingdom of Heaven.

CREED

CLOSING PRAYER
Lord Jesus, you chose the twelve apostles
to bring your message to the world.
You also chose to give each one of us life,
and to welcome us into the family of God.
Help us to share your message of love and truth
with the people we meet each day.

Love

Joy

GOODNESS

FORGIVENESS

Generosity

Bread of life

God's rules

Sixteenth Sunday of the Year
The shepherd and his flock

INTRODUCTION
A good shepherd always puts the needs of his flock first. Today we hear how Jesus, 'the Good Shepherd', put the needs of others before his own.

SIGN OF THE CROSS

LIGHT THE CANDLES
Light the candles and read this prayer:
The candle flame is warm and bright,
it changes darkness into light.
We feel its warmth and see its glow,
and when we look at it we know,
the light of Christ is burning bright,
for we are children of the light.

SORRY
Listen to this story Jesus told:

One day a shepherd found that one of his flock was missing, so he left the other ninety-nine sheep, and went off to look for it. He searched and searched until he found it, because every one of his sheep was precious to him.

If we have not been good, and have lost our way,
let us ask Jesus to forgive us
and to lead us back to his flock.

GLORIA

GOSPEL ACCLAMATION
To welcome today's Gospel sing Acclamation 3:
Alleluia, alleluia.

GOSPEL (cf Mark 6:30-34)
After preaching to the people and curing many that were sick, the apostles returned to Jesus, and told him everything that they had said and done. As usual, crowds of people had followed them; the apostles were feeling tired and in need of a rest. Jesus said to them, 'We will go somewhere quiet and spend some time alone.'

However when Jesus and his friends arrived, a crowd of people had already gathered to meet them. When Jesus saw them, he was filled with pity, because they were like sheep without a shepherd to care for them. He sat down on the hillside and began to teach them.

DISCUSSION
Where had the apostles been? (Recall last week's Gospel.)

When they returned to Jesus, what did they find? – Wherever Jesus travelled, news soon reached the local people, and it was not long before a crowd of people flocked around him. The apostles were tired after their journeys and eager to spend time telling Jesus about everything that had happened. Jesus was surrounded by people wanting his attention.

What did Jesus suggest that they do? – Jesus suggested that they sail off to find some peace and quiet.

Things did not go quite as planned! What did they find when they moored their boat? – People had guessed their plan and when they arrived a crowd had already gathered.

What did Jesus do? Did he grow impatient or angry? – Jesus felt a deep sense of love for his followers, and as always, put their needs before his own. The 'good shepherd' knew that these people were his flock. They relied on him to guide and look after them, just as a good shepherd guides and looks after his sheep. He would never let them down or turn them away.

ACTIVITY
Copy the adaptation of *Psalm 23* on to a large sheet of paper. Cut out a 'Good Shepherd' figure and enough sheep for each child. Use these to decorate the words of the prayer and encourage the children to illustrate the picture by drawing tufts of green grass, pools of water, a path etc. Alternatively hand out the colouring in picture.

CREED

CLOSING PRAYER
Read *Psalm 23* aloud together and discuss the words and illustrations with the children.

Psalm 23
The Good Shepherd takes care of all my needs:
He leads me to lush green meadows
and crystal clear pools.
He guides and protects me
and I grow strong in his care.
When night falls, I am not afraid,
for he is always beside me
to protect me from harm.
When he calls, I will follow,
knowing that his love for me
will last forever.

Seventeenth Sunday of the Year
Jesus feeds the people

INTRODUCTION
Jesus loved and cared for his followers; one day with only five loaves and two fish he was able to feed a crowd of five thousand people.

SIGN OF THE CROSS

LIGHT THE CANDLES
Light the candles and sing the Candle Song together.

SORRY
If we have wandered away from God's friendship and love, let us tell him that we are sorry and ask for his forgiveness as we sing Sorry Song 4.

GLORIA

GOSPEL ACCLAMATION
(All) Alleluia, alleluia.
(Reader) May we listen to your word, Lord and carry it in our hearts.
(All) Alleluia.

GOSPEL (cf John 6:1-15)
Jesus crossed the Sea of Galilee, and seeing that a large crowd had followed him along the shore, he turned to Philip and asked, 'Where can we buy some bread to feed these people?' Philip answered, 'Master, it would cost a fortune to give each person even a small piece of bread!'

Then a small boy, with five loaves and two fish was brought to Jesus. 'This is all the food we have!' the disciples said.

'Tell the people to sit down,' Jesus said, and taking the bread and fish, he gave thanks to God, then he gave the food out to as many as five thousand people, and there was plenty for everyone. When they had finished eating, they filled twelve baskets with the scraps that were left! These people saw and believed that Jesus was indeed the Son of God.

DISCUSSION
Last week we talked about Jesus as the 'Good Shepherd' who takes care of the needs of his flock. What did the people on the hillside need that day? – The people had walked many miles that day to be with Jesus, and they were tired and hungry. It was miles to the nearest town, and even then, Jesus and his disciples did not have enough money to buy food for so many! The people needed food, and Jesus provided it for them.

How many people were in the crowd that day? – The Gospel tells us that as many as five thousand people needed to be fed that day. The exact number does not really matter, because normally five loaves and two fish could not possibly feed them all.

Have you ever shared a meal with a large number of people? – At certain times of year, perhaps at Christmas or a birthday party, many friends and relatives gather together to share a meal. Usually a lot of planning and preparation takes place, to make sure that there is enough for everyone to eat and drink. Imagine how the disciples must have felt when Jesus suddenly decided that they should feed this huge crowd of people!

What did Jesus do with the loaves and the fish?

He thanked God for his goodness, blessed the food and then shared it with the people.

When does Jesus feed us? – Jesus said, 'I am the Bread of Life. If you eat this bread, I will live in you and you in me.' At the Eucharistic meal, Jesus shares himself with us in a very special way, so we can grow in God's love and be filled with joy and goodness.

ACTIVITY
Ask each child to draw a picture of a basket and then glue two cut-out fish and five loaves into place on their picture. After colouring, help them to write, 'Jesus feeds his people' on their completed picture.

CREED

CLOSING PRAYER
Lord Jesus,
you fed the hungry crowds that day,
and you feed us with the bread of life.
Through the gift of yourself
help us to become more like you.

Eighteenth Sunday of the Year
Manna from Heaven

INTRODUCTION
After the Israelites had fled from Egypt into the desert, God took care of his people and made sure that they did not go hungry.

SIGN OF THE CROSS

LIGHT THE CANDLES
Light the candles and pray:
The light of the candle
and the warmth of its flame,
remind us
that the light and warmth of your love
surrounds each one of us always.

SORRY
Ask a child to choose a sorry colour and after a few minutes of quiet reflection, read the prayer aloud together.

GLORIA

ACCLAMATION
Listen and know how much God loves you!

READING (cf Exodus 16:2-4, 12-15)
After escaping from Egypt, Moses led the Israelites through the desert. Soon they ran short of food and they became bad-tempered and ungrateful as they grew hungry.

'At least when we were slaves we had plenty to eat!' they grumbled. God heard his people complaining, and he said to Moses, 'I will make food fall from the sky, and my people can gather all that they need. I will send them meat, so they will be satisfied and content. Then they will know that I am their God who loves and cares for them.'

That evening a flock of quails settled around the camp and the people caught and ate them. In the morning the ground was covered with dew, and when it dried it left behind manna which God had sent. Moses told the people, 'God has heard our cries for help, and has sent us manna from heaven to answer our prayers.'

DISCUSSION
Why had the Israelites wanted to escape from Egypt? – For many years the Israelites had lived as slaves of the Egyptians. Life was hard there, and the Egyptians were cruel and harsh. The people prayed to God to save them from their misery.

Who did God choose to rescue the Israelites, and to lead them to the promised land? – God chose Moses to rescue his people from slavery and to lead them to freedom.

Why did the people begin to grumble and complain? – When they began to run out of food, they grew more and more hungry and began to complain to Moses.

Have you ever seen pictures of a desert? What is it like? Is there much to eat there? (Show the children any relevant pictures/ photographs you can.)

Deserts are often very hot by day and very cold at night. They can be sandy or stony but there is never very much soil, so few plants can grow there and few animals can live there. The Israelites could not find enough to eat.

What did God promise to send? – God promised to make food fall from the sky and to provide them with meat to eat.

What was the name given to the food which appeared on the ground each day? – The people called it 'manna'. The Bible tells us that manna was like small whitish/yellow coriander seeds (cf Numbers 11. 7-9). The people gathered these and pounded them to make flour. They mixed it with olive oil and made it into flat cakes or pancakes which tasted like bread. (If possible show the children some whole coriander seeds.)

What flew into the camp and provided the Israelites with meat to eat? – A flock of small game birds called quails flew into the camp.

When the Israelites were hungry, God provided food for them to eat. Can you remember when Jesus provided food for a large crowd of hungry people? – Last week we heard how Jesus fed the five thousand people with five loaves and two fish.

ACTIVITY
Draw the background for a desert scene on a large piece of paper. Make the foreground appear cracked to emphasize its dryness, and add a large and glaring sun to be coloured. Photocopy the quail shapes to be cut out and coloured by the children. Glue these onto the scene with some fine wisps of cotton wool to represent the manna.

CREED

CLOSING PRAYER
Dear Lord, you gave Moses and the Israelites manna to eat in the desert.
We ask you today to help all those people who are hungry in our world.
Help us to be generous
by sharing what we have with others.
We ask this through Christ our Lord.

Nineteenth Sunday of the Year
God feeds Elijah

INTRODUCTION
Over the past two weeks we have heard how God feeds his people and takes care of their needs. Today we listen to a story about the prophet Elijah, who lay weak with hunger, feeling totally hopeless, until God saved him.

SIGN OF THE CROSS

LIGHT THE CANDLES
Light the candles and read this prayer aloud:
Lord, at our baptism
we became children of the light;
help that light
to shine out in our lives,
so that others will be touched
by the love and faith
which you have given to us.

SORRY
Let us ask for God's forgiveness and help to make a fresh start as we sing together Sorry Song 2

GLORIA

ACCLAMATION
God our Father loves us and keeps us from harm.

READING (cf First Book of Kings 19:1-8)
The prophet Elijah listened to God and told the people what God had said. A man called Ahab, was King of Israel at that time, and he did not believe in God.

After Elijah and the king had a great argument, Elijah escaped to the desert, because he was afraid that the king would have him killed. After walking for a whole day under the glare of the desert sun, Elijah sat down under a shady bush and said, 'I can't go on, Lord! I have had enough and just want to die in peace!'

He fell asleep, until an angel woke him and said, 'Elijah, have something to eat and drink.' Beside him he saw a loaf of bread and a jar of water. He ate and drank and then fell asleep again. This happened a second time, and finally Elijah got up, and feeling much better, carried on with his journey.

DISCUSSION
Why did Elijah feel so fed up? – He had argued with King Ahab and upset him, and he believed that the King might have him killed.

Why did Elijah flee to the desert? – Elijah's life was in danger, so he set off into the wilderness where no-one could find him. Elijah had fled in panic, to escape from the King's soldiers. He was not properly prepared for such a journey through the desert, and carried little food or water. It was not long before he began to feel hungry, thirsty and very tired.

When you are hungry and thirsty, how does it make you feel? – We all know how miserable we feel when we need something to eat. We have no energy to do anything and we feel downhearted and unable to carry on.

What made Elijah feel better and lift his spirits? – God saw that Elijah needed something to eat and drink. He knew that after a nourishing meal Elijah would feel much better and be ready to pick himself up and carry on. God sees when we are in trouble or in great need, and always sends his spirit to help us and give us strength.

What food does Jesus share with us, to nourish us on our journey through life? – In the Holy Eucharist, Jesus gives us the gift of himself – the 'Bread of Life'. In this way he becomes a part of us and helps us to become one with him. It makes us grow in love and goodness, and gives us the strength to carry on when times are hard, just as God gave food and strength to Elijah.

ACTIVITY
Photocopy a picture of Elijah for each child to colour and take home.

CREED

CLOSING PRAYER
Lord Jesus,
you are the 'Bread of Life'
who shares everlasting life with us.
Fill our hearts with your love
and satisfy our hunger for you.

Twentieth Sunday of the Year
The Bread of Life

INTRODUCTION
Today Jesus tells the people that he is the 'Bread of Life' and that anyone who eats this bread will live forever.

SIGN OF THE CROSS

LIGHT THE CANDLES
Say together:
May the love of God burn in our hearts and light up our lives so that others will see and believe.

SORRY
Let us ask God to pour his love into our hearts and change them with his goodness, so that we become more like him as we pray: Our Father . . .

GLORIA

GOSPEL ACCLAMATION
To welcome today's Gospel sing Acclamation 4: *Praise the Lord.*

GOSPEL (cf John 6:51-58)
Jesus said to the people, 'I am the Bread of Life which has come down from Heaven. This bread is my body which will be given to save the world, and whoever eats it will live forever.'

'What nonsense is this?' asked the Jews angrily. 'Are we supposed to eat this man's flesh?'

Then Jesus said, 'Whoever eats my body and drinks my blood, will rise up on the last day to share everlasting life with God. They will live in me, and I will fill them with my life. This bread comes from Heaven, and it is not like the bread your fathers ate. They are all dead. But whoever eats the bread of life will live forever.'

DISCUSSION
Where does bread come from? – Bread is made with flour which comes from wheat which has been ground and milled. At the bakery it is mixed with yeast to make it rise, before it is baked and sold.

How did Jesus describe himself to the people?

Jesus described himself as the 'Bread of Life' which had come down from Heaven. Whoever ate this bread would share everlasting life with God at the end of time.

Did the people understand what Jesus told them? – Some thought that Jesus wanted them to eat his very flesh; others were confused because Jesus had told them that he had come down from heaven, yet they knew that he was the son of Joseph and Mary; others were confused because he offered them the gift of eternal life and they did not understand how this could happen.

Do you find what Jesus said a little confusing?

Sometimes when we find something confusing or we do not understand, it becomes clear after we have listened carefully from the very beginning through to the very end. We know the end of today's story because we know what Jesus gave to his friends at the Last Supper.

What did Jesus do with the bread and wine at the last supper? – Jesus changed them into his own body and blood. Through the power of the Holy Spirit they became Jesus himself, so that he could share himself in a very special way with his apostles.

How does Jesus share himself with us today? – At the offertory, we bring bread and wine to be changed through the power of God, into the body and blood of Jesus. We do not understand how this happens, but we *believe* it because we *know* that *nothing* is impossible for God. We receive the body and blood so that we can share in Christ's life and and become more like Jesus. It nourishes and feeds us, making us grow stronger in goodness and love.

Jesus said, 'Whoever eats the Bread of Life will live forever.' What did he mean? – We know that Jesus died and rose from the dead at Easter. The power of God is so great that he can raise someone from the dead to new life. Jesus promised that if we eat the bread which he gives, the gift of himself, then he will fill us with his life, and at the end of time we will rise from the dead to live with him forever in Heaven.

ACTIVITY
Using the picture as a guide, cut out the host complete with rays, and the chalice from stiff card. Allow the children to decorate the chalice and colour the rays. Hang these as a mobile or on a wall.

CREED

CLOSING PRAYER
Jesus, you are the Bread of Life
and I believe that you are really present
in the Eucharistic meal we share.
Fill me with your life
and make me become more like you.

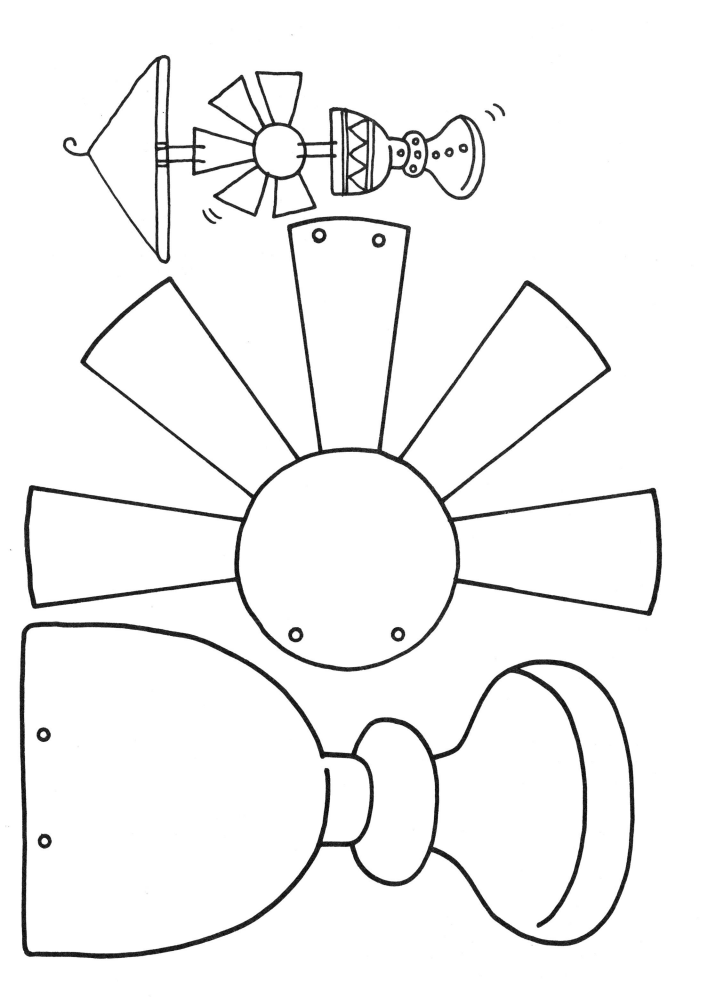

Twenty-first Sunday of the Year
We believe

INTRODUCTION

When Jesus had told the crowd that he was the 'living bread', many of them turned away and left because they did not believe in him.

SIGN OF THE CROSS

LIGHT THE CANDLES

Sing the Candle Song together.

SORRY

Read this prayer (cf Psalm 14:2-3):
Help us Lord to do what is right.
Make our words and thoughts true and sincere,
so that we harm no one by what we say or do.

Let's close our eyes and in our hearts ask Gods' forgiveness for anything we have done to hurt others by what we have said or done.

GLORIA

GOSPEL ACCLAMATION

(All) Alleluia, alleluia.
(Reader) Jesus is the living bread, who brings the message of eternal life.
(All) Alleluia, alleluia.

GOSPEL (cf John 6:60-69)

Jesus had told his followers that he was the 'Bread of Life', but many of them refused to believe what he had said. Jesus heard them arguing with each other and said to them, 'Many will not believe that I am the way to eternal life. I know that my heavenly Father has revealed this to only a few.'

After this some of the crowd left him and followed him no more. Jesus turned to the twelve he had chosen and asked, 'Will you choose to leave me too?'

Then Simon Peter stepped forward and said, 'Master, who would we turn to? We believe in your message of eternal life, because we know that you are the Son of God.'

DISCUSSION

Have you ever found that somebody didn't believe what you told them? – How did you feel?

Sometimes when we have something extraordinary to tell someone, they find it hard to believe. We have to try to convince them that it is really true, even though we might have no proof.

What was the extraordinary thing that Jesus had said? – Jesus had told his followers that he was the 'Bread of Life,' and that whoever ate his body and drank his blood would be filled with everlasting life.

Did all the followers of Jesus believe what he had told them? – God had revealed to them that Jesus was his Son, but many did not understand his message of eternal life. Their faith was weak, so they turned away from him and left.

How do you think Jesus felt when they left? – Jesus was probably sad and disappointed to find that so many people did not believe in him. He had come to share the special gift of his life with them, and they had chosen to turn away and leave him.

Did the twelve apostles choose to leave Jesus too? – Sometimes the apostles did not fully understand all that Jesus told them. Often things needed to be explained, and many things only became clear after Jesus had died and risen from the dead. It was Simon Peter who once again showed the strength of his faith. He stepped forward to declare his belief in Jesus, as the Son of God. The other apostles followed Peter's example and stayed with Jesus.

Do we choose to believe in Jesus and to follow him? – Peter said, 'Master who would we turn to?' Like Peter, we can turn to Jesus to guide us and lead us to his heavenly kingdom. He is our teacher and friend; he is always there to help us when we need him, and his love for us is all forgiving and unending. We trust and believe in him and all that he teaches. We know that he is indeed the 'Bread of Life.'

ACTIVITY

Use a large piece of coloured paper to make a banner. Cut out enough letters for the children to colour and make into the caption 'We believe in Jesus and follow him'. Help them to glue these into place.

CREED

CLOSING PRAYER

Jesus we believe in you
and choose to follow your way.
Give us the Bread of Life
to fill us with love and to make our faith strong.

Twenty-second Sunday of the Year
A clean heart

INTRODUCTION
The Pharisees and scribes had made many laws supposed to help the Jews obey God's law. After a time it became more important to obey their own laws than those of God. Today we hear how and why Jesus disobeyed one of these laws.

SIGN OF THE CROSS

LIGHT THE CANDLES
Light the candles and read:
At baptism
we received the light of Christ,
as a sign of his love.
May we always walk in the light of this love,
and share it with whoever we meet.

SORRY
Have you ever had a bright shiny apple and bitten into it only to find that it is rotten in the middle?

What is on the outside is not important, but what is inside really matters. St Matthew tells us (cf Matthew 12:34-35):

The words that we speak flow from our hearts. If our hearts are filled with goodness, our words and actions will be kind and loving too. But if our hearts are filled with darkness and hate, then our words and actions will be selfish and unkind.

Let us turn to God and speak to him in our hearts, asking for his help to chase away any darkness, and to fill our hearts with his goodness and love.

(Allow the children a few quiet moments to contemplate.)

GLORIA

GOSPEL ACCLAMATION
To welcome today's Gospel sing Acclamation 2: *Light up our hearts.*

GOSPEL (cf Mark 7:1-5, 14-15, 20-23)
One day the Pharisees noticed that Jesus and his disciples had not washed properly before eating. They asked Jesus, 'Why do you ignore the Jewish custom and eat your food with unclean hands?' Jesus answered, 'You have made the laws of men more important than the laws of God. You take great care to wash and keep your bodies clean on the outside. But you have forgotten that what is important is what lies inside – within your hearts.

Ordinary dirt cannot make our hearts and lives unclean! Only wicked words, thoughts and actions can do this. It is more important to God to have a good heart than clean hands.'

DISCUSSION
Why were the Pharisees angry with Jesus and his disciples? – They had disobeyed the custom of washing before a meal. Jewish laws expected people to wash their hands and faces before eating or praying.

Have you ever heard the saying: 'Cleanliness is next to Godliness'? – This sums up how the Pharisees felt about the importance of washing. It was very important to them to keep their bodies clean and free from stain, because they thought this brought them closer to God.

Why did Jesus not place such importance on these rules? – Jesus wanted to explain that dirt on the outside could not make a person unclean on the inside.

What do you think could make a person's heart unclean? (Encourage the children to make suggestions.)

When people have unkind thoughts, or act selfishly, or say something cruel, all these things make their hearts unclean. What goes on inside us is what really matters, and that is what matters most to God.

Another saying we often use is: 'You cannot judge a book by its cover.' Does this agree with what Jesus said? – A book may be old and grubby on the outside, but the story written inside could be the best story you've ever read. Just like books the outward appearance of people can be misleading. We have to look into their hearts, and see what is inside, to know whether they are filled with God's goodness.

ACTIVITY
Dress the figure in the illustration in some simple cut-out clothes, with a jacket that opens at the front. Cut out a large heart shape, and help the children to write on it some of the things which make a person good inside. Stick this onto the figure, and make sure his jacket opens so that they can look inside.

CREED

CLOSING PRAYER
Father, pour your goodness into our hearts.
Help us to try not
to judge others by their appearance,
but to look for your goodness inside them.

Fold

Fold

A.

A. Glue to back of boy.

waistcoat opens to reveal heart.

Twenty-third Sunday of the Year

Jesus cures a deaf man

INTRODUCTION
Unless we know someone who is deaf, we take the gift of hearing for granted. We never stop to imagine how different our lives would be if we could not hear. Jesus often changed the lives of the people he met. Today we hear how one deaf man's world would never be the same again.

SIGN OF THE CROSS

LIGHT THE CANDLES
Light the candles and say Candle Prayer 1: *Flicker, flicker little candle.*

SORRY
As we sing our sorry song together, let us ask God to change our hearts and help us to be good. Sing Sorry Song 3.

GLORIA

GOSPEL ACCLAMATION
To welcome today's Gospel sing Acclamation 5: *We have come to hear you, Lord.*

GOSPEL (cf Mark 7:31-37)
Jesus was returning to the Sea of Galilee when some people brought to him a man who was deaf and could not speak properly. They asked Jesus to help their friend.

Jesus was filled with pity and led the man away to a quiet place where he touched his ears and tongue with his hands, and looking up to heaven said, 'Be opened!' At once the man could hear and speak clearly!

The man and his friends were amazed, and they told everyone they met about the miracle Jesus had performed.

DISCUSSION
Ask the children to close their eyes, sit very quietly and listen to all the things around them. After a few moments ask them to describe some of the sounds they could hear.

Can you remember the very first sound you heard this morning?

If you had to choose a favourite sound what would it be and why?

Often we associate certain sounds with particular happy events:
- A car in the drive which means that Daddy is home from work.
- The sound of Happy Birthday being sung, before you open your presents.
- A cheering crowd when your team has just scored a goal!

Now ask the children to close their eyes and put their hands tightly over their ears.

What difference would it make to their lives if they could not hear?

They would not be able to:
- listen to music
- hear what others are saying.
- understand a television programme easily.
- hear the sound of traffic.
- hear the words 'I love you.'

(Encourage the children to make their own suggestions.)

How do deaf people today communicate with the world? – They use sign language and lip reading to hold a conversation. Some television programmes have subtitles, or write the words being spoken on the screen, so that deaf people can understand.

How do you think the deaf man must have felt when Jesus cured him? – Suddenly his silence was broken by the sounds of the world around him, sounds which he had never heard before! He found that he could speak clearly and make himself understood. Jesus had totally changed his life by his act of kindness, and it would never be the same again.

What do you imagine he might have heard and said first? – Perhaps the first thing that he heard was the sound of Jesus' own voice, and it would be nice to imagine that the first words he spoke were to thank Jesus for changing his life and enabling him to hear and speak.

ACTIVITY
Photocopy the series of pictures telling the story of today's Gospel. Help the children to arrange these in order to make a booklet.

CREED

CLOSING PRAYER
Dear God,
we thank you today
for the gift of hearing.
Help us to listen to and appreciate
all the wonderful sounds around us,
and to pray for all those
who only know the sound of silence.

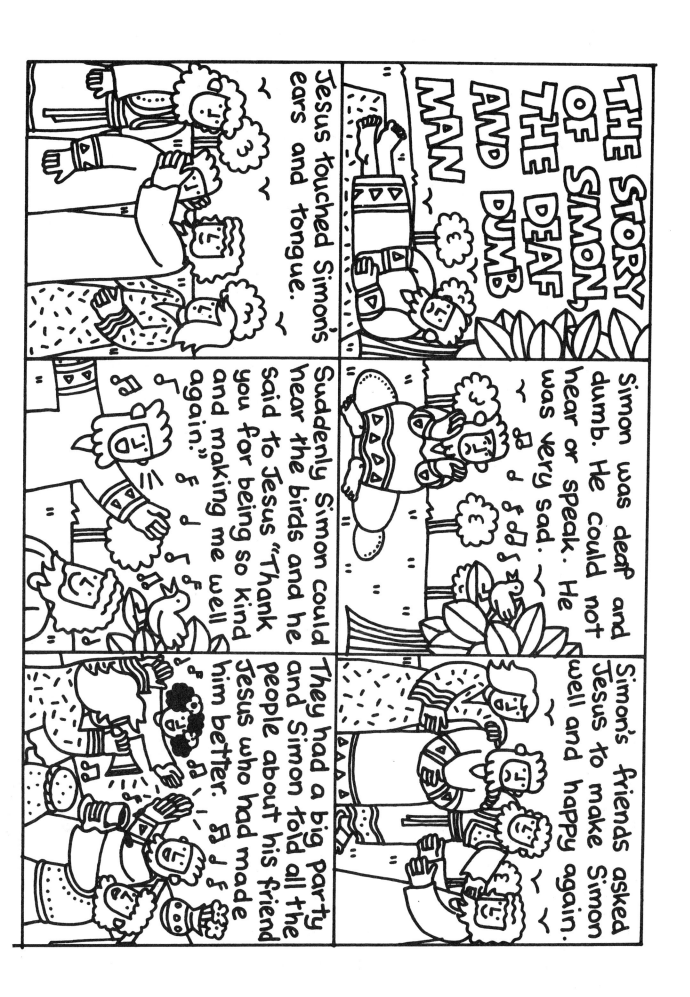

Twenty-fourth Sunday of the Year

Jesus is the Son of God

INTRODUCTION

Today we hear Jesus asking his followers a difficult question: 'Who do you think I am?' Listen carefully, and see which disciple gave the right answer.

SIGN OF THE CROSS

LIGHT THE CANDLES

Light the candles and read this prayer:
The candle flame is warm and bright,
it changes darkness into light.
We feel its warmth and see its glow,
and when we look at it we know.
The light of Christ is burning bright,
for we are children of the light.

SORRY

One day Jesus told this story (adapted from Matthew 18:23-35):

There was once a servant who owed his master lots of money. His master took pity on him and cancelled all his debts. Now the servant had a friend who owed him a small amount of money which he could not pay, so he had him thrown into jail. When his master heard this he sent for his unforgiving servant. 'Could you not forgive others as I forgave you?' he asked. Then he threw him into jail until he could repay all that he owed.

Help us Lord to remember this story so that we are always ready to forgive others just as you are always ready to forgive us. Amen.

GLORIA

GOSPEL ACCLAMATION

Alleluia, alleluia.
Open our ears to hear the 'Good News' which Jesus shared with the world.
Alleluia.

GOSPEL (cf Mark 8:27-35)

One day, while Jesus and his disciples were walking along, he asked them, 'Who do people say that I am?'

'Some say that you are John the Baptist, or Elijah or a prophet sent by God,' they answered.

Then Jesus asked them, 'Who do you think I am?'

It was Simon Peter who spoke up and said, 'You are Christ, the Son of God.'

After this, Jesus began to tell them how he would suffer and die, but would rise again after three days. Simon Peter argued with him, 'Lord we must not go to Jerusalem. These things must never happen!' Jesus said to him, 'Peter, we must do things God's way, even though it will not be easy.'

DISCUSSION

Why were people uncertain about who Jesus was?

Some people confused him with John the Baptist; some people had heard him preaching and thought that he was a prophet; to others he was simply the son of Joseph and Mary. Jesus appeared differently to different people.

Which apostle recognised who Jesus really was? What did Simon Peter say? – 'You are Christ, the Son of God.' The apostles had grown to know and love Jesus. On several occasions they had seen Jesus perform miracles which were only possible through the power of God.

If Jesus asked us the same question today, what would we say? – We know that Jesus is the Son of God, and saviour of the world. His love for us is unending and, he is our best friend.

Why did Simon Peter get upset and argue with Jesus? – When Simon Peter heard that Jesus would suffer and die in Jerusalem, he wanted to save him and protect him from harm.

How did Jesus answer Simon Peter? – Jesus told him that it is more important to follow God's way than the way we might choose, even though sometimes this can mean putting up with difficult times.

What does today's Gospel say to us? – We recognise Jesus as the Son of God. We are called to follow him like Simon Peter, but Jesus warns us that this will not always be easy. Just as he carried the cross for us before his death and resurrection, we will all have our own crosses or difficulties to bear in life. Our reward for this will be to share everlasting life with Christ Jesus.

ACTIVITY

Give each child a cross shaped badge. Help them to pin these on after they have been coloured or decorated.

CREED

CLOSING PRAYER

We ask you, O Lord,
to help us through difficult times
when our troubles seem almost too much to bear.
Give us the strength to carry on
and to always do our best.
We ask this through Christ our Lord.

Twenty-fifth Sunday of the Year
The last shall be first

INTRODUCTION
Often we call people great when they are very successful, or rich and powerful. Jesus explains that such things are not important to God. He measures our greatness by our goodness and willingness to think of others before ourselves.

SIGN OF THE CROSS

LIGHT THE CANDLES
Light the candles and say together:
May the light of God's love shine in our lives today and always.

SORRY
We ask Jesus to forgive our mistakes as we pray together:
Lamb of God, you take away the sins of the world: have mercy on us.
Lamb of God, you take away the sins of the world: have mercy on us.
Lamb of God, you take away the sins of the world: grant us peace.

GLORIA

GOSPEL ACCLAMATION
To welcome today's Gospel sing Acclamation 3:
Alleluia, alleluia.

GOSPEL (cf Mark 9:33-35)
After walking all day, Jesus and his disciples arrived in Capernaum. When Jesus asked the disciples what they had been talking about on the way, no-one looked at Jesus or answered his question, because they had been arguing about which one of them was the most important. Jesus told the disciples to sit down and then he said, 'Anyone who wants to be the greatest must become the servant of all, and make himself the least important.'

DISCUSSION
What were the disciples arguing about as they walked along? – Jesus had told them that he would be leaving them soon, and they were arguing about which one of them was the greatest and should take charge when he had gone.

If you said that someone was 'great' at something, what would you mean? – A boy who is 'great' at football, might score lots of goals, make brilliant tackles and be the best player in the team. They are chosen to play for the first team, because of their importance in helping them to win matches.

How did Jesus describe a truly great person? – A truly great person is not the one who draws attention to themselves or stands out in a crowd. They put the needs of others before their own, and stay quietly in the background without drawing attention to their goodness. They think of themselves last, and for this reason they will come first in the Kingdom of God.

God is not impressed by our power or wealth or riches! What is really important to him is our goodness. How should we live, if we want to be 'great' in a way which really matters to God?

By learning to put ourselves last and other people first! Instead of being bossy and taking charge in the playground, stand back sometimes and let someone else have a turn. When you want to watch something on the television, but your brother or sister doesn't, then let them watch the programme they choose. To put others first is not always easy, but with God's help we will succeed.

ACTIVITY
Hand out the colouring picture to the children that shows how the last will come first.

CREED

CLOSING PRAYER
Lord,
sometimes I find it hard
not to have things my own way!
To be expected to share
and to put others first.
Help me to be generous and thoughtful
as you would want me to.

Twenty-sixth Sunday of the Year

All goodness comes from God

INTRODUCTION
Anyone who loves Jesus and acts in his name, is filled with the goodness of God. Whatever our religion or race might be, God will see this goodness, and reward us with his love.

SIGN OF THE CROSS

LIGHT THE CANDLES
Light the candles and read aloud (cf Romans 13:12-13):
Live your lives as children of the light.
Do not hide in the darkness,
for there is nothing to fear.
Fill your lives with love and goodness,
and follow in the footsteps of Jesus.

SORRY
If we have shut out God's love and turned away from him, let us ask his spirit to change our hearts as we pray:
Lord Jesus,
you were always kind and caring;
forgive us if we have been selfish or unkind,
and help us to become more loving and thoughtful.
Lord in your mercy.
(Resp): Hear our prayer.

GLORIA

GOSPEL ACCLAMATION
To welcome today's Gospel sing Acclamation 2:
Light up our hearts.

GOSPEL (cf Mark 9:38-41)
One day John came to Jesus and said, 'Lord, we saw a man curing the sick in your name, and because we did not know him, we told him to stop!'

But Jesus said to him, 'Do not stop anyone who is using my name from doing something good. By their actions they show their love for me, and they can do no harm. Any person who acts kindly for my sake will be rewarded for their goodness in heaven.'

DISCUSSION
Why was John worried about the man who was curing the sick? – Although this man was a follower of Jesus, and cured people using his name, the disciples did not know him. John was worried that his actions might not please Jesus.

What did John try to do? – John tried to stop the man from curing the sick.

What did Jesus say about the man who acted kindly using his name? – As followers of Christ we are called Christians, and we try to live as Jesus did – filling our lives with kindness and love, and obeying God's commandments. This man was also a Christian who believed in Jesus and showed his love for God, by helping people who were sick. Jesus saw the goodness of this man who acted with kindness and love, and he was pleased.

How does God pour out his goodness into our hearts? – God's generosity is so great that he freely offers his love to *all* people of every race, colour and religion. He shares this love with the world through the gift of his Holy Spirit. The spirit brings us his gifts and guides our lives, so that we can share God's goodness with everyone we meet.

ACTIVITY
Copy the dove and the picture of the world onto a large sheet of paper to be coloured and pinned onto a board. See if the children can remember the seven gifts which the Holy Spirit shares with us. (See Pentecost Sunday.)

CREED

CLOSING PRAYER
Let us pray
that the spirit of God
will work through our lives,
so we can share
Christ's love with the world.

Twenty-seventh Sunday of the Year

The Children's friend

INTRODUCTION

Jesus loved to spend time with children, enjoying their laughter, talking to them, and listening to what they had to say. They have always been just as important to him as grown-ups.

SIGN OF THE CROSS

LIGHT THE CANDLES

Light the candles and say:
May Christ's love fill our lives with light and chase any darkness away!

SORRY

Help the children to spend some time reflecting on the events of the past week. Have they always been thoughtful and kind? Have they remembered to treat each person as though they were Jesus himself? After a few quiet moments, sing Sorry Song 4 together.

GLORIA

GOSPEL ACCLAMATION

(All) Alleluia, alleluia.
(Reader) Help us to listen to your word, Lord, and put your love into action in our lives.
(All) Alleluia.

GOSPEL (cf Mark 10:13-16)

People would often bring children to Jesus to be blessed by him. One day, the disciples sent the children away to let Jesus get some rest. But seeing this, Jesus scolded his disciples and said, 'Let them come to me, and do not stand in their way. Anyone wishing to enter the kingdom of God, must first become like one of these little children.' Then taking them in his arms, he blessed each one of them.

DISCUSSION

Why did the disciples want to send the children away? – Jesus had been preaching to the crowds all day, and his disciples knew that he was feeling tired. When they saw the group of children coming, and heard their excited chatter and laughter, they wanted them to go away and let Jesus have some peace and quiet.

What did Jesus do? – He scolded the disciples for trying to send the children away. Jesus wanted to spend time with them talking and listening to what they had to say. The children were just as important to him as grown-ups!

Have you ever found that sometimes grown-ups are too busy or tired to listen to you, and you just seem to be getting in their way?

At such times it can be very difficult to get their attention, and make them *really* listen to what you have to say.

Was Jesus ever too busy or tired to listen to children? – Even though Jesus felt tired, he did not send the children away and he was always ready to listen to them.

Why did Jesus say that grown-ups need to become more like children to enter the kingdom of God? – Children love Jesus and trust in his goodness. They listen to his message and are ready to try to live as he taught them. They know Jesus as a special friend who is never too busy to listen to them. Grown-ups should remember to love and to listen to Jesus like children do. If they do this, their lives will be pleasing to God, and they will share eternal life with him in the kingdom of Heaven.

ACTIVITY

Photocopy and cut out the figure of Jesus. Stick this in the middle of a large sheet of paper. Ask each child to draw a picture of themselves with their name, and help them to cut these out. Let each child stick their picture around the central figure of Jesus, and add the caption: 'Let the children come to me.'

CREED

CLOSING PRAYER

Lord Jesus, friend of little children,
you are always ready to listen
to what we have to say,
and to take care of us
in the grown-up world.
As we become adults,
help the special trust and friendship
we shared with you as little children
grow within us,
and draw us ever closer to you.

LET THE CHILDREN COME TO ME!

Twenty-eighth Sunday of the Year

The camel and the needle

INTRODUCTION

In today's Gospel, Jesus tells a young man what he must do if he wants to share everlasting life in the kingdom of God.

SIGN OF THE CROSS

LIGHT THE CANDLES

Light the candles and say Candle Prayer 2: *Show me, show me little candle.*

SORRY

If we have turned away from God, He is always ready to forgive us. Listen to this story:

Zacchaeus was a tax collector who was very rich because he cheated people out of their money. No-one liked him and he had no friends, but Jesus was ready to forgive Zacchaeus and to offer him his friendship. Zacchaeus had a change of heart, and was sorry for his dishonesty and selfishness. He promised Jesus that he would change his ways and try hard to be kind and loving to everyone.

Close your eyes as you say 'sorry' quietly in your heart, and ask Jesus to help us to change our ways and make a fresh start.

GLORIA

GOSPEL ACCLAMATION

To welcome today's Gospel sing Acclamation 1: *Share your word with us.*

GOSPEL *(cf Mark 10:17-25)*

A man came to Jesus and asked, 'Master, what must I do if I want to share everlasting life with God?'

Jesus said, 'First, you must obey all of God's commandments.'

'I have always tried to live according to the rules of God,' the man said. Jesus looked at the man kindly, and saw his goodness and love. 'Then you must sell everything you own, and give all your money away. By doing this you will have riches in heaven, instead of here on earth.'

The man left Jesus sadly, because he was a very wealthy man. Jesus said to his friends, 'It is easier for a camel to pass through the eye of a needle, than for a rich man to enter the kingdom of heaven!'

DISCUSSION

What did the man want Jesus to tell him? – The man wanted to know what to do to make sure that he would go to heaven when he died.

What answer did Jesus give? – First, Jesus told the man that he must obey God's commandments. These rules were given to us by God, to help us choose between right and wrong. Then Jesus told the man that he must give away all his money and everything he owned.

How did the man feel when he heard the words of Jesus? – The man went away feeling sad, because although he was a good man, he did not want to give away all of his riches. Everything he owned meant more to him than the message of Jesus.

Jesus said that it was easier for a camel to pass through the eye of a needle than a rich man to enter the kingdom of Heaven. Has anyone ever seen a camel? How big are they? How big is a needle?

What do we mean by the eye of the needle?

If you imagine how difficult it would be, for a large camel to climb through a needle, then you can understand what Jesus was trying to tell us!

(In this story Jesus was talking about a narrow gate leading into the city of Jerusalem, known as 'the Needle'. A camel could not pass through this gate easily, and in this way Jesus helped his followers to understand his message.)

Why did Jesus want the man to give up what he owned? – He wanted the man to understand that it is more important to have riches in heaven than riches on earth. Money can often make people greedy and selfish, and forgetful about the needs of others. God measures our wealth by our goodness, and whether we are generous and loving, and prepared to share what we have with others.

ACTIVITY

Photocopy the illustration. Give one of each to every child, and after colouring, help them to make a mobile.

CREED

CLOSING PRAYER

Lord, you see and remember
every act of kindness and generosity
and store them in your heart.
Help me to store up my treasure in heaven,
so that I can share everlasting life with you
at the end of time.

Twenty-ninth Sunday of the Year

A place in Heaven

INTRODUCTION

James and John went to Jesus to ask an important favour. They wanted Jesus to promise them a special place beside him in the kingdom of Heaven. Listen carefully to today's Gospel to hear whether or not Jesus granted their wish.

SIGN OF THE CROSS

LIGHT THE CANDLES

As we light the candles we listen to the words of the prophet Isaiah. *(cf Isaiah 9:2-3, 6-7.)*

The world was full of darkness and shadows, but now it is filled with light so everyone can see. God sent his only Son, Jesus, to fill our world with peace and love.

SORRY

Listen to this reading *(cf Psalm 16:11)*:
Lord you will show me the path that leads to everlasting life, and as you walk beside me on my journey, I will be filled with the happiness that lasts forever.
We turn to God and ask:
Heavenly Father,
guide me along your path
and never let me lose my way.
If I ever wander from your love,
because of what I say or do,
forgive me please,
and lead me back to you.

GLORIA

GOSPEL ACCLAMATION

To welcome today's Gospel sing Acclamation 4: *Praise the Lord.*

GOSPEL *(cf Mark 10:35-45)*

The two disciples, James and John, came to Jesus and asked him, 'Master, can we sit on either side of your throne in the kingdom of Heaven?' Jesus answered, 'Only my heavenly Father can decide this.' When the other disciples heard what James and John had asked, they were angry and began to argue with them. Jesus said to them, 'You must not quarrel with each other about which of you is the greatest! I have come as a servant and not as a king! Whoever thinks of others before themselves will be rewarded for their goodness, and they will have a place with me in the kingdom of Heaven.'

DISCUSSION

Why were the disciples angry with James and John? – James and John wanted Jesus to promise them a special place in heaven with him. The disciples argued about which one of them was the greatest, and deserved to have the best place.

What did Jesus remind them of? – *(See 25th Sunday of Year B.)* – That it is God the Father who will decide who deserves a place in Heaven. He will measure our 'greatness' by our goodness and willingness to think of others before ourselves. Jesus did not come as a king, but to serve all of mankind. He put our needs first, and died on the cross to save us from sin.

Can you think of anyone who puts the needs of others before their own?

(Encourage the children to make their own suggestions, for example their parents, their teachers, doctors and nurses etc.)

Has anyone ever heard of Mother Teresa?

What can you tell us about her?

Mother Teresa is a nun who truly puts the words of Jesus into action. Like him, she has made herself a servant of the people, and puts the needs of the poor and dying people in India first. She does all of this out of love for Jesus, and she expects no thanks or reward. Her goodness will make her truly great in the sight of God.

How should we live if we want to share a place in heaven with Jesus? – If we remember the words of Jesus: 'Whatever you do to others, you do to me', then we should always remember to treat other people with love and kindness, and to think of them before ourselves. By being unselfish and generous with our love, we will be assured of a place with Jesus in Heaven.

ACTIVITY

Photocopy the picture of God sitting on his heavenly throne, with a crowd of people in the foreground. Explain that only God will decide who shall be welcomed into his heavenly Kingdom.

CREED

CLOSING PRAYER

Jesus teach us
to be loving and caring,
and to think of other people
before thinking of ourselves.

Thirtieth Sunday of the Year
Master, let me see!

INTRODUCTION
God gives us the gift of our five senses: touch, taste, hearing, smell and sight. Often, we take these for granted and give them little thought. Today we hear how a blind man called Bartimaeus, begs Jesus to take pity on him, and cure his blindness.

SIGN OF THE CROSS

LIGHT THE CANDLES
Light the candles and read:
A blind person cannot see the candle flame flickering in the darkness, but they can feel the warmth of its glow. Jesus is the light of the world; we see him in the people around us and feel the warmth of his love in their lives.

SORRY
The words of St Paul remind us that as Christians we are called to follow Christ, and live as he taught us (cf Colossians 3:12-14, 23):
You are God's chosen people. Always be ready to care for others, and to be kind and gentle. Be patient and calm and never boast about or be proud of your goodness. Just as God always forgives you, so you must always be forgiving towards others. Fill your hearts with love, and whatever you do, do it for God.

Ask the children to close their eyes and then read this prayer to them slowly:
Father, forgive us if we have hurt anyone
by our thoughts or actions,
and help us to forgive those who have hurt us.
We ask this through Jesus our Lord.

GLORIA

GOSPEL ACCLAMATION
(All) Alleluia, alleluia.
(Reader) Open my eyes to see you in the world around me, Lord.
(All) Alleluia.

(Ask the children to close their eyes to listen to the Gospel.)

GOSPEL (cf Mark 10:46-52)
Jesus and his disciples were leaving Jericho with a crowd of followers, when they passed a blind beggar called Bartimaeus, sitting at the roadside. When he heard that Jesus of Nazareth had passed by, Bartimaeus began to shout loudly, 'Jesus have pity and help me!'
The crowd told him to calm down and be quiet, but Bartimaeus kept on shouting until Jesus heard his cries.
'Bring that man to me,' said Jesus, and they led Bartimaeus to him.
'What can I do for you?' he asked, and Bartimaeus said, 'Master, let me see!'
Then Jesus told him, 'Go. Because you believe in me your sight has returned.' Suddenly Bartimaeus could see clearly, and he set off at once to follow Jesus.

DISCUSSION
(Ask the children to open their eyes again)
Why was Bartimaeus begging at the roadside?
Because he could not see, Bartimaeus was unable to work to earn enough money to feed and clothe himself. He had to beg from passers by and rely on their kindness and generosity to save him from starvation.
What would you miss most if you could not see? (Encourage the children to share their thoughts.)
What did Bartimaeus do when he heard that Jesus was close by? – He believed that Jesus could cure his blindness, and save him from a life of misery. He shouted loudly to attract Jesus' attention, and did not give up even when the crowd told him to be quiet.
What did Jesus do when he heard Bartimaeus cry for help? – Jesus did not let him down; and his cry for help was answered.
What did Bartimaeus do when he had been healed? – He followed Jesus, because his heart and mind, as well as his eyes, had been opened by God's love. Because of his faith, he could 'see' with his heart that Jesus was indeed the Son of God.

ACTIVITY
Assemble photocopies of the story into mini-books to be read aloud and coloured by the children.

CREED

CLOSING PRAYER
Dear Jesus,
today we pray for blind people everywhere
and for those who help to care for them.
Thank you for the gift of sight,
allowing us to see the beauty of your world.

Thirty-first Sunday of the Year
The two great commandments

INTRODUCTION
The scribes were very religious and carefully obeyed every commandment of the Jewish Law, and spent much of their time studying the scriptures. One day, a scribe came to Jesus and asked him an important question.

SIGN OF THE CROSS

LIGHT THE CANDLES
Light the candles and read this prayer:
The candle flame is warm and bright,
it changes darkness into light.
We feel its warmth and see its glow,
and when we look at it we know,
the light of Christ is burning bright,
for we are children of the light.

SORRY
Lord, as we sing this song together, help us to be truly sorry and to change our hearts if we have not always been good. Sing Sorry Song 1

GLORIA

GOSPEL ACCLAMATION
To welcome today's Gospel sing Acclamation 1:
Share your word with us.

GOSPEL *(cf Mark 12:28-34)*
One of the scribes came to Jesus and asked, 'Which of God's commandments is the most important?' Jesus answered, 'To love God with all your heart, and all your mind and all your strength, and to love others as much as you love yourself. These commandments come before all others!' Then the scribe said to Jesus, 'What you have said is true, because nothing is more important than loving God and loving our neighbours.'

Seeing that the scribe was wise and good, Jesus said to him, 'My friend, what you have said will please God and keep you close to him.'

DISCUSSION
Which of God's commandments are the most important? – To love God and to love our neighbours as ourselves.

Who is our neighbour? – Jesus did not only mean the person living next door, or people that you know! Every person we meet is our 'neighbour', and Jesus expects us to treat them in the same way as we would like to be treated ourselves.

Why might the scribe have asked such a question? – Many of the scribes paid more attention to the rules and regulations of the law, rather than the things which were truly important – loving God and our neighbour. The scribe had listened to Jesus preaching, and was probably curious to know what was most important to Jesus.

Jesus wants us to put our love for God and for other people before anything else in our lives. What will happen if we do this? – Like the scribe in the story, our lives will be pleasing to God and we will stay close to his love as he leads us through life. At the end of time, the reward for our goodness will be to share everlasting life with him in heaven.

How can we show our love to God and to each other? (Encourage the children to share their ideas.)

Jesus once said, 'Love one another as I have loved you.' He showed his love by caring for everyone he met – spending time listening and talking to them; helping the sick; making the lonely feel welcome and loved; by being forgiving and not judging others. Jesus has shown us many ways to put the two greatest commandments into action in our lives.

ACTIVITY
Use large sheets of paper to make two banners. Cut out the individual letters which make up the words of the two greatest commandments. Ask the children to colour these brightly, and help them to assemble them in the correct order before sticking them onto the banners.

CREED

CLOSING PRAYER
Heavenly Father,
you know each one of us
and generously pour your love
into our lives.
Teach us
not to be selfish or greedy,
by returning your love
and sharing it willingly
with everyone we meet.

Thirty-second Sunday of the Year

The generous woman

INTRODUCTION
Today's Gospel story teaches us that it is not how much we give to others that is important, but how we give it and what is in our hearts at that moment.

SIGN OF THE CROSS

LIGHT THE CANDLES
Light the candles and sing the Candle Song together.

SORRY
Ask one of the children to choose a sorry colour for everyone to read aloud.

GLORIA

GOSPEL ACCLAMATION
(All) Alleluia, alleluia.
(Reader) Happy are the poor, because they will see the Kingdom of God.
(All) Alleluia.

GOSPEL *(cf Mark 12:41-44)*
When Jesus was in the Temple one day, he watched the people putting their money in a collection box as their offering. Many of the wealthy Jews gave large amounts of money. Then a poor old woman came into the Temple, and dropped two small coins, worth as little as one pence, into the box. Seeing this, Jesus turned to his disciples and said, 'This old woman has given more than any of the others! They gave money that they could spare, but she has given *all* the money that she had.'

DISCUSSION
Do you mind sharing what you have with other people? – It is easy to share when we have plenty, because we do not really miss what we have given away. It is much harder to give to others, when we have very little ourselves.

Imagine you have a large bag of sweets, and were asked to share it with everyone in this room. Would you find it hard to do? – Probably not, because there would be enough to give everyone a sweet, and still have plenty left.

Now imagine you had just one of your favourite sweets! How easy do you think it would be to give that precious sweet away to someone else?

What did Jesus say about the rich men? – The rich men had plenty of money, and like the large bag of sweets, it made little difference to them if they gave lots of it away.

The poor old woman only gave two small coins, and yet Jesus said that she had given the most. Why? – The old woman gave very little, but it was *all* she had, so she had given everything. She trusted in God to provide her with whatever she needed.

What message does today's Gospel have for us? – Today's Gospel teaches us about giving and sharing. It is not *how much* we give that is important, but *how* we give it, and what is in our hearts when we share something. Giving and sharing with a loving and sincere heart is what really matters to God.

What can you give and share with other people? (Encourage the children to suggest their own ideas.)
- your love
- your time
- your toys and possessions
- your happiness
- your friendship

ACTIVITY
Photocopy this picture showing the old widow putting all that she had into the offerings box. Encourage the children to draw Jesus and some rich men as part of the scene.

CREED

CLOSING PRAYER
Dear Lord,
teach us how to share
and never to be greedy,
because everything that we have
comes from you.

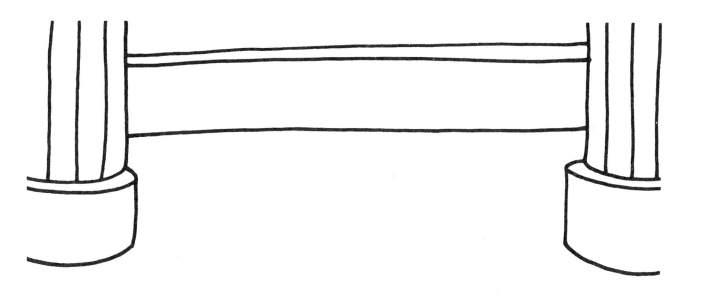

Thirty-third Sunday of the Year
Jesus will return

INTRODUCTION
At the end of time, Jesus will return in power and glory and will welcome all those who have been chosen to join him in the kingdom of Heaven.

SIGN OF THE CROSS

LIGHT THE CANDLES
Light the candles and say Candle Prayer 3: *The light of God.*

SORRY
One day Simon Peter asked Jesus, 'Master, how many times must I forgive someone? As many as seven times?' Jesus answered, 'Not just seven times, Peter, but seventy times seven! You must always forgive someone from your heart.' (*cf Matthew 18:21-22, 35*).

Lord, help us to be ready to welcome you whenever you might come. Teach us to say sorry and to forgive others as soon as a quarrel begins. We ask for your forgiveness as we pray:
Our Father . . .

GLORIA

GOSPEL ACCLAMATION
To welcome today's Gospel sing Acclamation 4: *Praise the Lord.*

GOSPEL (*cf Mark 13:24-29, 32*)
Jesus said to his disciples, 'One day I will return, and you will know that the time has come because of these signs: the sun will grow dark, the moon will lose its brightness, stars will fall to earth and even the sky will shake. Then the Son of God will appear in all his glory, and send his angels to gather his people together from all over the world. Only my heavenly Father knows when all this will happen, so stay awake and be ready!'

DISCUSSION
Jesus said that he will return at the end of time. When will that be? – No-one knows the date or time, except for God the Father, so we must always keep ourselves ready.

Can you think of a parable or story Jesus once told, explaining how we must be prepared for his return at any time? – The parable of the ten bridesmaids. (See the 32nd Sunday Year A).

What must we do to be ready to welcome Jesus? – If we try to live each day in the way Jesus showed us, then our lives will always be pleasing to God. God will judge us by the goodness and love we have shown to him and our neighbours each day of our lives.

What are the signs that will appear before the second coming of Christ?
- The sun will grow dark, filling the world with darkness.
- The moon will no longer shine.
- The stars will fall from the sky.
- The heavens or sky will be shaken, perhaps by thunder or lightning.

How should we greet Jesus when he comes?

Jesus will come to gather all the good people in the world, and to welcome them into the kingdom of Heaven. There, they will share everlasting life and happiness with God. The good will have nothing to fear, and they will join the angels as they rejoice at God's power and glory.

ACTIVITY
With the children's help, make a list of the signs which will appear before the second coming of Christ. With these in mind ask each child to draw a picture of what they imagine might happen when Jesus returns in glory. Hand out the photocopied text for the children to colour and take home.

CREED

CLOSING PRAYER
Lord,
may our lives always be rich
in love and goodness,
so we are ready to welcome you
whenever you return.

The ☀ will grow dark. The 🌙 will no longer shine. The ⭐⭐ will fall from the sky. ⛈ will shake the heavens.

The Feast of Christ the King
Jesus before Pontius Pilate

INTRODUCTION
The Jewish leaders were afraid that Jesus would lead the people to rise up against them, so they plotted to have him arrested and sentenced to death.

SIGN OF THE CROSS

LIGHT THE CANDLES
Light the candles and read (*cf Romans 13:12-13*):
Live your lives as children of the light. Do not hide in the darkness for there is nothing to fear. Fill your lives with love and goodness and follow in the footsteps of Jesus.

SORRY
Close your eyes and listen to this reading (*cf Psalm 14:2-3*):
Lord those who turn away from you do wrong, those who are wise worship you,
Lord you see all that we do,
help us to do what is right.
(Allow the children a few moments to think about these words before reading the following slowly:
If we have chosen the wrong way, and made a mistake,
Lord have mercy.
If we have forgotten to share your love with others,
Christ have mercy.
If we have spoiled our friendship with you and made you sad,
Lord have mercy.

GLORIA

GOSPEL ACCLAMATION
To welcome today's Gospel sing this Acclamation (to the tune of *Hickory, Dickory, Dock*):

Christ is the king of the world,
One day he will come back
And we will see his full glory,
Christ is the king of the world.

GOSPEL (*cf John 18:33-37*)
They brought Jesus before Pontius Pilate who asked him, 'Are you the king of the Jews?'
Jesus answered, 'My kingdom is not of this world.'
'So you do indeed claim to be a king!' said Pilate.
'You are the one who calls me king,' answered Jesus. 'I came into this world to share truth and love, and those who know and love the truth will listen to me.'

DISCUSSION
Who was Pontius Pilate? – Pontius Pilate was the Roman governor of Judaea. He was in charge of the Roman army and responsible for keeping the peace. He acted as judge when serious crimes were committed.

Why was Jesus brought before Pontius Pilate? – The Jewish leaders had seen the welcome given to Jesus as he entered Jerusalem, and they were afraid of his position and power. They wanted to get rid of Jesus by whatever means they could, so they took Jesus to Pilate and asked for him to be sentenced to death.

What question did Pontius Pilate ask Jesus? – Jesus tried to explain that he was not a king who belonged to this world, but that he had come into the world to share his kingdom of love and goodness.

Did Pilate listen to Jesus and understand what he had said? – Pilate knew that Jesus was harmless and had done nothing wrong, but he was more interested in keeping the peace and not upsetting the Jewish leaders, than in seeing that justice was done. He allowed the Jewish leaders to have their own way, and eventually handed Jesus over to be put to death.

What happened after Jesus had suffered and died on the cross? – Three days later on Easter Sunday he rose from the dead and showed the world that he is the king of the universe, with the power to conquer death and bring new and everlasting life.

ACTIVITY
Cut out crown shapes from card and write on each one 'Christ is our King'. Decorate these and staple the crowns so that they can be worn or carried by the children.

CREED

CLOSING PRAYER
God our Father
we thank you
for sending your only Son to be our saviour.
Help us to know and love your truth
and to listen to you always.

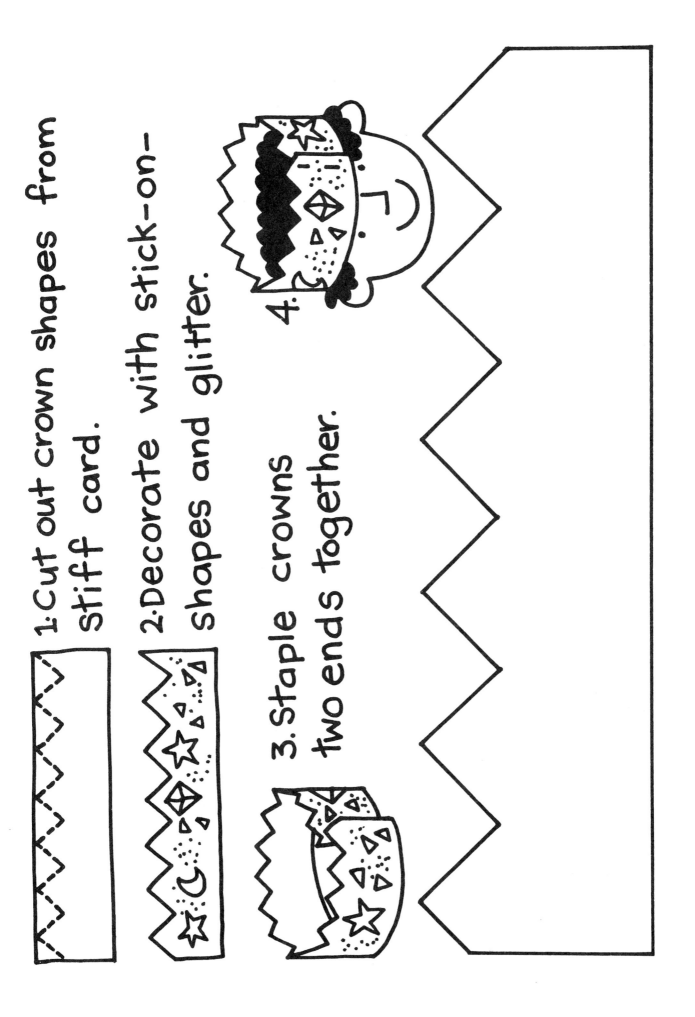

1. Cut out crown shapes from stiff card.

2. Decorate with stick-on shapes and glitter.

3. Staple crowns two ends together.

4.

Year C

First Sunday of Advent
Jesus will return

INTRODUCTION
Today we begin our preparation to celebrate the birthday of our saviour, Jesus Christ. During Advent we think about the past, our lives today and what will be in the future.

SIGN OF THE CROSS

LIGHT THE CANDLES
Light the altar candles and the first candle on the Advent wreath. Each Sunday the light will grow brighter as we draw closer to Christmas day when Jesus 'the light of the world' was born.

SORRY
During Advent we prepare to celebrate Jesus Christ's birthday, and we spend time thinking about how to welcome Jesus in our lives every day.

(Ask the children to close their eyes and listen carefully.)

Do we always remember to make a space for Jesus in our day? Do we remember to thank him for his goodness? Do we sometimes forget to share the love and happiness he gave to us with other people? Do we treat each person we meet as though they were Jesus himself?

Advent is a good time for us all to make a fresh start; to think of ways to welcome Jesus and to show how much we really love him. Spend a few moments talking to Jesus in silence, before singing Sorry Song 1 together.

GOSPEL ACCLAMATION
To welcome today's Gospel sing the Advent Song.

GOSPEL (cf Luke 21:25-28, 34-36)
Jesus said to his disciples: 'When you see the signs in the sun and moon and stars, you will know that the time has come for the Son of God to return. Do not be afraid when all these things happen, but be filled with joy to see the power and glory of God. Stay awake and be ready, because only my heavenly Father knows when this day will come.'

DISCUSSION
Begin by asking the children to describe what the sky looks like on a clear night, and what they can see. Do they know any names of the stars? What signs will show us that the time has come for Jesus to return?

'There will be signs in the sun and moon and stars.' No one knows what this means or what exactly will happen, but just as everyone on earth can see the sky, so everyone will know that the end of time has come.

Do we know *when* this will happen? – Only God the Father knows, so Jesus tells us that we must 'be ready' to welcome him at any time!

Everyone is very busy getting ready to celebrate the birthday of Jesus. What else must we be ready for? – Jesus is living in our world *today* and we know that he will return in glory at the end of time. We must be ready to welcome him into our hearts and lives today and every day.

How should we do this? – Jesus came to share his love, forgiveness, peace and happiness with the world. If we share these gifts of his love with the people we meet everyday, by small acts of kindness or goodness, then we will be ready to fully enjoy the celebrations which take place at Christmas and at the end of time.

ACTIVITY
Over the four Sundays of Advent as we prepare to celebrate the birth of Jesus, two different activity schemes are suggested *to be continued each week.* Choose whichever is more appropriate for your particular group or the facilities you have available.

1. The Jesse Tree.
A Jesse tree traditionally represents the family tree of Jesus, but here we have adapted it to show most of the important characters involved in the Christmas celebration. Construct a free standing tree from coloured card as shown in the diagram. Each week add more characters and discuss their importance with the children. Use the drawings as a guide or ask the children to do their own. The pictures can be stuck directly onto the tree, or drawn onto 'bauble' shapes and hung as decorations. Be imaginative!

On Christmas morning place a silver star on top of the completed Jesse tree.

2. An Advent Frieze.
The frieze should illustrate the characters and events leading up to Christmas day, beginning with the angel Gabriel appearing to Mary and ending with the joyful scene at Bethlehem on Christmas day when the Holy Family is added to the frieze.

CREED

CLOSING PRAYER
Lord Jesus,
help us to get ready
to greet you at Christmas
and at the end of time.

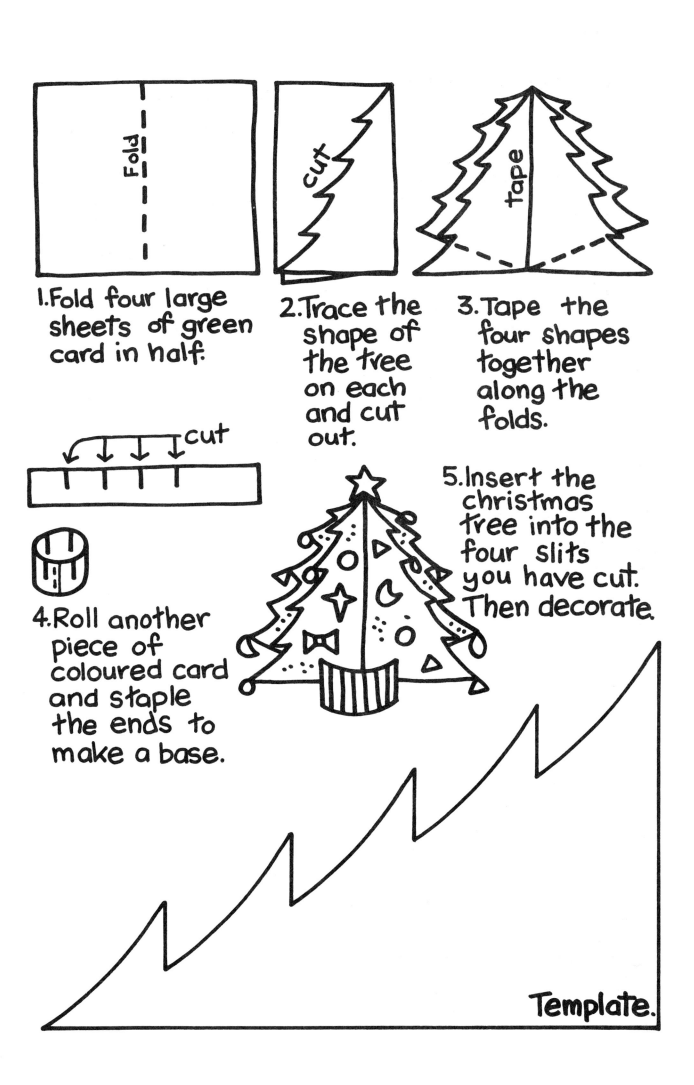

1. Fold four large sheets of green card in half.

Fold

2. Trace the shape of the tree on each and cut out.

cut

3. Tape the four shapes together along the folds.

tape

cut

4. Roll another piece of coloured card and staple the ends to make a base.

5. Insert the christmas tree into the four slits you have cut. Then decorate.

Template.

Second Sunday of Advent
Prepare my people

INTRODUCTION
The people of Israel had turned away from God and his love. He had promised to send them a saviour, but first he sent someone to prepare the people to welcome the Son of God.

SIGN OF THE CROSS

LIGHT THE CANDLES
Light the candles, and also light two candles on the Advent wreath. Say together:
May the light of Jesus shine in our hearts.

SORRY
John the Baptist told the people of Israel to turn back to God and ask for his forgiveness. Today we do the same as we sing our sorry song together. Sing Sorry Song 1.

GOSPEL ACCLAMATION
To welcome today's Gospel sing the Advent Song.

GOSPEL (cf Luke 3:1-6)
When Pontius Pilate was the Roman governor of Judaea, a man appeared in the desert and began to preach the word of God; his name was John. He told the people to turn away from their sins and to ask for God's forgiveness. He baptised the people who were truly sorry and wanted to make a fresh start in their lives, and so he came to be known as 'John the Baptist.'

DISCUSSION
What was the name of the man who appeared in the desert?

What did he tell the people to do? – He wanted them to turn back to God and ask for his forgiveness. Then they could make a fresh start and try to lead better lives.

Why was John called 'the Baptist'? – Water is used in many ways, but most importantly it keeps us *alive* and makes us *clean*. John baptised all the people who were truly sorry as a sign that they wanted to wash away all their sins and so begin a new life, with a fresh start.

What was so special about John the Baptist? – God sent John to prepare the people for the coming of his son, Jesus. He was filled with the Holy Spirit and had the courage to stand before the crowds and the Jewish priests and preach to them. He came to turn them away from sin and to change their hearts so that they were ready to listen to the words of Jesus when he came.

Ask the children to tell you what they know about John the Baptist. Read the following passage to tell them more about his family and how he was specially chosen by God (cf Luke 1:5-17):

Zacchariah and Elizabeth (Mary's cousin) had been married for many years and had no children. They were good people who lived according to God's rules. Zacchariah worked as a priest in the Temple, and it was while he was there that the angel Gabriel appeared to him and said, 'Do not be afraid! You and Elizabeth will have a son and you will call him John. He will be filled with the Holy Spirit and be remembered for his greatness. He will lead the people of Israel back to God and prepare them for the Lord.'

Who came to visit Elizabeth when she was expecting her baby, John? – Mary, the mother of Jesus, came to visit her cousin Elizabeth after the angel Gabriel had appeared to her.

ACTIVITY
Continue decorating the Jesse tree or adding scenes to the Advent frieze.

CREED

CLOSING PRAYER
Help us, Lord
to be like John the Baptist,
filled with your spirit and brave enough
to say and do what is right.
Give us the courage to choose the right way,
despite what others might say or think,
because we believe in you
and love you with all our hearts.

Third Sunday of Advent
Lead lives filled with goodness

INTRODUCTION
John the Baptist told the people to ask for God's forgiveness for their sins and to change their hearts. They did not know how to please God or to make him welcome in their lives, so John showed them the way.

SIGN OF THE CROSS

LIGHT THE CANDLES
As you light the altar candles and three candles on the Advent wreath, sing together *See the light.*

SORRY
Christmas is a time of joy and peace, and for wishing goodwill to everyone. As St Matthew reminds us *(cf Matthew 5:23-26)*:
'If you are about to come before God to pray and then remember that you have quarrelled with someone, go away first, settle your argument and make your peace with them.'

Listen to the words of this prayer:
Lord Jesus,
please forgive us
if we have said
or done something wrong,
and give us the courage
to forgive others
as you forgive us.

GOSPEL ACCLAMATION
To welcome today's Gospel sing the Advent Song.

GOSPEL *(cf Luke 3:10-18)*
The people listened to John the Baptist's message and asked him, 'What must we do to be ready for the Lord?'

John answered, 'Be generous and kind, and always ready to share whatever you have with others. Be honest and fair and be happy with whatever you have.'

The people grew excited and many began to think that John might be the Messiah, promised by God. So John told them, 'I baptise you with water, but someone is coming who will baptise you with the Holy Spirit. He is filled with the power of God, and I am not good enough to undo his sandals.'

DISCUSSION
The crowds wanted to be ready to welcome the Lord. Can you remember what John told them they should do?

– to be generous and kind.
– to be willing to share whatever they had.
– to be honest and fair.
– to be content with whatever they had.

John was preparing the way for someone else. Who was that person?

John came to prepare the people to listen to and act upon Jesus' message of love. The words of John the Baptist are just as important for us today, as they were for the crowds long ago, so that we, too, will be ready for the Lord.

Today is the third Sunday of Advent, and we have lit three candles in the wreath. Today's candle is pink, does anyone know why it is pink? – The pink candle is a symbol of 'joy', as we rejoice and look forward to Christmas. The crowds listening to John the Baptist were filled with excitement and joy as they prepared and waited for the coming of their saviour.

Christmas is a very special time of year, an important celebration of Christ's birthday. Jesus came to share his love and happiness with everyone, and we try to do the same by giving presents and sending cards to each other. There are many people who spend Christmas alone or unhappy.

Think about the words of John the Baptist, and then can you suggest some ways we can put them into practice this Christmas?
– By giving what we can to local charities.
– By bringing a card or small gift to someone who lives alone.
– By giving the toys which we have outgrown to local children's homes.
(Encourage the children to share any suggestions and ideas.)

ACTIVITY
Continue decorating the Jesse tree using these figures or adding scenes to the Advent frieze. Discuss the work completed so far with the children.

CREED

CLOSING PRAYER
As Christmas draws closer,
help us to remember anyone
who is sick or lonely
at this time of year,
the homeless and sad,
those who are hungry or at war.
May the peace and joy of Christmas
reach out and touch their lives.

Fourth Sunday of Advent
Blessed are you

INTRODUCTION
Mary was chosen to be the mother of Christ, and so became the mother of Christians everywhere. Filled with the Holy Spirit and understanding that nothing is impossible for God, she set off to visit her cousin Elizabeth to share her joy and wonder.

SIGN OF THE CROSS

LIGHT THE CANDLES
As the candles are lit, read this prayer to the children:
If we keep our eyes on the light,
we need never feel afraid.
Jesus will walk before us,
guiding us through life
towards the kingdom of Heaven.

SORRY
We too are filled with the Holy Spirit. He breathed 'new' life into us at our Baptism, and shares his peace and love with us always. If we have turned away from God, let us ask him to work in our lives, so that we can follow Jesus more closely every day.
If I have made mistakes and chosen the wrong way.
   Father, forgive me.
If I have been unloving or selfish.
   Jesus, forgive me.
When I find it difficult to choose God's way.
   Spirit, give me your strength.

GOSPEL ACCLAMATION
As we welcome the Gospel, sing the Advent Song.

GOSPEL (cf Luke 1:39-44)
After the angel Gabriel had appeared to Mary, she set off at once to visit her cousin Elizabeth. When Elizabeth saw Mary coming she ran to welcome her, and the baby inside her leapt for joy at the sound of Mary's greeting. Elizabeth was filled with the Holy Spirit and said to Mary, 'Of all women you are the most blessed, and blessed is the child you will have, because you believe in the power of God and he has chosen you to be the mother of our saviour.'

DISCUSSION
When Gabriel appeared to Mary, what had he told her about Elizabeth? – That Elizabeth and her husband Zacchariah were expecting a baby.

Why was Mary surprised by this news? – Because both Elizabeth and her husband were quite old and had never been able to have children, but Mary knew that nothing was impossible for God! *(See the discussion for the Second Sunday of Advent.)*

What did Mary do after the angel's visit? – Immediately she set off to visit Elizabeth. Mary's first thoughts were for her cousin, and being generous and kind she was always ready to help in whatever way she could.

What happened when Elizabeth and Mary met? – Elizabeth was filled with understanding by the Holy Spirit and she too knew that nothing is impossible for God. She knew that God had chosen Mary to be the mother of his son in a very special way.

What do you think Mary and Elizabeth would have talked about together? – They probably talked about the angel who brought them both such good news, and marvelled together at the power of God. Both of them were expecting their first child, and probably shared their feelings of excitement and joy as they waited for them to be born. Elizabeth and Mary knew that they had been chosen by God, and that their children would be blessed by God in a very special way.

Which prayer do we say which includes the words which Elizabeth spoke that day? – The 'Hail Mary'. (If possible have a large copy of the prayer for the children to look at, and see if they can pick out the words of Elizabeth.)

ACTIVITY
Put the finishing touches to the Jesse tree or Advent frieze so that they will be completed for Christmas day. Make a star for the tree or a picture of the Holy Family together, but do not add them to the activities until Christmas morning!

CREED

CLOSING PRAYER
Let us thank Mary for becoming the mother of Jesus and for sharing her son with the world as we say together:
'Hail Mary, . . .'

The Feast of the Holy Family
Jesus is lost

INTRODUCTION
Every year the Jews celebrated the Feast of the Passover, and remembered how God had saved them from slavery in Egypt. When Jesus was twelve years old Mary and Joseph took him with them to Jerusalem.

SIGN OF THE CROSS

LIGHT THE CANDLES
Light the candles and say Candle Prayer 2: *Show me, show me little candle.*

SORRY
On the Feast of the Holy Family let us think about our own families. Read the following questions slowly, pausing for thought between each.

Do we show everyone in our family how much we love them by our words and actions? – Do we sometimes take them for granted, without realising how lucky we are to feel loved and cared for?

Do we always treat our brothers and sisters thoughtfully? – Are we obedient and good for our parents?

As brothers and sisters in the one family of God we know that our heavenly Father loves us and is always ready to forgive and forget the mistakes we make.

Sing Sorry Song 1 together.

GLORIA

GOSPEL ACCLAMATION
To welcome today's Gospel say together:
Alleluia, alleluia,
Lord Jesus open our ears and minds so that we hear and understand your word.
Alleluia, alleluia.

GOSPEL (*cf Luke 2:41-52*)
Every year Joseph and Mary went to Jerusalem to celebrate the Jewish Passover. When Jesus was twelve years old, he made the journey with them. After the feast, Mary and Joseph set off for home. But that evening, they realized that Jesus was missing, and at once they returned to Jerusalem to look for him.

After searching for three days, they finally found Jesus in the Temple. He sat listening and asking questions of the Jewish teachers who were filled with admiration for this child. Mary and Joseph were overcome when they saw him and said, 'Son, we have been so worried for three days! Why have you done this to us?'

But Jesus answered, 'Why were you looking for me? Did you not realise that I would be in my Father's house?' But they did not understand what his answer meant. The family returned to Nazareth, and Mary kept all these things in her heart. Jesus grew in height and wisdom, and was loved by God and all who knew him.

DISCUSSION
Have you ever been lost before? – What happened and how did you feel? How did your parents feel?

How do you think Mary and Joseph felt when they lost Jesus in Jerusalem?

Often people travelled in separate groups and they thought that Jesus was with the other group. When they realised that Jesus was missing they set off at once to look for him, filled with a feeling of panic and concern.

Did they find Jesus straight away? – They spent three long days searching before they found him.

Where did Mary and Joseph eventually find Jesus and what was he doing? – They found him in the Temple, sitting with the elders and the teachers, discussing the scriptures. Mary and Joseph were delighted and relieved to have found Jesus safe and well. They had been so worried, but Jesus did not appear to be at all troubled by everything that had taken place.

What did Jesus say when his parents told him of their deep concern? – Jesus had not felt 'lost' because he was perfectly at home in the Temple. To him it was an obvious place to be, in his heavenly Father's house. Mary and Joseph did not understand the special relationship that Jesus had with his heavenly Father. But under their guidance, and with their love and help, Jesus prepared for his mission of bringing the Good News to the world.

ACTIVITY
Using the illustration as a guide, help the children to make a banner depicting the Holy Family.

CREED

CLOSING PRAYER
We thank you, Lord,
for our families and each other.
Please bless them and help them
to be loving and forgiving,
and always there for us
in times of trouble or need.

First Sunday of Lent
Temptation in the desert

INTRODUCTION
The season of Lent begins on Ash Wednesday, and we remember the forty days which Jesus spent fasting and praying in the desert. We are called to turn away from our selfishness and to grow closer to God's love.

SIGN OF THE CROSS

LIGHT THE CANDLES
As we light the candles we listen to the words of the prophet Isaiah (cf Isaiah 9:2-3, 6-7):

The world was full of darkness and shadows, but now it is filled with light so everyone can see. God sent us his only Son, Jesus, to fill our world with peace and love.

SORRY
Ask the children to close their eyes and to make the words of this prayer their own:
Do not be afraid,
God will always love you.
Whatever you have done,
God will always love you.
As a Father loves his child,
He will always love you.
Come back to him and know,
God's love lasts forever.

GOSPEL ACCLAMATION
To welcome today's Gospel sing Acclamation 4: *Praise the Lord.*

GOSPEL (cf Luke 4:1-13)
Filled with the Holy Spirit, Jesus went into the desert to pray and be close to God.

He stayed there for forty days and during that time he had nothing to eat because he was fasting. He looked at the stones around him and knew that he could change them into bread; but he chose not to.

As he walked through the desert he knew that he could make himself king over all the land; but he chose not to.

When the forty days had past Jesus went to the Temple in Jerusalem and climbed the stairs to the rooftop. He knew that if he jumped from the top, God would save him from harm, but he chose not to.

DISCUSSION
How many days did Jesus spend in the desert?

Forty days is a long time! How many weeks are there in forty days? – There are almost six full weeks in forty days.

Jesus went into the desert to be close to God and to think. What do we call the time of year when we spend six weeks looking carefully at our lives and trying to grow closer to God? – Lent is the time when we stop and think about our lives, and turn back to God if we have wandered away from his love. During the six weeks of Lent we try to do something for God, to show how much we love him. It is a chance to say sorry for any mistakes we have made, and to make a fresh start.

Did Jesus find it easy in the desert? – On several occasions Jesus was tempted to take the easy way out, but he chose not to. During Lent we too will find it hard when we feel tempted to give up, but we must try not to.

Can you remember the three temptations which Jesus refused?
1. To turn the stones into bread. Jesus knew that God would provide him with everything he needed, and that he had been sent to take care of the needs of other people.
2. To become king of all the land. God is the king of all creation, and Jesus knew that his kingdom was more important than anything on earth.
3. To jump off the roof of the Temple and test God's love. Jesus trusted in his Father's great love; he did not need to ask God to prove it.

What can we learn from today's Gospel? – Jesus showed us the importance of spending some time looking at the good and bad things in our lives, and growing closer to God through prayer. Like us, he did not always find it easy to do, but with God's help he was able to choose to do the right thing, and to turn away from temptation. With help from our heavenly Father we can do the same!

ACTIVITY
Photocopy the illustration and help the children to complete the temptations which Jesus had to face.

CREED

CLOSING PRAYER
Lord Jesus, you never gave up
even when you found it most difficult.
During the six weeks of Lent,
help us to be strong
and to keep our promises
as a sign of our love for you.

1. Turn the stones into _ _ _ _ _ .

2. To become " _ _ _ _ " of all the land.

3. To _ _ _ _ off the Temple walls and test " God's love. "

Second Sunday of Lent
Jesus shines like the sun

INTRODUCTION
Today we hear how Jesus allowed his closest friends to glimpse the power and brilliance of God's glory.

SIGN OF THE CROSS

LIGHT THE CANDLES
As children of the light we will never hide in the darkness.

SORRY
Listen to the words of St Paul who tells us to *(cf St Paul's Letter to the Ephesians 4:23-32)*:
'Make a fresh start and change your heart. Tell the truth and do not let your anger spoil your friendship with others and with God. Speak words of kindness and act with love and goodness towards each other. Above all, be ready to forgive others as God forgives you.'

Heavenly Father,
during the season of Lent
help us to turn back to you
and to make a fresh start.

GOSPEL ACCLAMATION
Jesus said: 'Follow me and love each other, and you will be a sign for all to see that you are children of my love.'

GOSPEL *(cf Matthew 17:1-10)*
One day Jesus asked Peter, James and John to come and pray with him. He led them to the top of a steep mountain, where it was peaceful and quiet, and they could be alone. Jesus began to pray to his heavenly Father when suddenly he appeared to change! His face and clothes shone with a brilliant light, as dazzling as the rays of the sun. Then the disciples saw Moses and Elijah on either side of Jesus, talking to him. Peter jumped up with excitement and said, 'Lord, this is wonderful! I could make three shelters – one for each of you!' At that moment a cloud streaming with light appeared above them, and a voice said, 'This is my Son, whom I love very much. Listen to what he says.' The disciples were so terrified that they threw themselves to the ground and hid their faces. Then Jesus said gently, 'Get up my friends, do not be afraid.' When they looked up, Jesus was standing alone.

DISCUSSION
What did Peter, James and John see on the mountain top that day?

Jesus was 'transfigured'! This means his appearance changed as his face and clothes shone like the sun.

What happens if the sun shines in our eyes?

We are dazzled by its brightness and the strength of its light. The light shining from Jesus was as bright as the sun. These rays of light were shafts of God's glory, and a glimpse of his power and might.

If we lived in a world where there was no light, what would it be like? – It would be a cold and frightening place, full of darkness and gloom. (Encourage the children to share their thoughts and ideas. Have they ever had a power cut at home? What happened?)

Why is 'light' so important in our world? – By day the natural light of the sun warms the earth and makes things grow, and at night we use artificial light so that we can see, and find our way in the darkness.

On the mountain the disciples saw a change in Jesus as the brightness of God's glory shone out from him. Do you think the disciples were changed by what they had seen that day? – Just as light chases away the darkness so that we can see, the light shining out from Jesus that day made the disciples 'see' that he was indeed the Son of God. Their lives had been touched by the brilliance of God's power and love, and they were filled with the light of faith.

ACTIVITY
Cut out several large candle shapes from card. You may be able to photocopy the illustration onto thin card. Using coloured squares of paper ask the children to glue these onto the candles to make mosaic patterns. The candles can then be hung from a mobile with the caption, 'Jesus fills our lives with light.'

CREED

CLOSING PRAYER
Jesus, fill me with the light
of your love and faith.
Make me shine in the darkness,
and touch the lives of others
with the light of your goodness.

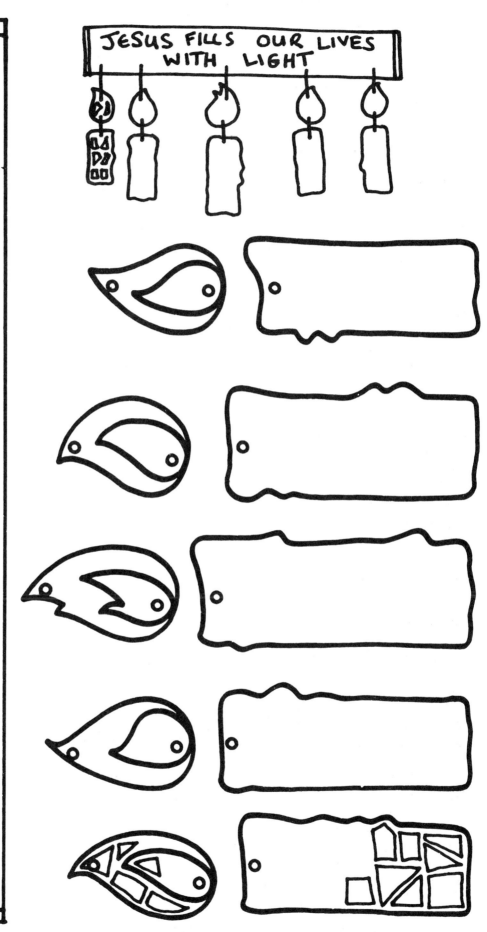

JESUS FILLS OUR LIVES WITH LIGHT

JESUS FILLS OUR LIVES WITH LIGHT

Third Sunday of Lent
God gives us another chance

INTRODUCTION
Sometimes when we are ready to give up, we decide to give something one more chance and then find that we finally succeed! God is always ready to give us another chance, even when we get things wrong time and time again.

SIGN OF THE CROSS

LIGHT THE CANDLES
Say together:
May the light of God's love shine in our lives for everyone to see.

SORRY
Jesus wanted us to know that God will always give us another chance to change for the better. When we ask for his forgiveness, he is ready to help us to make a fresh start.

Listen to this story:

Zacchaeus was a tax collector who cheated people out of their money. No-one liked him and he had no friends; but Jesus was ready to forgive Zacchaeus and to offer his friendship. Zacchaeus had a change of heart, and was sorry for his dishonesty and selfishness. He promised Jesus that he would change his ways, and try hard to be kind and loving to everyone.

Close your eyes and spend a few moments thinking of anything you want to say sorry for before we sing our sorry song together.

Sing Sorry Song 4

GOSPEL ACCLAMATION
To welcome today's Gospel sing Acclamation 5: *We have come to hear you, Lord.*

GOSPEL (*cf Luke 13:6-9*)
One day Jesus told his people this parable:

'A man went to check how many fruits were growing on a tree in his orchard, but he found that there were none. So he sent for his gardener and told him, "This tree has grown no fruit for the last three years. Cut it down and plant another tree in its place!"

But the gardener said to him, "Master give the tree one more year so I can feed and care for it. Then if it still has no fruit on it, cut it down." '

DISCUSSION
Why did the man want to cut the tree down? – Because it had grown no fruit for three years, and he wanted to plant another tree in its place.

What did the gardener ask his master to do? – He asked his master to give the tree one more chance to prove itself.

What was the gardener willing to do to help the tree to produce some fruit? – The gardener would feed the tree with manure and make sure it was well watered and cared for. The gardener was ready to do whatever he could, to help the tree to grow some fruit, and to save it from being destroyed.

Jesus often told parables or stories with a message. What do you think the message of today's parable is? – That God is always ready to give us another chance to change, and to grow the fruits of his love. Just as the gardener was ready to care for the tree and help it to fruit, so Jesus will help us to be kind, loving, generous and forgiving, and able to bear the fruits of God's life and love in us.

ACTIVITY
Copy the activity sheet and ask each child to draw a picture in the space provided.

CREED

CLOSING PRAYER
Lord, take my hand and show me the way.
Help me to get up when I fall
and to try again,
knowing that you will always give me
another chance.

Healthy tree,
lots of fruit.

A kind and
loving person.

Another
Chance

Another
Chance

Diseased tree
with no fruit.

A selfish and
unkind person.

Fourth Sunday of Lent
The son who came back

INTRODUCTION

We all know how good we feel when we say sorry and make up after a quarrel. Jesus told a story to show that when we forgive, and are forgiven, we are filled with great joy and a feeling of peace.

SIGN OF THE CROSS

LIGHT THE CANDLES

Read these words (cf Proverbs 4:18-19):
The path to our heavenly Father is like the rising sun, getting brighter and brighter as we draw closer to God.

SORRY

God calls us to love each other and to change our hearts if we have been unkind or selfish. He will always forgive us when we are sorry, and expects us to forgive each other. Say together:
'Our Father . . .'

GOSPEL ACCLAMATION

Your word, Lord, is a light for my path, a lamp to guide me closer to you.

GOSPEL (cf Luke 15:11-24)

One day Jesus told this story. 'There was a man who had two sons and the younger one came to his father and said, 'Father, give me everything that will one day belong to me, so I can enjoy my riches now.'

The father did this, and the younger son set off to look for adventure. He travelled to a distant land and spent all his money enjoying himself.

There was a famine in that land, and the young man found himself penniless and hungry. 'If I stay here I will surely starve,' he thought, so he decided to return to his father and ask for his forgiveness. The father saw his son coming and ran to welcome him. As he hugged him, the young man said, 'Father I am *so* sorry. I no longer deserve to be called your son.' But his father told his servants to prepare a feast and to bring the finest clothes, and they began to celebrate.'

DISCUSSION

Why did the son decide to leave home? – He wanted to enjoy himself and to see the world while he was young.

How do you think his father felt? – His father was probably very sad. He loved his son and wanted to make him happy, so he was ready to give him what he asked for and to watch him leave.

Do you think the son was selfish? – The young man thought only of his own needs and happiness. He did not worry about the unhappiness he would cause.

Why did the young man decide to return home? – When he was starving, he realised that he would always be welcomed and cared for at home. When we are having a bad time, we know that we can turn to our families at home for help and support because they love and care for us.

The father saw his son coming in the distance and ran to greet him. What does this tell us about him? – The father was looking out for his son and hoping that one day he would return. He never stopped loving him and ran to welcome him and show how pleased he was to have him home again.

What did the son say to his father? – The son asked his father to forgive him for being foolish and selfish. The father forgave him at once and celebrated his return.

Why did Jesus tell this story? – Jesus wanted us to understand that whatever we do wrong, we can always come back to our heavenly Father to ask for his forgiveness and know that he will welcome us with open arms. God feels sad and waits patiently for our return when we turn away from him.

When do we come to God and ask for his forgiveness in a special way? – In the sacrament of Reconciliation we come to make our peace with God. We ask for God's forgiveness and his help to become more loving and caring people. Like the son who returned to his father, we are filled with happiness and joy when we make peace with God our Father.

ACTIVITY

Photocopy the pictures telling the story of 'The son who came back' and help the children to make and colour their mini books.

CREED

CLOSING PRAYER

Lord, you gave your love and peace to us.
Help us to make our world a happier place
by sharing that love and peace
with each other.

Fifth Sunday of Lent
Jesus forgives a woman

INTRODUCTION
Jewish laws were very strict and everyone was expected to obey them; those who did not could expect to be punished. Today we hear how Jesus shows mercy to a woman without disobeying the law.

SIGN OF THE CROSS

LIGHT THE CANDLES
Sing the Candle Song.

SORRY
Jesus said, 'Do not point out the mistakes of others before doing something about your own.' (cf Luke 6:41-42).
It is not easy to admit when we have made mistakes and done something wrong. Let us spend a few moments in silence, asking Jesus to forgive our faults, and to help us to forgive the faults we find in others.

Say together: Our Father . . .

GOSPEL ACCLAMATION
To welcome today's Gospel sing Acclamation 6: *Jesus here we are.*

GOSPEL (cf John 8:1-11)
Jesus was teaching in the Temple when the Pharisees brought a woman to stand before him. 'This woman has been caught doing something wrong, and the law says that she should be stoned,' they said. 'What do you think?' they asked, because they wanted to trick Jesus.

After a few moments Jesus stood up and said, 'Let the person who has never done anything wrong throw the first stone at her.'

The crowd that had gathered began to leave one by one, until Jesus and the woman stood alone. Jesus said to her, 'Has anyone thrown a stone at you?' 'No sir,' she answered. ' Then I have forgiven you,' he said. 'Now go and make a fresh start.'

DISCUSSION
Why did the Pharisees want to stone the woman? – According to their law, stoning was the punishment required for her wrong-doing.

How did they mean to trick Jesus? – The Pharisees wanted to see whether Jesus would disobey the law and show the woman mercy.

What did Jesus say to them?

He told the people that anyone who was completely pure and good, and who had never done anything wrong, should throw the first stone. The crowd had been ready to punish this woman, but Jesus made them realise that no one is perfect and we all make mistakes.

There was *one* perfectly good person there that day. Who was it? – Jesus.

Was Jesus ready to punish the woman? – Jesus understood that people are often weak and do things wrong. He was always ready to give them another chance to change their hearts and their lives. He showed the woman mercy and sent her away to try again.

What can we learn from this story?
1. That Jesus is merciful and forgiving. He is ready to forgive our mistakes and give us another chance.
   Can you remember the name of a tax-collector, who was given the chance to change his heart and make a fresh start? – Zacchaeus (see the 31st Sunday Year C).
2. Often we see the mistakes and faults of other people before we notice our own. We should be ready to forgive others, just as others forgive our own faults.
   Can you think of a story Jesus told about an unforgiving servant? – (See the 31st Sunday Year A.) Help the children to recall these stories, or re-tell them briefly in your own words.

ACTIVITY
Photocopy the activity sheet and help the children to fill in the blanks.

CREED

CLOSING PRAYER
Merciful Jesus,
help us to be understanding and forgiving,
and to remember
that we all make mistakes sometimes.

We all make mistakes sometimes!

Jesus showed us how to be forgiving.

Things that annoy me about other people.

_____
_____
_____
_____
_____

Things that annoy other people about me.

_____
_____
_____
_____
_____
_____

Second Sunday of Easter
Peace be with you

INTRODUCTION
After the Resurrection, Jesus appeared to the disciples and offered them the gift of his peace. At the same time he sent them out into the world to preach the Gospel and to share this peace with others.

SIGN OF THE CROSS

LIGHT THE CANDLES
Light the candles and say Candle Prayer 3: *The light of God.*

SORRY
Before making peace with God, Jesus told us to make peace with each other when he said (*cf Matthew 5:23-26*):
'If you are about to come before God to pray and then remember that you have quarrelled with someone, go away first, settle your disagreement and make your peace with them.'

Offer each other a sign of peace and then close your eyes as we pray:
Father forgive me
if I have done wrong
and help me to make a fresh start,
sharing your love and peace
with everyone I meet.

GLORIA

GOSPEL ACCLAMATION
Alleluia, alleluia.
Jesus is risen from the dead to be with us always.
Alleluia.

GOSPEL (*cf John 20:19-23*)
The disciples were gathered together in one room when suddenly, Jesus appeared among them. Seeing their fear he said to them, 'Peace be with you,' and he showed them the wounds in his hands and his side.

The disciples were overjoyed to see Jesus again and to know that he was alive! Then Jesus said to them, 'I give you my peace, and as my Father sent me, so I am sending you.'

Breathing gently on them he said, 'Be filled with the Holy Spirit, and know that whoever you forgive, will be forgiven by me.'

DISCUSSION
What were the first words Jesus spoke to the disciples? – 'Peace be with you.'

What does the word 'peace' mean? – The word peace can be used in many different ways. Jesus wanted his disciples to feel calm and unafraid; but it can also be used in other ways, to be free from disturbance or war; not quarrelsome but friendly, and also to mean silence, with little noise to disturb you.

Why do you think Jesus said these words? – The disciples had run away and left Jesus when he was arrested. Even Peter had denied knowing him three times. But Jesus had no quarrel with them, he had forgiven them and wanted to reassure them. They need not be afraid any more because Jesus would be with them always.

What else did Jesus say to them? – He sent them out to carry on his work with the help of the Holy Spirit, and to share the Good News with the rest of the world. He gave them the power and authority to forgive sins, and to share his peace and forgiveness with other people.

Jesus has shared his gift of peace with each one of us, as a sign of his love. How can we share his peace with others?
- by being understanding and forgiving instead of quarrelsome.
- by being kind and friendly.
- by smiling or shaking someone's hand.

(Encourage the children to share their own ideas.)

ACTIVITY
Help the children to make a 'Peace' banner as illustrated.

CREED

CLOSING PRAYER
Lord Jesus,
just as you shared your peace with us,
help us to share it with each other;
So that our world may be filled
with love and friendship.

Third Sunday of Easter
Breakfast on the shore

INTRODUCTION
There are many different ways to show people that we love them; a kiss, a smile, an act of kindness. Jesus appeared to his disciples and prepared a meal to share with them as a sign of his love and friendship.

SIGN OF THE CROSS

LIGHT THE CANDLES
Light the candles and say Candle Prayer 2: *Show me, show me little candle.*

SORRY
As we say our sorry prayer together, let us ask for God's forgiveness, and his help to try again.

Ask one of the children to choose a sorry colour, and read the corresponding prayer aloud together.

GLORIA

GOSPEL ACCLAMATION
To welcome today's Gospel sing Acclamation 3: *Alleluia, alleluia.*

GOSPEL (cf John 21:1-17)
Peter and some of the disciples had been fishing all night but had caught nothing. As daylight dawned, they noticed a man on the shore who called out to them, 'Have you caught anything?'

As they shook their heads, the stranger said, 'Try once more over there!'

They threw their nets back into the water and caught so many fish that their nets were ready to burst. At that moment Peter recognised Jesus, and jumping into the water, he swam to meet him.

On the beach, Jesus had made a fire and was cooking breakfast for Peter and his friends. After they had eaten, Jesus turned to Peter and asked, 'Do you love me?'

'Yes, Lord, you know that I love you,' Peter said.

Jesus asked Peter this question three times and after he had answered, Jesus told Peter about the work he wanted him to do.

DISCUSSION
What made Peter recognise Jesus that day? – Jesus told Peter and the other disciples to cast their nets again, and suddenly they found them full of fish. Peter knew that only the son of God had the power to work such a miracle.

When the disciples found Jesus on the shore, what was he doing? – Jesus was preparing breakfast for them as a sign of his love and friendship. He wanted to share a meal with his friends, just as he had done many times before, to prove to them that he was truly alive.

Have you ever prepared a meal for a special occasion to show how much you cared for someone? – Perhaps you have helped to bake a birthday cake, or brought breakfast in bed for one of your family.

When they had finished eating, what did Jesus ask Peter? – Jesus asked Peter the same question three times, 'Do you love me?' Each time Peter answered, 'Yes, Lord, you know I love you.'

Why do you think Jesus might have asked this on three occasions? – When Jesus was arrested, Peter was asked three times whether he was a friend of Jesus, and each time he said, 'No'. Jesus gave Peter another chance to prove his love for him. He wanted Peter to know that he trusted in his love, and wanted Peter to share this love and faith with the rest of the world.

When do we share a special meal with Jesus? – When we celebrate the Eucharist we gather together at a special meal, where Jesus shares himself with us in a very special way, as the 'Bread of Life'.

ACTIVITY
Help the children to re-tell today's Gospel story in their own words and to imagine the scene. Ask them to draw a picture of Jesus preparing breakfast for his friends that morning on the shore.

Alternatively they can rewrite the story in a mini-book using the picture strip drawings.

CREED

CLOSING PRAYER
Lord Jesus,
help us to recognise you
in the world around us
and to show how much we love you
by our words and actions.

Fourth Sunday of Easter
You are my sheep

INTRODUCTION

Jesus knows and loves each one of us just like a shepherd with his sheep; he is the 'Good Shepherd' who came to care for us and to show us the way to everlasting happiness.

SIGN OF THE CROSS

LIGHT THE CANDLES

Jesus, you are the Good Shepherd
who takes care of all our needs.
Help us
to follow you wherever you lead.
Sing *See the light.*

SORRY

Jesus is the Good Shepherd who will lead us to the Kingdom of Heaven if we follow him. Listen to this story Jesus told:

One day a shepherd found that one of his flock was missing, so he left the other ninety-nine sheep, and went off to look for it. He searched and searched until he found it, because everyone of his sheep was precious to him.

Let us ask Jesus to forgive us if we have wandered from his love, as we sing Sorry Song 2 together.

GLORIA

GOSPEL ACCLAMATION

Alleluia, alleluia.
Lord help us to listen and to recognise your voice.
Alleluia, alleluia.

GOSPEL (*cf John 10:27-28*)

Jesus said: 'My sheep know my voice and they follow me, as I lead them to everlasting life. I know each one of them by name, and they can always trust me to take care of them and to protect them from harm.'

DISCUSSION

Does anyone have a pet dog or cat?

What happens if you call their name?

Hopefully they come when you call them!

What makes them come? – They recognise their name and the sound of your voice. They know that you care for them and they follow you because they trust in your love.

Who are the 'sheep' that follow Jesus? – Jesus is the 'Good Shepherd' and anyone who follows him belongs to his flock. Jesus used the idea of a shepherd and his flock to make the people understand how he would guide and look after his people. He knows each one of us by name, and called us to follow him when we were christened or baptised into the family of God.

Who can we turn to in times of trouble or when we feel afraid or alone? – A good shepherd is always there when his sheep need him, just as Jesus is always there for us in times of need. He will never abandon us and is always watching over us. We can place all our trust in his love and care, knowing that he was ready to die for us so that we could be with him forever.

ACTIVITY

Copy the activity sheet and ask the children to find a way for the sheep to follow their shepherd.

CREED

CLOSING PRAYER

Ask the children to sit quietly with their eyes closed and listen to the words of Psalm 23:
The good shepherd takes care of all my needs;
He leads me to green meadows
and crystal clear pools.
He guides and protects me,
and I grow strong in his care.
When night falls, I am not afraid,
for he is always by my side
to protect me from harm.
When he calls, I will follow,
knowing that his love for me
will last forever.

Fifth Sunday of Easter

Love one another

INTRODUCTION
Jesus and his apostles gathered to celebrate the Jewish Passover and share their Last Supper together. When they had finished, Jesus explained that soon he would be leaving them.

SIGN OF THE CROSS

LIGHT THE CANDLES
Light the candles and read this prayer aloud:
The candle flame is warm and bright,
it changes darkness into light.
We feel it's warmth and see it's glow,
and when we look at it we know,
the light of Christ is burning bright,
for we are children of the light!

SORRY
Jesus told his disciples to 'love one another.' St Paul reminds all Christians that if we do this, then our lives will always be pleasing to God. Listen to these words of St Paul:
'If you love one another as you love yourself, then you will never harm another person, and will live according to the rules given by God.' (cf Romans 13:8-10)

Heavenly Father,
help us to be loving and forgiving,
so that our lives are always pleasing to you.

GLORIA

GOSPEL ACCLAMATION
To welcome today's Gospel sing Acclamation 2: *Light up our hearts.*

GOSPEL (cf John 13:33-35)
When Judas had left them, Jesus turned to his apostles and said, 'It will soon be time for me to leave you my friends, and you cannot come where I am going. When I have gone, I want you to love each other as I have loved each one of you. If you live by this rule, other people will see your goodness and love and they will know that you are my disciples.'

DISCUSSION
Jesus said that he was going to leave his apostles. Where was he going? – Jesus knew that the time had come for him to suffer and die, before rising from the dead and returning to his Father in Heaven.

What did Jesus tell his disciples to do when he had gone? – He gave them a new commandment, to love one another as he had loved them.

Jesus loved and cared for all people, and wanted to put right whatever was wrong in their lives. Can you remember some of the times he showed how much he cared?
- when he fed five thousand hungry people.
- when he cured the lepers.
- when he brought a little girl back to life.
- when he changed the water into wine at the wedding feast.
- when he cured the crippled, and made the blind see.

(Encourage the children to suggest their own favourite examples.)

What was the greatest sign of his love for us? – Jesus loved us so much that he was willing to suffer and die for us, so that we could share everlasting life with him at the end of time.

How do other people know that we are followers of Jesus? – When we love and care for others as Jesus taught us to, then we become more like Jesus, and people see his goodness working in our lives and know that we are his followers.

ACTIVITY
Give each child a copy of the activity sheet and ask them to fill in the blank spaces and to draw a picture of someone they love or care about.

CREED

CLOSING PRAYER
Lord Jesus,
you showed us how we should love
and care for one another.
May our love be a sign
to bring others to know
and love you too.

What can I do to show I care?

When someone is sad,

When someone feels left out,

When someone is hurt,

"Love one another"

Sixth Sunday of Easter
I give you my peace

INTRODUCTION
All of us know how good it feels to get away once in a while from the hustle and bustle of our everyday lives, and enjoy some peace and quiet. Jesus gave us the gift of his peace which comes from God himself.

SIGN OF THE CROSS

LIGHT THE CANDLES
As we light the candles today, let us remember the words of Jesus who said *(cf John 8:12)*:
'I am the light of the world;
whoever follows me will have the light of life and will never walk in darkness'.

SORRY
Close your eyes and listen carefully to the words of this prayer:
Lord, forgive us our impatience,
or when we've not been true,
for when we did not listen,
or turned away from you.
Give us lots of courage
to make a fresh new start.
Help us to be sorry,
we ask this from the heart.

GLORIA

GOSPEL ACCLAMATION
To welcome today's Gospel sing Acclamation 5:
We have come to hear you, Lord.

GOSPEL *(cf John 14:23-27)*
Jesus said: 'If you love me, my Father will love you and the Holy Spirit will live in your hearts and fill you with wisdom and goodness. I leave you the gift of my peace, a peace which comes from God alone. Remember, do not be afraid, because I will be with you always.'

DISCUSSION
What was the gift that Jesus gave to his followers? – The gift of his peace.

What does the word 'peace' mean? – It means to be calm and quiet, and free from disturbance or trouble.

What was special about the peace which Jesus shared with his disciples? – The peace which Jesus shared was the special feeling which comes from being filled with the spirit of his love and goodness. Being close to God gives us a wonderful feeling of well-being and happiness. Jesus offered this peace to anyone who chose to follow him.

Stop and think for a few moments, which part of your normal day is most peaceful and quiet? (Encourage the children to share their thoughts and ideas).

For many people, the most peaceful time of day is at bedtime, just before they fall asleep! It is a good time to think about everything that has happened that day, and to spend a little time talking to God.

Why is it important to make time for peace and quiet in our lives? – Many people find it easier to pray and feel close to God when they can sit quietly without noise and distraction. At such moments we can talk to God and he can speak to us in our hearts. Then we know the peace which Jesus promised us, as we are filled with the spirit of God.

ACTIVITY
Photocopy these doves and make individual badges for the children to decorate and wear.

CREED

CLOSING PRAYER
Come, Holy Spirit,
and fill our hearts
with your love and peace.
Help us to make time
in our busy lives,
to spend some time
talking quietly to God.

Seventh Sunday of Easter
Proclaim the Good News

INTRODUCTION
Jesus asked his heavenly Father to unite his disciples in love and to give them the courage to proclaim the Good News to the world.

SIGN OF THE CROSS

LIGHT THE CANDLES
Light the candles and sing the Candles Song.

SORRY
Let us ask God to pour his spirit into our hearts and to change them with his goodness as we sing Sorry Song 4

GLORIA

GOSPEL ACCLAMATION
Alleluia! Alleluia!
Go out to the world and proclaim the Good News. Alleluia!

GOSPEL (cf John 17:20-26)
Looking up to heaven Jesus prayed, 'Heavenly Father, take care of my disciples and everyone who comes to believe in you because of them. Unite them in love and make them one just as you and I are one. Through me they have come to know you, and will share what they know with the whole world. They have seen your glory on earth, let them share it with you forever at the end of time.'

DISCUSSION
What did the apostles do after Jesus had returned to his heavenly Father? – Filled with the Holy Spirit, they put the love of God and other people first in their lives, and began to tell everyone about Jesus and to cure people in his name. Soon their numbers grew as more and more people came to believe in Jesus.

What do we know about the early Church?

The early Christians loved one another and shared everything they had, taking care of each other's needs, just as Jesus had taught them to. They met together to pray and celebrate the breaking of bread, and to share with each other all the things which Jesus had said and done.

How did the teachings of Jesus spread outside Jerusalem? – Through the Holy Spirit the disciples were filled with the joy of Christ and with his life. Urged by the spirit, some of them set off on missionary journeys to bring their faith to others. They shared the words and teachings of Jesus, and through them many came to believe in him.

In which part of the Bible can you read about the lives and actions of those who first believed in Jesus? – After the Gospels of Matthew, Mark, Luke and John, there is a book called the Acts of the Apostles, which tells how the early followers of Jesus were guided by the Holy Spirit to share Christ's message with the whole world.

The early Christians were drawn together by their love and their belief in Jesus, just as Christians are today. What prayer do we say every week in which we proclaim our faith just as the first disciples did? – In the 'Creed' we tell each other, and the world, that we believe in God who is all powerful and full of love and goodness.

ACTIVITY
Photocopy the activity sheet and read the 'Little Creed' together, before colouring the illustrations.

CREED

CLOSING PRAYER
Spirit of God,
fill us with faith and joy,
so that through us
others may come to know you.

We believe in God our Father,
who made the world in which
we live.
We believe in Jesus Christ,
the Son of God.
He was born by the power
of the Holy Spirit and Mary
was his mother. Jesus was
crucified and died for us,
but after three days he rose
from the dead. Jesus returned
to heaven and lives with God
and one day he will come
again.

Second Sunday of the Year
The miracle at Cana

INTRODUCTION
A miracle is a sign of God's power and glory; a remarkable and amazing event that cannot be explained. Today we hear how Jesus performed his first miracle by changing water into wine.

SIGN OF THE CROSS

LIGHT THE CANDLES
Light the candles and read:
Jesus is the light of the world
who chases away the darkness with his love.

SORRY
Let us ask Jesus to forgive our mistakes and to lead us back to his love as we sing Sorry Song 1.

GLORIA

GOSPEL ACCLAMATION
To welcome today's Gospel sing Acclamation 2: *Light up our hearts.*

GOSPEL (cf John 2:1-11)
Jesus and his mother, along with his disciples, were invited to a wedding in a town called Cana. There was food to eat and wine to drink, and the celebrations carried on throughout the evening. Then Mary came to Jesus and said, 'Son, there is no more wine for the guests to drink.'

'Why do you ask for help when my time has not yet come?' Jesus asked, but Mary turned to the servants and said to them, 'Do whatever Jesus tells you.'

Nearby stood six very large water jars, and Jesus told the servants to fill them with water! 'Now pour some out and take it to the head waiter,' he said.

The water had been changed to wine, and after tasting it, the head waiter went to the bridegroom and said, 'Sir, you have certainly saved the very best wine until last!'

The celebration carried on and there was plenty of wine for everyone. Those who knew what Jesus had done were filled with wonder by this sign of his power.

DISCUSSION
Who was invited to the wedding at Cana? – Jesus and his mother Mary, the disciples, and many other guests.

Has anyone here ever been to a wedding?
After the bridegroom and bride have been married, there is usually a joyful celebration or party, when there is plenty for everyone to eat and drink.

What happened at the wedding in Cana? – They ran out of wine in the middle of the celebration.

How would you feel if you invited lots of people to a party and then ran out of food or drink? – The celebration would be spoilt and you would feel disappointed and embarrassed.

What did Mary do when she heard about the wine? – Mary turned to Jesus for help in this time of difficulty. She believed and trusted in his kindness and goodness, and knew that somehow he could save the day from disaster.

What did Jesus do? – Jesus performed his first miracle by changing the water in the jar into wine.

How do you think the head waiter and the disciples felt? – The bridegroom and the guests did not realise what had happened, but the disciples of Jesus and the servants had seen for themselves that ordinary water had been changed into wine. They were the first to catch a glimpse of the power of Jesus, and they must have been amazed.

In today's Gospel what do we learn about Mary? – Mary acted out of kindness and concern when she learned that the wine had run out. She asked Jesus to help, and showed complete trust in his goodness telling the servants to do whatever he said. Like Mary, we should be kind and caring about others, and always ready to turn to Jesus in times of difficulty. Jesus listens to his mother, and when we pray, we can ask Mary to pray with us for all our needs.

ACTIVITY
Cut out the shape of a water jug from a large sheet of paper. Copy and cut out several smaller jars, the pictures of the servants/disciples, the figures of Jesus and the bride and groom. Ask the children to colour these and stick them onto the large jar shape to be displayed on a board. Using the pictures, help them to tell the story of Christ's first miracle.

CREED

CLOSING PRAYER
Lord Jesus, help us to turn to you
in times of difficulty
and place our trust in your goodness and love.

Third Sunday of the Year
We belong to one body

INTRODUCTION
Sometimes when we hurt ourselves, we realise just how often we use that particular part of our body. Today St Paul reminds us that one body is made up of many parts, and that all of these are important in their own way.

SIGN OF THE CROSS

LIGHT THE CANDLES
Light the candles and pray together:
May the light of Jesus fill our lives with love.

SORRY
Encourage the children to listen carefully to the words of this prayer:
Do not be afraid,
God will always love you.
Whatever you have done,
God will always love you.
As a father loves his child,
He will always love you.
Turn back to him and know,
God's love lasts forever.

GLORIA

GOSPEL ACCLAMATION
To welcome today's reading, sing Acclamation 4: *Praise the Lord.*

READING (cf 1 Cor 12:12-30)
Just as your body has many different parts, so it is with the Christian family. Each part of your body has a special job to do, and without that part, your body could not work properly. Without your legs you could not stand up and walk. Many different parts make up one body, and every part is just as important as another. Each one of us belongs to the one family of God, and has special gifts which God has given to us. We must use these gifts to make sure that the one body of Christ works properly and is full of life.

DISCUSSION
Ask the children to point to each part of their body as you read this list: head, toes, elbow, mouth, knee, nose, back, ear.
Which one of these parts is most important? – Each part of the body does its own particular job, which only it can do. You cannot see with your ears, nor smell with your knees! The whole body relies on the eyes for sight, and on the ears to hear, and on the legs to carry it about. No part can manage without the others, and they are all equally important.

St Paul compared us to parts of the one body of Christ. What did he mean? – At baptism each of us became a member of the family of God and was invited to share in the life of Jesus who rose from the dead. Although there are many Christians in the world today, together we make up one Church, or one body which believes in and follows the teachings of Jesus.

As many parts belonging to the one body of Christ, what jobs can we do in the church and in our ordinary lives? – We can put whatever talents we have to good use in lots of different ways. Many people help us to celebrate at church on Sunday – the musicians and choir, the flower arrangers, the readers, the people who welcome us at the door. They do all these jobs on behalf of everyone. In the same way, in our ordinary lives, our acts of kindness and love, work on behalf of everyone else who belongs to the family of God.

ACTIVITY
Cut out the various parts of the body as illustrated. Punch holes in the relevant places (take care if you are doing this with the children) and ask the children to assemble a body from the various parts using butterfly pins!

CREED

CLOSING PRAYER
Lord Jesus,
you call each one of us
to belong to one people,
the family of God.
Help us,
together with our brothers and sisters,
to share your love
with the world.

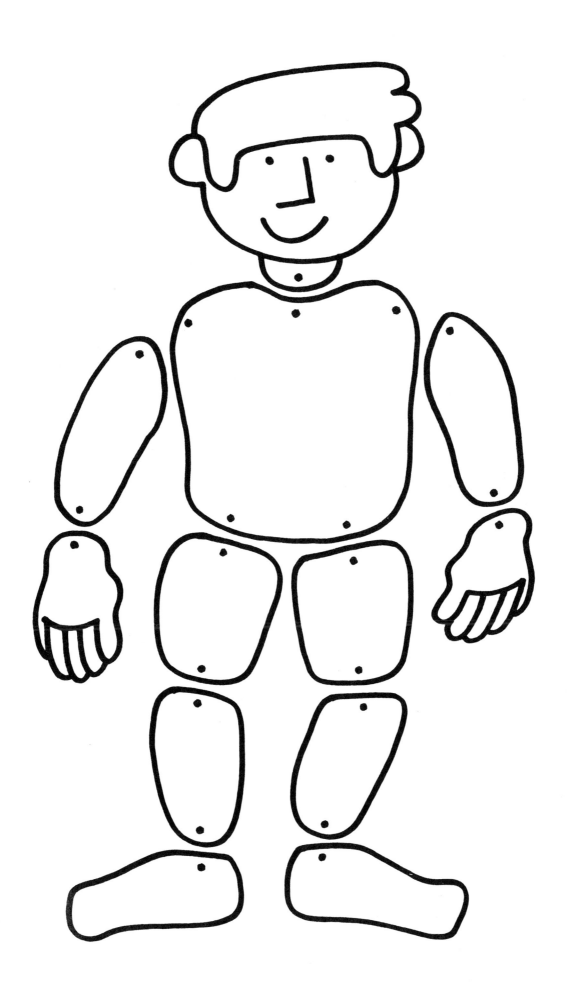

Fourth Sunday of the Year
God's Good News

INTRODUCTION

Jesus returned to Nazareth where he had lived as a child and learned the skills of a carpenter. While he was there, he went to the Temple and began to read from the Scriptures.

SIGN OF THE CROSS

LIGHT THE CANDLES

Light the candles and sing the Candle Song together.

SORRY

Ask the children to close their eyes and listen carefully to the words of this reading (cf St Paul's Letter to the Ephesians 4:23-32):

Make a fresh start and change your heart. Tell the truth, and do not let anger spoil your friendship with others and with God. Speak only words of kindness, and act with love and goodness towards each other. Above all, be ready to forgive others as God forgives you.

In a few moments of silence, let each of us talk to God in our hearts, and ask for his forgiveness and help to make a fresh start.

GLORIA

GOSPEL ACCLAMATION

Alleluia, alleluia,
Jesus is the light of the world who has come to bring the Good News to all people.
Alleluia, alleluia.

GOSPEL (cf Luke 4:20-30)

Jesus began to read the words of the prophet Isaiah to the people in the Temple. 'The spirit of God is with me and he has sent me to bring the Good News to the poor. I have come to bring freedom and to show people a new way.'

After Jesus had finished reading from the scriptures he looked up at the crowd who were listening and said, 'Everything you have heard is coming true today, for I have been sent to bring the Good News to the world.'

The crowd grew angry when they heard this and said, 'Surely this is the son of Joseph the carpenter. He has no right to say such things!' Then they dragged him out of the Temple and away from the town, but Jesus slipped away before they could do him any harm.

DISCUSSION

What did Jesus say to the people after he had finished reading from the scriptures? – Jesus told the crowd that the words of the prophet Isaiah were coming true that very day. God's spirit was with him and he had come to share the message of God's love and mercy with all people.

Why did the crowd become angry? – Jesus was well known to many people in the crowd that day, because Nazareth was his home town where he had grown up. They all knew him as Mary and Joseph's son, an ordinary carpenter. They became angry when they heard him announce that he was the special one that the prophet Isaiah had foretold would come. They did not believe that there was anything special about this man.

What did they do to Jesus? – They dragged him from the Temple and bustled him out of town.

How do you think Jesus felt? – Jesus knew that his own villagers and neighbours would find it hard to accept him as anything other than an ordinary carpenter. He probably felt sad and disappointed that they were not willing to listen and believe in his message.

Had Jesus been sent to bring the Good News to the Jewish people alone? – Jesus brought the message of God's love to be shared with *all* people, whatever their race or colour might be. God knows and loves each one of us, and we are all of equal importance to him. Jesus was always ready to welcome and love everyone, and we must be ready to do the same.

ACTIVITY

Photocopy the illustration to be coloured and pinned onto a display board.

CREED

CLOSING PRAYER

Lord Jesus, open our ears to hear
the Good News of God's love
for each one of us.
Increase our faith and love for you,
we ask this through Christ our Lord.

Fifth Sunday of the Year
The marvellous catch

INTRODUCTION
Peter and his friends James and John had been fishing all night without any luck! Jesus told them to sail out again and cast their nets one more time. Listen to hear what happened!

SIGN OF THE CROSS

LIGHT THE CANDLES
Light the candles and read these words *(cf St Paul's Letter to the Philippians 2:15):*

You are the children of God who shine out in the darkness like the stars which light up the sky at night.

SORRY
Let us spends a few quiet moments talking to God in our hearts. If we have made mistakes, we ask for forgiveness and make our peace with him again.

GLORIA

GOSPEL ACCLAMATION
To welcome today's Gospel sing Acclamation 1: *Share your word with us.*

GOSPEL *(cf Luke 5:1-11)*
Jesus was preaching by the Sea of Galilee, when crowds of people gathered all around to listen to him. Jesus noticed two fishing boats tied up near by. He climbed aboard one which belonged to Peter and asked him to sail a little way from the shore. When Jesus had finished talking to the crowds he turned to Peter and said, 'Sail out to the deep water and cast out your nets.'

'Master, we have been fishing all night and have caught nothing,' Peter said, 'but I will do whatever you say.'

That day they caught so many fish that their nets were ready to burst. Peter and his friends James and John were filled with wonder by this marvellous sight and fell to their knees. Then Jesus said, 'Do not be afraid; come and follow me.' So they left their boats and became his disciples.

DISCUSSION
Why did Jesus climb into Peter's boat? – So many people had come to listen to Jesus teaching that there was little space left on the shore. Many of the crowd could not see or hear Jesus properly, so he sailed a little way from the shore.

After he had finished speaking, what did Jesus tell Peter to do? – Jesus told Peter to sail out to deeper water and to lower his fishing nets into the sea.

Why did Peter not think this was a good idea? – Peter, James and John had been fishing all night but had caught nothing. They were probably feeling tired and disappointed, and eager to get home.

What did Peter do? – Peter did as Jesus had said, and sailed out to the deeper water where he cast out his nets. Although he felt unsure, Peter already trusted Jesus, and was ready to do what he asked.

Did Peter and his friends manage to catch any fish that day? – When they began to pull in their nets, they had caught so many fish that their nets were ready to burst.

How do you think they felt? – They were probably overjoyed by this marvellous catch after their long and disappointing night's fishing. They were amazed by what they had seen, and they began to realise that Jesus was no ordinary man.

What did Jesus ask them to do when they returned to shore? – Jesus invited these fishermen to follow him and become his disciples. They left their boats and nets, and went with him, to help Jesus tell the people about the Good News of God's love.

ACTIVITY
Using an old box help the children to make an underwater scene of the Sea of Galilee

CREED

CLOSING PRAYER
Lord Jesus,
you called Peter and his friends
to follow you,
and you have also called each of us.
Help us to trust in you, as Peter did,
and make our faith grow stronger every day.

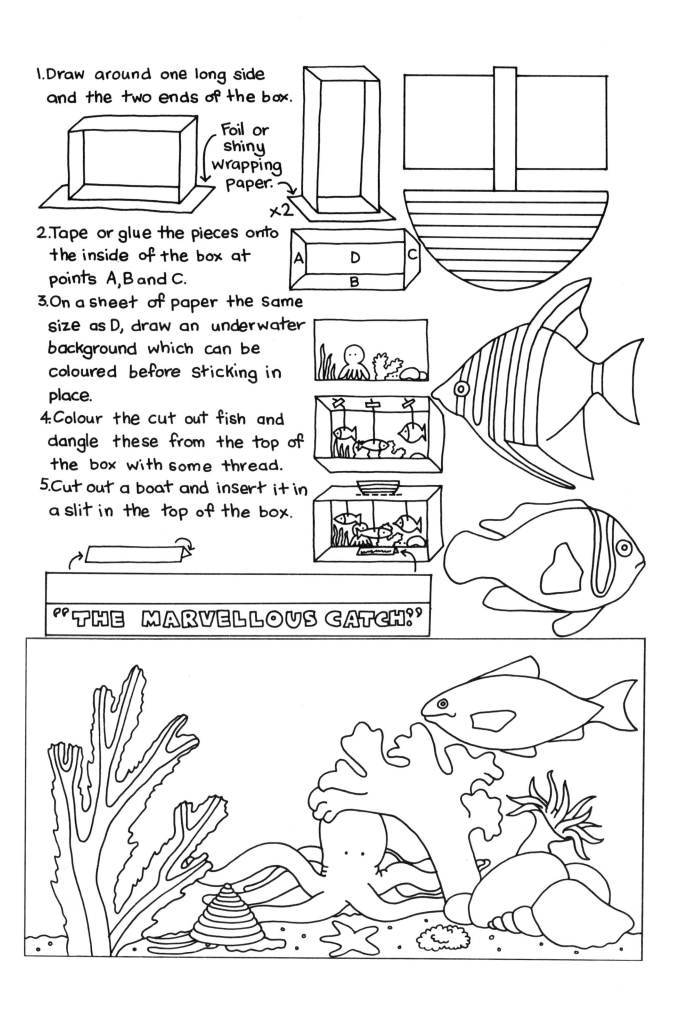

1. Draw around one long side and the two ends of the box.

Foil or shiny wrapping Paper.

×2

2. Tape or glue the pieces onto the inside of the box at points A, B and C.

3. On a sheet of paper the same size as D, draw an underwater background which can be coloured before sticking in place.

4. Colour the cut out fish and dangle these from the top of the box with some thread.

5. Cut out a boat and insert it in a slit in the top of the box.

"THE MARVELLOUS CATCH"

Sixth Sunday of the Year
Happiness is . . .

INTRODUCTION
Someone who has everything they want is not always a happy person. Jesus explained to the crowds that true happiness comes from trusting God, and allowing his love to fill our lives.

SIGN OF THE CROSS

LIGHT THE CANDLES
Light the candles and say Candle Prayer 3: *The light of God.*

SORRY
God our Father is always ready to take care of all our needs, because we are his children and he loves us. When we do something wrong, he will see our sorrow and forgive us time and time again. For a few quiet moments let us speak to God in our hearts, asking his forgiveness and his help to make a fresh start.

Say together: Our Father . . .

GLORIA

GOSPEL ACCLAMATION
To welcome today's Gospel sing Acclamation 6: *Jesus we are here.*

GOSPEL *(cf Luke 6:17-23)*
A large crowd of people had gathered to listen to Jesus who sat down and began to speak:
'Happy are the poor,
for their riches are stored in heaven.
Happy are the hungry,
because God will take care of their needs.
All who weep and are sad
will know only joy and laughter.
Be happy when people are cruel
or unkind because you follow me,
for your reward will be great in heaven.'

DISCUSSION
Why had the crowd followed Jesus that day? – They wanted to listen to him teaching, and many had come hoping to be cured of their illnesses.

Jesus sat down and began to preach to them. Do you know what name is given to the sermon which he gave that day? – Today's passage is called 'The Sermon on the Mount' because Jesus spoke to the crowd as they gathered on a hillside or 'Mount' beside the Sea of Galilee.

St Luke tells us that Jesus gave four examples of true happiness.

Can you remember what they were? – (Help the children to recall the words)
1 Happy are the poor . . .
2 Happy are the hungry . . .
3 All who weep and are sad . . .
4 Be happy when people are cruel or unkind . . .

What was Jesus telling us in this this sermon? – When we know that we are loved so much by God, that love brims over into our lives, we cannot help but share it with each other. It is through giving that we receive. So by sharing God's love which makes us so happy, with others, we make other people happy in turn, and our own happiness increases even more.

Worldly possessions and riches do not last forever, but God's love does and it is worth more than anything else. If we open our hearts and lives to God's love then we will know the true happiness that Jesus spoke of.

ACTIVITY
Photocopy and cut out a shape for each child. Ask them to draw themselves on the blank, and pin all the figures on a board with the caption 'Jesus makes us happy.'

CREED

CLOSING PRAYER
Teach us, Lord,
that true happiness comes from you
and is worth more
than all our worldly possessions.

JESUS MAKES US HAPPY

Seventh Sunday of the Year
Love your enemies

INTRODUCTION
After David, the shepherd boy, had killed the giant Goliath, he went to live at King Saul's palace. Everyone loved David because he was brave and good, and before long, King Saul became jealous and decided to kill him. David managed to escape into the desert, but King Saul and his army followed him there.

SIGN OF THE CROSS

LIGHT THE CANDLES
Read this prayer aloud:
Heavenly Father,
may the light of your love
shine out in our lives
and show others the way to you.

SORRY
Ask a child to choose a sorry colour and after a few moments of quiet reflection, read it aloud together.

GLORIA

ACCLAMATION
Lord, fill our hearts with love and forgiveness.
Open our ears, and help us to listen.

READING (cf 1 Samuel 26:2-23)
King Saul and his army set off into the desert to look for David. One night while Saul and his soldiers slept, David crept into the King's tent. Stuck in the ground by the sleeping King was a spear, but David did not strike his enemy. Taking the spear with him he crept out of the enemy camp. In the morning, David called out in a loud voice, 'King Saul, where is your spear?'

The spear had gone, and the King knew then that David had spared his life. Feeling sorry and ashamed, King Saul led his army home and left David alone.

DISCUSSION
Why did King Saul want to kill David? – David was popular and well-liked by everyone, and Saul became jealous and afraid that David would take his place as King. He decided that he would get rid of David by killing him.

What did the King do when David escaped into the desert? – King Saul and his army followed David to hunt him down and kill him.

What did David do when he had the chance to kill his enemy? – David always tried to live in God's way, being ready to forgive others and being kind even when they treated him badly. King Saul was his enemy but David wished him no harm. By showing Saul his mercy, he hoped that they could make peace.

When King Saul realised that David had spared his life, what did he do? – The forgiveness and love which David had shown, made the King feel ashamed of his own jealousy and wickedness. Because David had been merciful and ready to love his enemy, King Saul was ready to make peace and follow his example.

How did Jesus tell us to treat our enemies? – Jesus told us to love our enemies and do good to those who hate us. We must try to see some goodness in them and surprise them with our kindness. Just as we treat others with forgiveness and without judging them, so will our heavenly Father treat us.

ACTIVITY
Photocopy the pictures depicting the story of David and King Saul. These can be cut up to make booklets or used as a single sheet.

CREED

CLOSING PRAYER
Lord, help us to be brave
and merciful like David,
who was ready to forgive his enemy
and show him a new way.
Give us the courage and strength
to do what we know is right.

Eighth Sunday of the Year
The fruits of goodness

INTRODUCTION

Just as we can recognise an apple tree by the fruit which grows on it, so too can people recognise us as Christians by the way we act and the things we say.

SIGN OF THE CROSS

LIGHT THE CANDLES

Sing the Candle song.

SORRY

Have you ever had a bright shiny apple and bitten into it only to find that it is rotten in the middle?

What is on the outside is not important, but Jesus wants our hearts to be filled with goodness. St Matthew tells us (cf Matthew 12:34-35):

The words that we speak flow from our hearts. If our hearts are filled with goodness, our words and actions will be kind and loving too. But if our hearts are filled with darkness and hate, then our words and actions will be selfish and unkind.

Let us turn to God and speak to him in our hearts, asking for his help to chase away any darkness, and to fill our hearts with his goodness and love.

(Allow the children a few quiet moments to contemplate)

GLORIA

GOSPEL ACCLAMATION

To welcome today's Gospel sing Acclamation 2: *Light up our hearts.*

GOSPEL (cf Luke 6:43-45)

One day Jesus told this parable: 'Fruit that is rotten and bad can never grow on a strong and healthy tree, just as good fruit cannot grow on a tree that is sick and diseased.

Different fruits grow on different trees, and everyone knows which fruit belongs to which type of tree. Like the tree and its fruit, a good person will speak and act kindly, because of the goodness in their hearts.'

DISCUSSION

Does anyone have a fruit tree growing in their garden?

What type of tree is it?

What is the easiest way to tell the difference between an apple and a pear tree?

At certain times of the year, trees can be identified by the fruit growing on their branches. Apples only grow on apple trees, and pears only grow on pear trees!

(Show the children some pictures of different fruit trees and their fruit; a good gardening book should provide these.)

What do you need to get a good crop of tasty healthy apples? – An apple tree that is healthy and well cared for, will usually produce lots of good fruit. A tree which is attacked by disease or pests, or whose branches and trunk become rotten, will produce only a few poor apples.

What is the message of today's parable? – Just as you can tell whether a tree is good or bad by the fruit it grows, so the words and actions of people reveal the state of their hearts. If we are healthy and strong, and full of God's goodness, then that goodness will show in our lives. If our hearts are selfish and unkind, then we will be selfish and unkind people.

How can we make sure our lives are filled with God's love and goodness? – Jesus comes to each one of us in a very special way when we receive the Holy Eucharist. Just as a tree needs to be nourished to produce good fruit, so we need the 'Bread of Life' to nourish us. Jesus shares his love and goodness by giving himself to us. We invite Jesus into our lives and the goodness he shares with us overflows into our daily words and actions.

ACTIVITY

The children can cut out the good apples and stick them in the tree. Help them to assemble the pictures on a background after they have been coloured, and add the caption:
The Fruits of Goodness.

CREED

CLOSING PRAYER

Lord Jesus,
may people see the fruits of your love
and goodness in our words
and the way we treat other people.

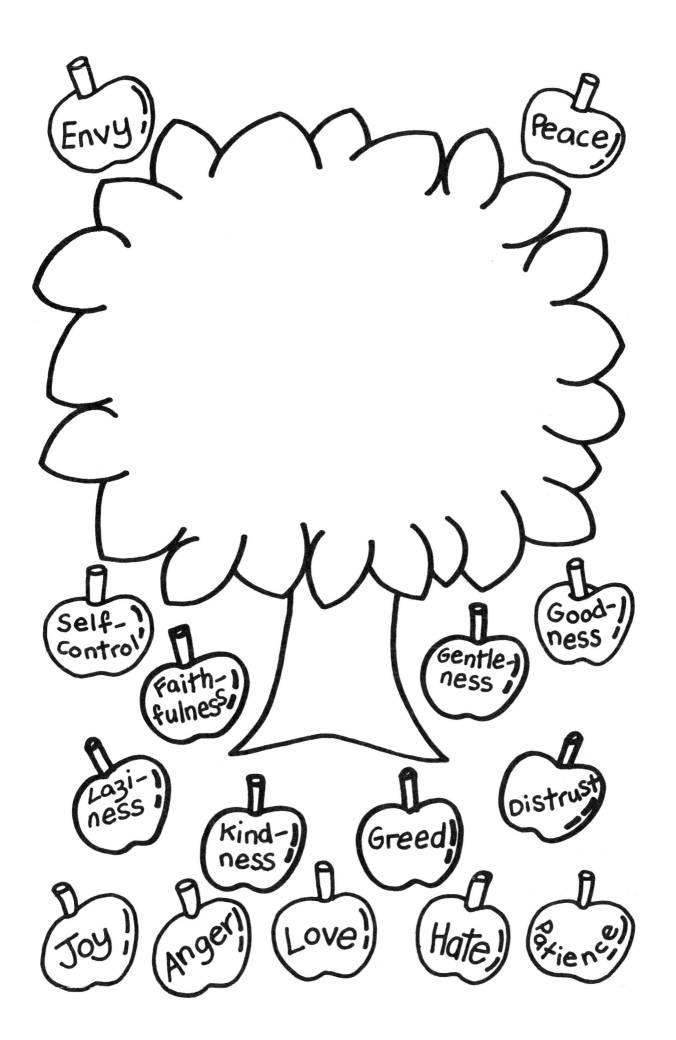

Ninth Sunday of the Year
The faithful centurion

INTRODUCTION
Everyone, including the Roman soldiers, had heard of the marvellous things which Jesus of Nazareth had done. One of these soldiers, a centurion, asked Jesus one day to help his favourite servant who was dying.

SIGN OF THE CROSS

LIGHT THE CANDLES
Light the candles and say Candle Prayer 3: *The light of God.*

SORRY
Lord,
you are always there when we need you,
whatever we have done wrong.
Please forgive us and help us to try again
because of our love for you.

(Allow the children a few moments to speak to God in their hearts.)

GLORIA

GOSPEL ACCLAMATION
Alleluia, alleluia,
Come to us, Lord, and open our ears and our hearts to hear and understand your word.
Alleluia.

GOSPEL (cf Luke 7:1-10)
While Jesus was in Capernaum, some of the Jews came to him to ask for help. They had been sent by a Roman centurion whose favourite servant was very ill and close to death.

'Jesus, please help this man, because he has always been fair and kind to us,' they said. Jesus went with them, but on the way they were met by some of the soldier's friends with a message for Jesus from the centurion which said: 'Jesus, do not put yourself to any trouble for my sake, because I am not good enough to expect you to come to me. I am a soldier, and I obey my orders just as my men obey me. Whatever I tell them to do, they will do it. If you will just give the order, I know that my servant will be well again.'

Jesus was amazed by the centurion's faith in his power and said, 'Few people have shown such great trust in me.'

When the centurion's friends returned to his house they found great rejoicing because the servant had completely recovered.

DISCUSSION
At the time when Jesus lived, who ruled Palestine? – The Romans had conquered Palestine about sixty years before Jesus was born. They had made it part of the great Roman Empire.

What was a Roman centurion? – A centurion was an officer in the Roman army who commanded a unit of one hundred soldiers. Whatever orders he gave were carried out by his men. (If possible show the children a picture of some Roman soldiers).

What did the centurion want from Jesus? – He wanted Jesus to help his favourite servant who was dying.

What did Jesus do when he knew that someone needed him? – Without hesitating Jesus went at once to help the dying servant. He was always ready to help *anyone* who needed him whatever nationality they happened to be.

What message did the centurion send to Jesus? – The centurion told Jesus that he did not deserve to have a man of such goodness coming to him, and he felt humble and unworthy.

How much did the centurion show that he believed in Jesus? – The centurion trusted in Jesus so much that he believed a simple command would cure his servant.

Do you recognise in which part of the Mass we remember the story of the faithful centurion? – As we prepare to receive communion we ask Jesus to forgive us and to come to us in a special way as we pray together, 'Lord, I am not worthy to receive you, but only say the word and I shall be healed.' Like the centurion we feel humble and undeserving of Jesus' goodness, but we trust and believe that Jesus has the power to make us better people and to fill us with his love and goodness.

ACTIVITY
Copy or trace the picture of the Roman centurion for the children to colour and keep.

CREED

CLOSING PRAYER
Lord,
whenever we need you,
you are always there to help us.
May our faith be as strong
as the Roman centurion
who placed all his trust in you.

Lord, I do not deserve your goodness, but only say the word and it shall be done

Tenth Sunday of the Year
Do not be sad

INTRODUCTION
We are God's children, and he wants each one of us to be happy. Jesus could not bear to see us sad and unhappy, and always tried to change tragedy into celebration.

SIGN OF THE CROSS

LIGHT THE CANDLES
Light the candles and read (cf Revelation 22:5):
There will be no more night, and we will not need lamps or sunlight, because the Lord God will be our light!

SORRY
Ask one of the children to choose a sorry colour and to read the corresponding prayer aloud to the group.

GLORIA

GOSPEL ACCLAMATION
To welcome today's Gospel sing Acclamation 6:
Jesus here we are.

GOSPEL (cf Luke 7:11-17)
A large crowd had followed Jesus and his disciples to a town called Nain, where they met a funeral procession outside the gates of the town. A widow's only son had died, and she walked behind the procession crying sadly. Seeing this, Jesus was filled with great pity and said to the woman, 'Do not cry.'

Then he stopped the procession and said loudly, 'Young man, get up!' At once the young man sat up and began to talk, and Jesus brought him to his mother. The woman and the crowd were filled with wonder and began to praise God, and soon everyone had heard about the marvellous thing which Jesus had done.

DISCUSSION
Why did Jesus take pity on the woman? – The woman was a widow, and so her husband had already died. The young man had been her only child, and now that he was dead too she was completely alone. Jesus saw her suffering and sadness and wanted to make her happy again.

What did Jesus do? – Jesus commanded the young man to get up, which is exactly what he did.

Imagine if you were in the crowd of mourners and saw this happening, what would you think?

(Encourage the children to share their thoughts.)

Friends of the young man and his mother had joined the procession of sad people, or mourners, who were taking the dead man to be buried. They must have been surprised when this stranger stopped the procession, and filled with disbelief when he brought the dead man back to life!

Can you remember any of the other times when Jesus changed the sadness of death into the joy of new life?
– when he brought Lazarus out of the tomb.
– when he brought a little girl back to life.
– when he rose from the dead on Easter Sunday, the joyous event we remember at every Mass.

ACTIVITY
Photocopy the activity sheet and cut out and fold the happy/sad faces. Staple them together at the top. Show the children how to place a pencil at the bottom of the paper and roll the top piece around it tightly. Move the pencil up and down to make the face change.

CREED

CLOSING PRAYER
Let us pray for all those who have died, and their families and friends who are feeling sad.

Lord hear us.
All: Lord graciously hear us.

Let us pray for anyone who is unhappy or alone; may Jesus touch their lives with his joy and love.

Lord hear us.
All: Lord graciously hear us.

(Ask the children if there is anyone they know who needs a special mention or prayer.)

1°

2°

3°

A

B

Jesus makes us happy

Eleventh Sunday of the Year
Jesus forgives a sinner

INTRODUCTION
It is never easy to say sorry, to admit our mistakes or to ask for forgiveness. Jesus showed us that he will always welcome us back to the joy of his love, whatever we have done wrong.

SIGN OF THE CROSS

LIGHT THE CANDLES
Sing *See the light* as the candles are lit.

SORRY
Read the following prayer:
Do not be afraid,
God will always love you.
Whatever you have done,
God will always love you.
As a Father loves his child,
He will always love you.
Come back to him and know,
God's love lasts forever.

GLORIA

GOSPEL ACCLAMATION
Alleluia, alleluia!
Jesus said 'Love one another as I have loved you.'
Alleluia!

GOSPEL *(cf Luke 7:36-50)*
One of the Pharisees called Simon invited Jesus to dinner. A woman who had done many things she was ashamed of, heard that Jesus would be there and came to find him. She knelt at his feet and began to cry, wiping his feet dry with her long hair before covering them with kisses and perfumed ointment.

Simon was annoyed that Jesus would allow such a person near him. But Jesus knew what Simon was thinking and asked him, 'If one servant owed his master fifty pounds and another owed his master five thousand pounds, which one would love his master more if the debts were cancelled?' 'The one who owed more,' Simon answered.

Then Jesus said, 'Simon, you did not offer me water to wash with, a kiss as a greeting, or perfume to refresh me. This woman has done all these things and more. Surely everything she has done wrong has been forgiven, for her to show such great love.'

Then Jesus said to the woman, 'Your faith has saved you! Go now, your sins have been forgiven.'

DISCUSSION
Who was the Pharisee who invited Jesus to dinner?

How did Simon feel when Jesus did not send the woman away? – As a Pharisee Simon was very religious and took great pride in obeying the laws. He felt annoyed and embarrassed to have a sinful woman in his own home. He could not understand why Jesus allowed this sinner to stay, instead of sending her away.

How did the woman show Jesus that she loved him and was sorry for everything she had done wrong? – She cried so much that she washed his feet with her tears and then dried them with her own hair. Finally she covered them with kisses and perfumed ointment as a sign of her love.

Jesus treated the woman with kindness and pity. How did he explain God's forgiveness to Simon? – However bad we have been, God is ready to forgive us when we are truly sorry. Jesus came to save sinners and to bring them back to God's love. Those who need God's forgiveness most, feel the greatest joy when they are forgiven. Jesus compared this woman to the servant with the huge debt who loved his master all the more because he had been pardoned so much.

What prayer can we say to tell God that we are sorry for all our mistakes? – Everyone learns an 'Act of Contrition' which is a special prayer for saying sorry and making peace with God. We use this prayer in the Sacrament of Reconciliation, but it is also a good prayer to say every night before we go to sleep.

ACTIVITY
Copy the Act of Contrition for each child to colour and to use at home.

CREED

CLOSING PRAYER
Help us Lord,
to come to you
and ask for your forgiveness
so that we will know the joy
of making our peace with you.

Read the Act of Contrition together.

O my God
I am sorry for
having sinned
against you.
Because you
are so good,
and with your
grace,
I will try not
to sin again.
Amen.

Twelfth Sunday of the Year
The Son of God

INTRODUCTION
Sometimes when we are asked a question and feel unsure of the answer, we find it easier to say nothing. Jesus asked his disciples a difficult question, which none of them answered until Peter bravely decided to speak up.

SIGN OF THE CROSS

LIGHT THE CANDLES
Ask the children to repeat:
May the light of Christ's love shine in our lives.

SORRY
All of us make mistakes sometimes and do things which we regret, but God always reaches out a forgiving hand. Let us spend a few moments making our peace with God, and asking for his forgiveness and help to change our hearts and try again.

Sing Sorry Song 5.

GLORIA

GOSPEL ACCLAMATION
To welcome today's Gospel sing Acclamation 1:
Share your word with us.

GOSPEL (*cf Luke 9:18-21*)
Jesus was praying quietly with his disciples when suddenly he asked them, 'Who do people say that I am?'

The disciples answered, 'Some believe you are John the Baptist, some say Elijah and others think that you are a prophet who has come back to life.'

'But tell me, who do you say that I am?' asked Jesus.

Then Peter spoke, 'Master, you are the Son of God.'

Jesus told them not to tell anyone about what they had heard that day.

DISCUSSION
If I asked you 'Who are you?' what would you say?
- perhaps you would tell me your name.
- you might say that you are someone's sister or brother.

What did the disciples say when Jesus asked them, 'Who do people say that I am?'

The disciples told Jesus what other people had said about him, and who he might be. They themselves seemed uncertain and confused. They all knew that he was the son of Mary and Joseph, an ordinary carpenter and yet they also knew that there was something extraordinary about him.

Which of the disciples spoke when Jesus pressed them for an answer? – Peter was the one who spoke and declared that Jesus was the Son of God.

How did Peter know that Jesus was God's son? – Peter had listened to Jesus preaching, and seen how he taught people to live according to God's love. He had seen Jesus heal the crippled and sick, bring the dead to life and perform many miracles, and these had touched his heart. In this way God had revealed to Peter that Jesus was no ordinary man, but his beloved son.

If someone asked you today, 'Who is Jesus?' what would you say?
- that Jesus is the son of God.
- that Jesus is the light of the world who shows us the way to God, and helps us on our journey to heaven.
- that Jesus is our friend, the Good Shepherd.
- that Jesus is the saviour of the world who saved us from sin so that we could share everlasting life with him in Heaven.

(Encourage the children to share their thoughts and ideas.)

ACTIVITY
Jesus has been described in many different ways:

Jesus is – the Son of God
         – the Good Shepherd
         – the Light of the World
         – the True Vine
         – the Bread of Life
         – King of the Universe.

Help the children to think of any other examples and then write them down on the worksheet. Ask each child to draw a picture of their favourite image of Jesus.

CREED

CLOSING PRAYER
Lord, help us to know you
as Peter did,
as a friend,
as a teacher,
and as the only Son of God.

JESUS IS:

The Son of God

The Good Shepherd

The Light of the world

The true vine

The Bread of Life

King of the Universe

Thirteenth Sunday of the Year
Welcome Jesus

INTRODUCTION

Everyone likes to feel welcomed and to be treated kindly. Sometimes Jesus and his disciples were treated unkindly by people who were unwilling to welcome them into their homes and their lives.

SIGN OF THE CROSS

LIGHT THE CANDLES

Light the candles and read aloud *(cf Romans 13:12-13):*

Live your lives as children of the light. Do not hide in the darkness for there is nothing to fear Fill your lives with love and goodness, and follow in the footsteps of Jesus.

SORRY

While St Paul was in prison in Rome, he wrote a letter to some of the early Christians and reminded them how important it is to ask for God's forgiveness, and to be ready to forgive others *(cf Ephesians 4:23-32):*

'Make a fresh start and change your heart. Tell the truth and do not let anger spoil your friendship with each other and God. Speak kindly and act with love and goodness. Above all, be ready to forgive other as God forgives you.'

Now we will spend a few quiet moments speaking to God in our hearts and telling him that we are sorry if we have done wrong.

GLORIA

GOSPEL ACCLAMATION

To welcome today's Gospel sing Acclamation 6: *Jesus here we are.*

GOSPEL *(cf Luke 9:51-55)*

Jesus set out for Jerusalem, intending to stop and rest at a Samaritan village on the way. The people there had heard that he was coming and drove Jesus and his followers away. Some of his disciples grew angry when this happened, but Jesus scolded them, and quietly led them away, to find another village where they would be made to feel welcome.

DISCUSSION

Why were Jesus and his disciples going to Jerusalem? – They were going to Jerusalem to celebrate the Jewish Passover together, after which Jesus would be arrested and put to death.

What made the Samaritans drive them away from their village? – The Samaritans and the Jews had been enemies since Old Testament times. When they heard that a crowd of Jews planned to stay in their village before travelling on to Jerusalem, they became angry and drove them away. They were not ready to welcome Jesus or willing to listen to his message of love and peace.

The disciples grew angry themselves when they saw how Jesus had been treated. What did Jesus say to them? – Jesus told them off for getting angry and wasting their time and energy. Instead he led them to another village where they might be welcomed. Jesus knew that there was much work to be done, and that they should waste no time on those who would not listen to the Good News they brought.

Jesus wanted to share his love and his message with anyone who made him welcome. How can we welcome Jesus into our lives today?

Jesus said, 'Whatever you do to others you do it to me.' When we treat other people with love and kindness, and make them feel welcome at home, at school or wherever we are, then we are doing the same to Jesus.

ACTIVITY

Photocopy the template onto some coloured card. Cut out the circles and ask the children to colour the letters and draw a smiling picture of themselves in the middle. These can then be hung from a mobile or attached to a handle for each child to carry.

CREED

CLOSING PRAYER

Lord Jesus,
may I see you in the people around me,
and welcome you with a warm smile
and a loving heart.
Help me to listen to your message
of love and peace:
the Good News which you came
to share with our world.

MAKE JESUS WELCOME

←a straw.

Fourteenth Sunday of the Year
Jesus shares his message

INTRODUCTION
Jesus wanted to reach everyone with his message of eternal life, and touch all lives with his love, so he sent his disciples out into the world so that through them others would come to know him.

SIGN OF THE CROSS

LIGHT THE CANDLES
As we look at the light from the candle flames let us remember that Jesus is 'the light of the world.'

SORRY
Encourage the children to close their eyes and listen to the words of this prayer:
Dear God,
help us to forgive anyone who has hurt us,
because we must be ready to forgive others,
just as you forgive us.
If we have done wrong,
by our words or our actions,
we ask your pardon
and will try to be good.

GLORIA

GOSPEL ACCLAMATION
Alleluia, alleluia!
Help us to understand your message Lord, and to share it with others.
Alleluia.

GOSPEL (cf Luke 10:1-12, 17-20)
Jesus chose seventy-two disciples and sent them out in pairs to all the towns and villages he would visit saying, 'Take nothing with you, and wherever you are welcomed, make the first words you speak, 'Peace be with you'. Stay if you are invited to, and eat and drink whatever you are given. Cure the sick and share the Good News of God's love with everyone. If you find people unfriendly or unkind, leave them and their village and go elsewhere.'

Soon the disciples returned and told Jesus about the marvellous things they had seen and done. Jesus said to them. 'Be happy indeed because your names are written in heaven.'

DISCUSSION
Why did Jesus send seventy-two disciples out to visit the surrounding towns and villages? – Jesus knew that he would need help to take the message of God's love to people throughout the world. He sent the disciples out to prepare the people for him to come into their lives.

What were the first words they were to speak? – 'Peace be with you'. Jesus wanted them to offer his peace and love so that they would know they had nothing to fear.

Ask the children to arrange themselves into pairs. If Jesus sent seventy-two disciples out in twos, how many pairs does this make? – There were thirty-six pairs altogether, and they probably visited more than one village each. In this way the teachings of Jesus were heard by many more people than Jesus could have reached on his own.

Imagine you were being sent on a journey by Jesus, what do you think you might need?
  – something to eat and drink
  – clothes
  – a map
  – protection from the weather
  – insect repellent!

What did Jesus tell them to take? – Jesus told them to take few belongings for their journey, but to trust God to take care of them. People would see their goodness and would treat them with kindness and generosity.

What did Jesus want the disciples to do? – To share the love and peace of God through their actions and words. He told them to cure the sick and to teach the people about the goodness of God, so that they would let him into their hearts. As Christians, and followers of Jesus we take his love and peace out to the people we meet today, just as the seventy-two disciples did so long ago.

ACTIVITY
Today's activity is designed to make the children appreciate how difficult it was at the time of Jesus to travel, and communicate with other people.

Cut out a series of circles and write one of the following on each: sailing boat, aeroplane, on foot, telephone, horse and cart, car, donkey, train, television, power boat, helicopter, bus.

Ask each child to choose a circle and draw a picture illustrating their particular word. Then pin them on a board under the relevant heading, and compare the differences between then and now.

Alternatively, use the worksheet for the same activity.

CREED

CLOSING PRAYER
Lord,
we pray for everyone
who shares your message
of love and peace
with the world.

"GO OUT TO THE WHOLE WORLD AND SHARE THE GOOD NEWS"

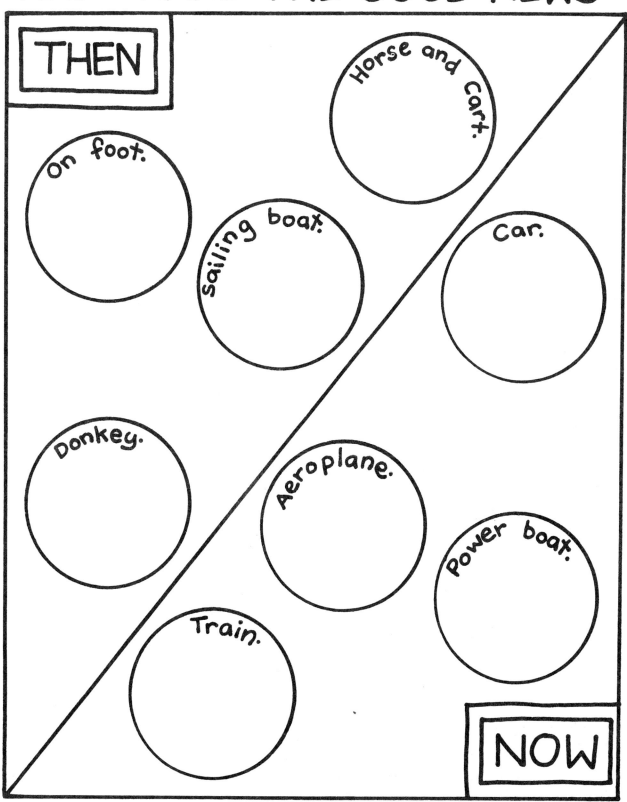

Fifteenth Sunday of the Year
The good Samaritan

INTRODUCTION
If someone stumbled and fell in the street would you help them, or feel embarrassed and walk on by? Jesus tells us that we must be ready to help whoever needs us, because everyone is our neighbour.

SIGN OF THE CROSS

LIGHT THE CANDLES
Light the candles and then read: *(cf Matthew 5:16-17)*
Jesus said: 'Let your goodness shine out like a light in the darkness, so that through you, the love of our heavenly Father will touch the lives of others.'

SORRY
After a few moments of quiet contemplation and prayer sing Sorry Song 1.

GLORIA

GOSPEL ACCLAMATION
Alleluia, alleluia.
Jesus said, 'Love one another as I have loved you.' Alleluia.

GOSPEL *(cf Luke 10:29-37)*
A man once said to Jesus, 'I know that I should love God with all my heart, and love my neighbour too. But who is my neighbour?'

Then Jesus told him this story: 'One day a man was travelling from Jericho to Jerusalem, when a gang of robbers attacked him. They beat him up, and after stealing everything he had, they left him lying injured by the roadside. A short time later one of the temple priests passed that way, but he crossed the road and walked on by. Soon, another traveller came, but he too passed on by. Then a Samaritan happened to pass, and when he saw the injured man he took pity on him. He bandaged his wounds, and carried him on horseback to a nearby inn. There he cared for him and when the time came to leave, he left the innkeeper enough money to pay for the man's room until he was better.' Jesus then asked the man, 'Which man in the story was a good neighbour?'

'The one who helped the wounded traveller', he answered. 'Go then and do the same for anyone who needs your help,' said Jesus.

DISCUSSION
This story is often called the 'good Samaritan'. What was a Samaritan?

A Samaritan was someone who came from a region of Palestine called Samaria. The Samaritans and the Jews had been enemies since Old Testament times. The good Samaritan did not worry about the injured man's religion or race, instead he saw someone who needed his help, and was filled with a sense of love and pity. Even today when someone does a good deed for another person, we often call them a 'good Samaritan.'

What did the other men do when they saw the injured traveller? – They crossed the road and walked on by. They were not prepared to put themselves to any trouble, and ignored the needs of the man lying on the roadside. Today, too many people are in a hurry, and are unwilling to stop and offer help to someone who needs it.

(Perhaps you or the children have had such an experience?)

From the story which Jesus told, who is our neighbour? – Our neighbour is whoever we meet, whatever their race, religion or colour might be. When a fellow human being is suffering, or needs our help, then we should show the same loving concern and compassion as the good Samaritan.

Jesus told the man to go away and be a good Samaritan. How can we do the same? – By treating everyone with kindness and love, whether it is at school, at home or when playing with friends. By loving one another as we love ourselves then we will please our heavenly Father.

ACTIVITY
Either photocopy the story of the good Samaritan for each child, or copy each picture onto a separate sheet of paper to be coloured and displayed.

CREED

CLOSING PRAYER
Lord,
today we pray for anyone
who needs a good Samaritan;
give each of us the courage
to stop and help
when our neighbour needs us.

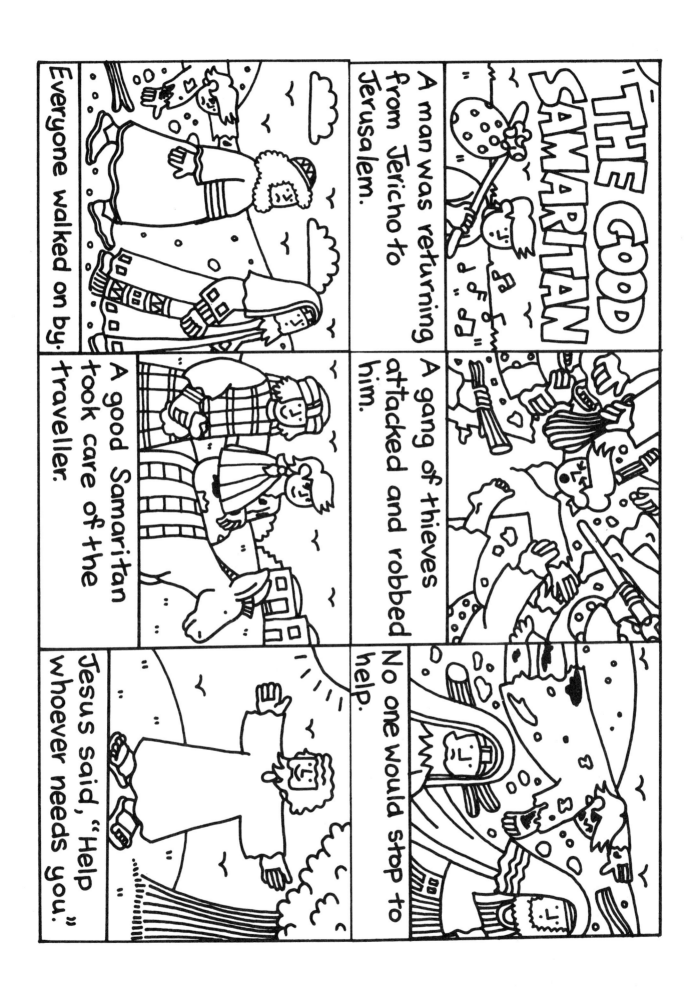

Sixteenth Sunday of the Year
Make time to listen

INTRODUCTION
Martha and Mary lived in Bethany, a small village near Jerusalem. They were close friends of Jesus, who often came to visit them when he passed that way.

SIGN OF THE CROSS

LIGHT THE CANDLES
As the candles are lit, the children listen to this reading by the prophet Isaiah *(cf Isaiah 60:1-3):*

The glory of God is shining on you! You will always have God's light to chase away the darkness, so others will look at you and see God's love shining out!

We ask Jesus to be a light in our lives as we sing the Candle Song together.

SORRY
Close your eyes and listen carefully to the words of this prayer:
God our Father,
you sent your son Jesus
because you love us so much.
When we do something that makes you sad,
help us to remember your love,
to ask for your forgiveness,
and to make a fresh start.
Say together: Our Father . . .

GLORIA

GOSPEL ACCLAMATION
To welcome today's Gospel sing Acclamation 5:
We have come to hear you, Lord.

GOSPEL *(cf Luke 10:38-42)*
One day Jesus and his disciples came to the village called Bethany where his friends Martha and Mary lived. They welcomed Jesus and his followers and invited them to stay for a meal.

While Martha busied herself preparing and serving the food, her sister Mary sat calmly beside Jesus and listened to him talking. Martha worked hard, and all the while Mary sat and listened to Jesus. Finally Martha got upset and said to Jesus, 'Lord must I do all this work on my own? Tell Mary to come and help me!'

'Martha, Martha,' Jesus said. 'Do not let these things upset you, they are not important. Mary has chosen to listen to me and that is the most important thing of all.'

DISCUSSION
Martha was very busy and had a lot to do. What do you imagine she had to do?

Jesus and his disciples had been invited to stay for a meal, so Martha had to prepare a lot of food. The travellers were thirsty after their journey, and Martha had to organise drinks for everyone.

What did Mary do while Martha was so busy?

Mary sat down beside Jesus and simply listened to his words.

How did Martha feel about this?

Martha became angry with Mary, perhaps because she thought that she was being lazy leaving her to do all the work. Martha may also have felt a little jealous of her sister, because she too wanted to sit at Jesus' feet and listen to him.

What did Jesus say when Martha complained?

Jesus told Martha that Mary had chosen to do the right thing. He was grateful for all the work that Martha had done for them, but what really made him happy was making time to listen to the word of God; nothing was more important!

What does this story teach us?

We all lead hectic and busy lives, and sometimes we forget what is really important: to make time for Jesus in our lives and to listen as he speaks to us.

ACTIVITY
Ask each child to draw a picture of themselves listening to God's word at Church, or making time for Jesus as they say their prayers.

CREED

CLOSING PRAYER
Lord Jesus, we pray
that we will always make you welcome
and be ready to spend time
listening to the word of God.

Making Time For Jesus

LISTENING TO GOD'S
WORD AT CHURCH

TALKING TO GOD AT
PRAYERTIME

Seventeenth Sunday of the Year
Teach us to pray

INTRODUCTION

Jesus taught us how to pray to God our Father, who will always listen to what we say and do whatever is best for us.

SIGN OF THE CROSS

LIGHT THE CANDLES

As we light our candles we thank God for sending Jesus his son to be a light in the darkness, and lead us to everlasting life.

SORRY

Jesus taught us to pray 'forgive us our trespasses as we forgive those who trespass against us,' and so we say:
Lamb of God, have mercy on us,
Lamb of God, make us merciful to others,
Lamb of God, fill us with your love and your peace.

GLORIA

GOSPEL ACCLAMATION

To welcome today's Gospel sing Acclamation 3:
Alleluia, alleluia.

GOSPEL (*cf Luke 11:1-4, 9-10*)

One day when Jesus had finished praying, one of his disciples said, 'Master, teach us how to pray!'
So Jesus taught them to say:
Our Father, who art in Heaven
hallowed be thy name.
Thy kingdom come,
thy will be done
on earth as it is in heaven.
Give us this day our daily bread
and forgive us our trespasses
as we forgive those
who trespass against us.
And lead us not into temptation
but deliver us from evil.
Amen.

Then Jesus said, 'Anyone who asks, will be answered; anyone who looks, will find, and anyone who knocks will have the door opened.'

DISCUSSION

What do we call the prayer which Jesus himself taught us?

'The Lord's Prayer' or the 'Our Father'.

The prayer that Jesus taught was very different from any thing the Jews had heard before. Do you know why?

Jesus taught the disciples to think of God as someone who was loving and protective, just like a 'father' to all people. This changed the whole idea of God from being someone all powerful and mighty, to someone who is a close friend.

What sort of things do you pray for? – (Encourage the children to share their thoughts and ideas.)

Jesus told them to pray:
'God our Father, you are everywhere,
and we bless your Holy name.
Help us to choose to share
the love and joy of your kingdom.
Help us to know and do your will.
Provide us with all our needs
because we depend on you.
Forgive our mistakes
as we forgive the mistakes of others.
Help us when we are put to the test
and keep us safe from harm.
Amen.'

Does God always seem to answer our prayers?

Jesus told us to ask and God will answer us; to look and we will find him. God always answers our prayers but in his own way, and not necessarily as we expect him to. Whatever happens we know that we can always rely on God's continuous concern and fatherly love for each one of us.

ACTIVITY

Either photocopy the Lord's Prayer for the children to decorate and hang up at home or ask the older children to write a prayer of the own.

CREED

CLOSING PRAYER

Ask the children to read out their own prayers
or
read aloud:
Father you know and love us so well,
you take care of all our needs
and we are never alone.
Help us to remember this as we pray
Our Father . . .

Eighteenth Sunday of the Year
The rich man

INTRODUCTION
Today Jesus explains that money and belongings cannot bring us the happiness of everlasting life in heaven.

SIGN OF THE CROSS

LIGHT THE CANDLES
Light the candles and read aloud: *(cf 2 Samuel 22:29)*
You, Lord are the light in my life who chases away any darkness.

SORRY
Ask one of the children to choose a sorry colour and to pin the corresponding prayer on a board for the children to read aloud together.

GLORIA

GOSPEL ACCLAMATION
Alleluia! Alleluia!
Lord help us to listen, and to follow you.
Alleluia!

GOSPEL *(cf Luke 12:16-21)*
One day Jesus told this parable: 'Once there was a rich man who owned many farms. One year the harvest was so good that the man could not store it all in his many barns. 'I will build bigger and better barns,' he said, 'and then I will be so rich that I will have nothing to worry about.'

But God said to the man, 'You are a foolish man! When you die, what use will your worldly riches be, because in the eyes of God you are poor indeed.'

DISCUSSION
Why did the rich man need to build bigger and better barns? – That year there was a bumper harvest and he could not fit all the crops into his barns to be stored.

If he had been a kind and generous man, what could he have done with the extra food he had? – The man was already rich, and did not really need to worry about storing the extra harvest. Instead of being selfish and greedy he could have stored up his treasure in heaven by giving some of the food to people who needed it more than he did.

What kind of treasure did the rich man store up for himself? – He busied himself making money, and thought that if he had enough then he would be a truly happy man.

What sort of riches should the man have stored up for himself? – Money and possessions do not make us rich in the eyes of God. By living as Jesus taught us and sharing in God's kingdom now, we will store up our treasure in heaven. Every good deed and word of kindness, are more precious to God than money can ever be. When we die, whatever money or possessions we have are left behind us, but our goodness will last forever and bring us everlasting happiness.

Can you remember another parable Jesus told to explain how important it is to know what really makes us rich in the eyes of God? – The parables of the treasure and the pearl (see 17th Sunday of Year A). Remind the children briefly of these stories in your own words.

ACTIVITY
Give each child a copy of the maze and ask them to show the rich man the way to heaven.

CREED

CLOSING PRAYER *(cf Psalm 119:36-37)*
Lord, help me
to store up my riches in heaven
and not just on earth,
and to know what is truly important
so that I do not waste my time
on worthless things.

Nineteenth Sunday of the Year

Jesus trusts us

INTRODUCTION

Have you ever trusted someone to do something and then been disappointed to find that it has not been done? Jesus trusted his disciples to carry on his work when he had gone.

SIGN OF THE CROSS

LIGHT THE CANDLES

Light the candles and then read: *(cf John 3:19-21)*
The light has come into the world, but wicked people who do wrong, love the darkness and hide from the light. Whoever is honest and good is not afraid of the light, because they live as God wants them to and have nothing to hide.

SORRY

Lord Jesus,
St Peter denied you three times
but you forgave him.
We ask your forgiveness
for the times we deny you
and turn away from your love.

(Allow the children a few moments of quiet prayer.)

GLORIA

GOSPEL ACCLAMATION

To welcome today's Gospel sing Acclamation 2: *Light up our hearts.*

GOSPEL *(cf Luke 12:41-48)*

One day Jesus told this story: 'A man gave orders to his two servants, and trusted them to be carried out while he was away. One servant did what his master had told him, even though he did not know when his master would return. The other servant betrayed his master's trust and did not carry out his wishes.

When the master returned unexpectedly, the good and trustworthy servant was generously rewarded, but the other servant was punished and sent away.'

DISCUSSION

What did the master ask his servants to do? – The master trusted his servants to carry out his orders while he was away.

Did the servants deserve their master's trust? – One of the servants did what his master asked. The other servant was lazy, and without his master to watch him, he avoided the work he had been given to do. The first servant deserved his master's trust but the second servant did not.

Before Jesus returned to his father in Heaven, what work did he trust his disciples to do when he had gone?

Jesus said *(cf John 15:14-16, 27)*: 'You are my friends if you do what I command. I chose you to go out and bear fruit which will last forever. You will be my witnesses because you have been with me from the beginning.'

Jesus trusted his disciples to carry on his work when he had gone: curing the sick, forgiving sinners, performing miracles in his name. Sharing the teachings of Christ with the world and the Good News of God's love for all people.

Did the disciples deserve Jesus' trust? Did they do what he had asked? – After the Holy Spirit came to the disciples at Pentecost, they went out and began to teach the Gospel to the world. They did what Jesus had asked them to do, and shared everything they had seen and heard, with others.

Who is trusted to do the work of Jesus today? – Each one of us, in our own way, has a part to play in sharing the Good News of the Gospel with other people. As Christians, we are followers, or disciples of Christ. Just as the first disciples were trusted, so Jesus trusts each one of us to carry on his work.

How can we do this in our everyday lives? – In our own way we can share Christ's message with others, by our words and actions and by being kind, forgiving and loving, just as Jesus was.

If we have been trustworthy what will happen at the end of time when Jesus returns? – We will be generously rewarded for our loyalty and goodness by sharing in the joy and happiness of everlasting life in Heaven.

ACTIVITY

Photocopy the activity sheet and if necessary help the children to fill in the blanks.

CREED

CLOSING PRAYER

Lord Jesus,
send your Holy Spirit to each one of us
so that we can carry on the work
with which you trust us.

Write down the first letter of each object to find out what Jesus trusts us to do.

_ _ _ _ _

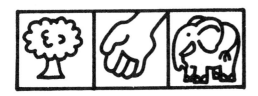   

_ _ _ _ _ _ _ _

_ _ _ _ _ _

_ _ _ _

_ _ _ _

Twentieth Sunday of the Year
Jeremiah in the well

INTRODUCTION
God's people had turned away from him, to worship false gods and lead wicked lives. God sent the prophet Jeremiah to tell the people to turn back to him or their lives would end in disaster.

SIGN OF THE CROSS

LIGHT THE CANDLES
Sing together *See the light.*

SORRY
The prophet Jeremiah tried to get God's people to turn back to him and change their hearts. We turn to God now to ask for his forgiveness, and to make our hearts more loving as we sing Sorry Song 5

GLORIA

ACCLAMATION
Change our hearts, Lord, and bring us back to you.

READING (cf Jeremiah 38:3-6, 8-13)
Jeremiah went to see the king of Judah with a message from God.

'The king of Babylon and his army will capture Jerusalem and destroy the city, and many of your people will be killed.'

When the army commanders heard what Jeremiah had been saying, they went to the king and said, 'This man does not want to help us! He is making the people and our soldiers afraid, and must be put to death!' The king agreed to their request so they took Jeremiah to a deep well and threw him in.

There was no water in the well, but Jeremiah sank into the deep mud at the bottom. When one of the king's servants heard what had happened, he went to the king to plead for Jeremiah's life to be spared, 'Your Majesty, he has done nothing wrong,' said the servant. So the king ordered the servant to take some men and to pull Jeremiah out of the well before he died.

DISCUSSION
What was the name of the prophet sent by God?

(Remind the children that a prophet was someone who spoke in the name of God and made his plans known to the people.)

Why was Jeremiah treated so badly and thrown down the well? – Jeremiah foretold that the king of Babylon would capture the city of Jerusalem and destroy it. He tried to prepare them for disaster before it happened, but no-one believed him. The army commanders did not want him to spread fear and doubt among the people and their army, so they decided to kill him.

Do you know what happened when the people did not listen to Jeremiah's message? – Everything happened as Jeremiah had said, and the people began to realise that they had lived badly and had to change their ways. Through Jeremiah, God invited them back to his love and a new way of life.

Those chosen by God have often been persecuted and had to suffer for his sake, because others would not believe them. What difficulties and hardships did the disciples of Jesus meet as they shared the Gospel message? – Many disciples were imprisoned for their belief in the teachings of Jesus, and sometimes they were even put to death. Like Jeremiah, they were full of courage and did whatever they had to, so that they would change people's lives and bring them back to God.

How easy is it to stand up and show others that we believe in Jesus?

We show others that we believe by going to Mass on Sundays and receiving the Blessed Sacrament; by what we say and what we do, and living as Jesus taught us to. Sometimes people laugh or ridicule us because we do what we know is right. They might call us names if we walk away from a fight in the playground, or treat someone kindly. Like Jeremiah and the disciples, we can overcome any hardship because we have God to love and take care of us.

ACTIVITY
Photocopy the picture of Jeremiah and stick it onto some stiff card. Help the children to tape a stick or straw onto the figure. Fold a piece of card or paper as illustrated, to make a well, and after placing Jeremiah inside, staple the bottom. Jeremiah can be moved up and down to peep out of the well!

CREED

CLOSING PRAYER (cf Psalm 11:7)
God is goodness itself
and he loves those who share his goodness
with others, by their words or actions.
He will surround them with his love
and always watch over them.

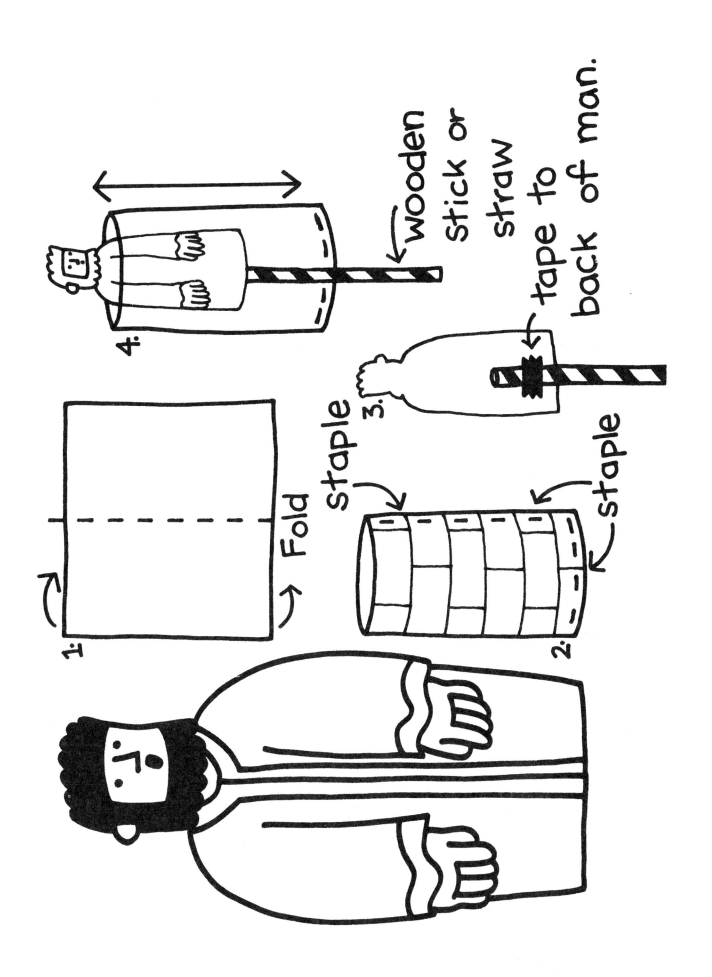

1.

Fold

2.

staple

staple

3.

tape to
back of man.

4.

wooden
stick or
straw

Twenty-first Sunday of the Year
Few will be chosen

INTRODUCTION

At the end of time, God will welcome all those who have been chosen to take their place with him in Heaven.

SIGN OF THE CROSS

LIGHT THE CANDLES

As we light the candles we listen to the words of the prophet Isaiah. *(cf Isaiah 9:2-3, 6-7):*

The world was full of darkness and shadows, but now it is filled with light so everyone can see. God sent us his only Son, Jesus, to fill our world with peace and love.

SORRY

God will forgive us just as we forgive others. The number of times he will forgive us cannot be counted because his forgiveness is never-ending. In the following reading Jesus reminds Peter of this *(cf Matthew 18:21-22, 35):*

One day Peter asked Jesus, 'How many times must I forgive someone who wrongs me? Would I have to forgive as many times as seven in a row?' Jesus answered, 'Not just seven times Peter, but more than seventy times seven, for you must forgive from your heart.'

GLORIA

GOSPEL ACCLAMATION

Alleluia! Alleluia!
Proclaim the Good News to the world.
Alleluia.

GOSPEL *(cf Luke 13:22-30)*

On the way to Jerusalem, someone stopped Jesus and asked, 'Master, will many be saved at the end of time?'

Jesus answered, 'Many will try to enter the kingdom of God but few will succeed; some will leave it too late and find they have missed their chance of everlasting happiness. So take care and be ready! At the end of time, people will be called from far and wide to rejoice in God's heavenly kingdom.'

DISCUSSION

Why will many try to enter the kingdom of God but not succeed? – Jesus showed us the way to God's kingdom by his actions and words. If we live in God's way then we will share everlasting happiness with him at the end of time. This is not easy to do, and throughout our lives we will often fail and make mistakes. With God's help we can carry on, but many will turn away or give up altogether.

Why will some people leave it too late to claim their place in Heaven? – No one knows when Jesus will return, and he told many parables to explain that we must always be ready for this moment.(e.g. The parable of the watchful servants, *Luke 12:35-40.* The parable of the wise bridesmaids, *Matthew 25:1-13.)* We must make each day of our life pleasing to God, instead of promising to be good tomorrow, or next week, or sometime after. If we do not try *now*, then we might miss our chance of happiness.

Can *anyone* belong to the kingdom of God? – Jesus taught us that God is 'our Father' and that we are all brothers and sisters in the one family of God. At the end of time, God will gather his children from all the nations, whatever their colour or language, to take their place in his Kingdom. They will deserve their place because of the goodness and the love in their lives.

What must each of us try to do today and every day? – To be ready to greet Jesus when he returns, by living each day as well as we possibly can! One good way of doing this is to say a 'morning offering', when we offer all our thoughts and actions of the coming day to God.

ACTIVITY

Photocopy the morning offering prayer to be read aloud together before being coloured.

CREED

CLOSING PRAYER

Lord Jesus,
help us to live in God's way
and always be ready to greet you.
Though we make many mistakes,
grant us your forgiveness
and pour your grace into our hearts
to make us strong again.

MORNING OFFERING

Father in Heaven
I give you today,
all that I think,
and do, and say.
I give you the good times
as well as the bad,
the times when I'm happy,
the times when I'm sad.
Fill me with grace
and make me strong.
With you at my side
I won't go wrong.

Amen.

Twenty-second Sunday of the Year

The first will be last

INTRODUCTION

When Jesus was invited for a meal, he took the opportunity to remind people that, in the sight of God, whoever puts themselves first will be last.

SIGN OF THE CROSS

LIGHT THE CANDLES
Say together:
May the light of Jesus burn in our hearts.

SORRY

If Christ's spirit is living in us then everyone will see the fruits of his presence: love, happiness, forgiveness, generosity and honesty. Let us all sit quietly for a few moments and answer these questions in our hearts:

Have other people seen the fruits of the spirit in my life?

Have I been generous and kind, or thoughtless and selfish?

Have I been ready to forgive the mistakes of others or carried grudges against them?

Heavenly Father,
the fruits of your Holy Spirit
are not always obvious in our lives.
Prune away the parts of our lives
which stop us from growing strong,
and fill us with your life and your love.

GLORIA

GOSPEL ACCLAMATION
To welcome today's Gospel sing Acclamation 4: *Praise the Lord.*

GOSPEL (cf Luke 14:1, 7-14)

One day Jesus went to the house of a Pharisee to share a Sabbath meal. Many guests had been invited and, noticing how they rushed to take the best seats, Jesus said to them: 'When you are invited for a meal, do not take the best place because a more important guest might be there. You will be embarrassed when the host asks you to move and give up your seat. Instead, always sit in the least important place, so that when you are moved to a better seat others will see how much you are respected.'

Then Jesus said, 'Do not invite people to eat with you because you know they can invite you back. Be generous and invite those who cannot repay your kindness. You will be rewarded for your goodness at the end of time.'

DISCUSSION

Have you ever rushed to get the 'best seat' before someone else?

– perhaps to get a particular seat on the school bus.
– to get a seat with the best view at a film or show.
– to sit closest to the food at a party.

All of us have done this at one time or another! Jesus wanted us to realise that when we do such a thing, we put ourselves before others, thinking that we are more important than other people.

What did Jesus tell us to do instead? – We should try to put others first and act without selfishness or pride. God is not impressed by greatness or rank, but by someone who acts humbly and shows kindness towards other people.

In what other way did Jesus suggest that we could be considerate? – Jesus used the example of inviting someone for a meal without expecting to be invited back. Often we do a 'good turn' for someone but expect them to repay our kindness in some way. Jesus taught us that if we act with unselfish kindness in this life, then God will repay our goodness in the next.

How can we put the words of Jesus into practice? – Instead of pushing to the front or grabbing the best seat, think of others first, and act thoughtfully instead of selfishly. Don't invite someone to play just so that they can invite you back; or share a toy because you expect one in return. Jesus said, 'those who are last will be first and those who are first will be last!' If we put other people first and recognise their importance, then we will be first in the eyes of God.

ACTIVITY

Jesus calls us to be less selfish and more loving. Colour the pictures which put others first, and cross out the pictures which show selfish and thoughtless actions.

CREED

CLOSING PRAYER
Jesus,
help me to put others first,
and to be generous and kind
without counting the cost.

Twenty-third Sunday of the Year

Consider the cost

INTRODUCTION
If we are really determined to do something, even though it might be difficult, then we can succeed. Jesus tells us that it is never easy to follow him, but we can succeed if we decide we really want to.

SIGN OF THE CROSS

LIGHT THE CANDLES
Light the candles and say Candle prayer 3: *The light of God.*

SORRY
It is hard to be good all the time, and God our Father knows and understands this. Let us ask for forgiveness as we sing Sorry Song 4.

GLORIA

GOSPEL ACCLAMATION
To welcome today's Gospel sing Acclamation 1: *Share your word with us.*

GOSPEL (cf Luke 14:28-33)
Jesus said to the crowd, 'If a man plans to build a house, he works out how much it will cost before he begins. Otherwise he might lay the foundations and then find that he cannot afford to finish the work. If a king's army of ten thousand men is preparing to fight an army of twenty thousand men, would the king not consider whether he might win or lose? If defeat is likely then he will send out messengers to make peace with his enemy.'

Then Jesus said, 'If anyone plans to follow me, then he must count the cost of being my disciple and belonging to the kingdom of God.'

DISCUSSION
What would a wise man do before starting to build a house? – He would first consider the cost of everything he might need – cement, wood , bricks, roof tiles and so on. If the total cost was more than he could afford, then he would be foolish to begin.

What did Jesus say about the king and his army? – The king thought about the 'cost' to his army of being outnumbered in battle. He could not win and was not prepared to have his soldiers killed, so he decided not to fight the battle at all, and to make peace instead.

What message does Jesus give us in today's Gospel? – It is not easy to be a follower of Jesus and to live as he taught us to. He wants us to think carefully about what is expected of us if we are to be his disciples – to love one another; to keep God's rules; to be kind and forgiving and all the other qualities of being truly Christian.

Although it can be hard and the costs are sometimes high, why do we choose to follow Jesus? – Each of us wants to find true happiness, to be filled with a sense of peace and to be loved. By following Jesus, we can belong to the Kingdom of God, where we will know enough love, peace and happiness, to make any 'costs' worthwhile.

ACTIVITY
Copy the activity sheet and discuss each picture with reference to today's Gospel story and its message.

CREED

CLOSING PRAYER
Lord,
help us to follow you always,
and give us the strength
to carry on when we are struggling.
Help us to make the effort
to do things God's way,
so we will be able to share
in your Glory
at the end of time.

Twenty-fourth Sunday of the Year

The lost coin

INTRODUCTION

Have you ever lost something which is very important or precious? Perhaps a favourite book or a particular toy. Today Jesus reminds us that God knows and loves each one of us, and will search until he finds us if we should lose our way.

SIGN OF THE CROSS

LIGHT THE CANDLES

Sing the Candle Song.

SORRY

If we do something wrong and wander away from God's love, he is always ready to forgive us and lead us back to him. Listen to this story Jesus told:

'One day a shepherd found that one of his flock was missing, so he left the other ninety-nine sheep, and went off to look for it. He searched and searched until he found it, because every one of his sheep was precious to him.'

If we have not been good,
and have lost our way,
let us ask Jesus to forgive us
and to lead us back to his flock.

GLORIA

GOSPEL ACCLAMATION

Alleluia! Alleluia!
Jesus came to forgive sinners and share his love.
Alleluia!

GOSPEL (cf Luke 15:1-3, 8-10)

After overhearing the Pharisees complaining about him spending so much time with tax collectors and sinners, Jesus told a parable: 'Once there was a woman who had ten silver coins. One day as she counted her savings, she realised that one of the precious coins was missing! The woman was poor, and to lose even one small coin made her very sad. So she lit her lamp and looked under all the furniture. She swept every corner of the house and searched until finally she found it! Picking up the coin she ran to tell all her friends the good news.'

Then Jesus said, 'God will search for anyone who is lost, and rejoice when he finds them.'

DISCUSSION

Why did the Pharisees complain about Jesus?

The Pharisees were very proud of their 'goodness' and their obedience of the law. They would not associate with people they considered to be sinners, and yet Jesus welcomed sinners! All too often for the Pharisees, Jesus was to be found spending his time with 'sinners' instead of people like themselves.

What happened in the parable which Jesus told? – (Encourage the children to retell the story in their own words.)

Did the woman give up searching for the coin? – The coin was very precious to the woman, and even though she could not find it at first, she carried on looking until her efforts were rewarded. In the same way, God our Father will search for anyone who has wandered from his love because each one of us is precious to him. Jesus came to forgive the sinners who had 'lost their way', and welcome them back to God's love.

How did the woman react when she found what she had lost? – Her sadness turned to joy, and she ran to share the good news with her friends. When we sin and turn away from God's love, he is filled with sadness. This sadness turns to joy when we change our ways and come back to our heavenly Father.

ACTIVITY

Photocopy the house shape on to thin card. You could enlarge it as well. Give a copy to each child. The older children can cut out the windows themselves. Ask the children to draw the woman looking for the lost coin inside.

CREED

CLOSING PRAYER

Turn back to me
and I will reach out and save you,
because you are my children
whom I love.

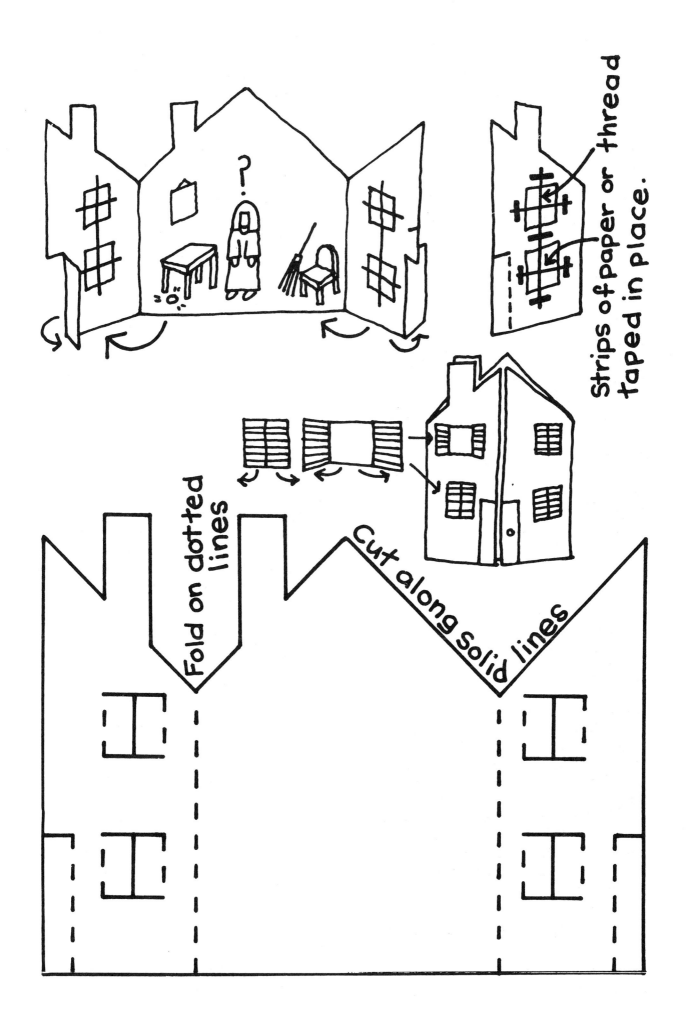

Fold on dotted lines

Cut along solid lines

Strips of paper or thread taped in place.

Twenty-fifth Sunday of the Year

Always be honest

INTRODUCTION

Have you ever heard the saying, 'Honesty is the best policy'? This means that it is always better to be honest rather than tell lies. If we are honest about the little things in life, we will be honest about everything else too.

SIGN OF THE CROSS

LIGHT THE CANDLES

Light the candles and pray:
In a world where there is so much dishonesty,
may our goodness shine out
like a light in the darkness to give others hope.

SORRY

Close your eyes and think about all the things which have happened over the past week. Have we always been as kind and thoughtful as we should have been? Have we done anything to make God feel sad or disappointed with us? If we are truly sorry in our hearts, then God our Father will always forgive us.

Listen carefully to the words of this reading (cf Psalm 25:11-16):

God is full of kindness and love, and wants to show us all the path we must follow. He leads us with patience and understanding, and forgives us when we stray and lose our way. When we look to him for help, he rescues us from harm and helps us to try again, for he is full of love and forgiveness.

GLORIA

GOSPEL ACCLAMATION

To welcome today's Gospel sing Acclamation 6: *Jesus here we are.*

GOSPEL (cf Luke 16:10-11)

Jesus said, 'When a person is honest about the small things in life, then they will be honest about more important things too. If you cannot be trusted with something as unimportant as money, how can you be trusted with the most precious treasure of all.'

DISCUSSION

If you saw someone dropping a pound coin without noticing, what would you do? – You would have to choose between being honest, and giving the coin back, or dishonest, and keeping the coin yourself. When a person is filled with the spirit of God's goodness, they can be trusted to make the right choice. A good person will always be honest, however great or small the amount of money may be.

Listen to this short story:

Peter had been saving his pocket money for a long time and just needed one more pound to afford the football he wanted so much. One day while shopping with his mum, he noticed that an old lady had dropped some money as she struggled to put it in her purse. The coin rolled across the floor and lay unnoticed. Peter picked it up and found to his delight that it was a pound, just what he needed! (At this point ask the children what they think Peter should do, before reading on to see if they were right!)

. . . Peter took the coin over to the old woman who thanked him for his kindness and honesty. Peter smiled, feeling very good inside.

Why do you think Peter felt good inside? – Peter had chosen God's way, by being honest and truthful. His actions had made the old woman very happy, and seeing her happiness made him feel good inside. We all know how wonderful we feel when we show someone that we care about them. Peter felt the joy of sharing God's love and knowing that God was pleased with him.

What is the most precious treasure of all which Jesus trusts us with? – The most precious treasure of all is the love of our heavenly Father which means more than all our worldly possessions. Money cannot make us happy, because true happiness comes from loving God. We are free to live as we choose, because God trusts us to do what we know is right.

ACTIVITY

Either use the activity sheets or help each child to fold a sheet of paper in half to find the middle. On one half, ask them to draw a picture of themselves in the playground, with a £1 coin they have found at their feet. Give each child a 'choice wheel' and a butterfly pin and help them to pin it on the other half of the paper. Get the children to draw an arrow and, turning the wheel, to point to whatever choice they think they should make. Discuss!

CREED

CLOSING PRAYER

Lord, help us to be truthful and honest with each other and to be guided by your goodness.

"Be Honest"

Take it to my teacher
Put it in my Pocket
Turn →
Buy some Sweets
Tell no-one
← Turn

Twenty-sixth Sunday of the Year

Lazarus and the rich man

INTRODUCTION
In today's Gospel story Jesus reminds us that the way we live our lives will decide whether or not we share everlasting happiness with him at the end of time.

SIGN OF THE CROSS

LIGHT THE CANDLES
Light the candles and say Candle Prayer 2:
Show me, show me little candle.

SORRY
The book of proverbs tells us (*cf Proverbs 3:27-29*):
Whenever you get the chance to help someone, do it willingly. Never turn someone away until tomorrow, when you can do a good deed today.

(Think about these words for a few moments before reading the prayer.)
Lord, whatever I have done to others,
I have done the same to you.
Please forgive me
if I have been selfish or unkind,
and put my own needs and happiness first.
Help me to make a fresh start
and to put your goodness
into action in my life.

GLORIA

GOSPEL ACCLAMATION
Alleluia! Alleluia!
Your words Lord will guide me closer to you.
Alleluia.

GOSPEL (*cf Luke 16:19-31*)
One day Jesus told this story: 'Once there was a rich man who had fine clothes, and the best of everything that money could buy. He spent his time enjoying himself and feasting with his rich friends.

'On the street outside his house lay a poor man called Lazarus who was thin and hungry, and covered in sores. Lazarus would gladly have eaten the rich man's scraps, if they had been offered to him.

'Lazarus died and went to heaven where he was truly happy at last. When the rich man died he went to hell, and seeing Lazarus so happy, he cried out to him for help. But God asked the rich man, "Did you help when Lazarus cried out for food? Did you care for him when he was ill and had nowhere to go? You thought only of yourself, and gave up the chance of everlasting happiness with me."'

DISCUSSION
How did the rich man spend his time and his money? – All his time was spent on himself and doing the things which made him happy.

Who lay unnoticed outside the rich man's house? – Lazarus had no home and no money. He sat outside the rich man's house, and begged for food.

Have you ever seen anyone begging? – Many poor people beg for money to buy food and clothes. Often they are homeless and have nowhere to sleep, and we want to help them but don't quite know how. There are many homes and hostels where donations of food, clothes and even toys are gratefully received. Each of us in our own way, however small, should help wherever we can.

What did the rich man do about Lazarus? – The rich man did absolutely *nothing!* He was so concerned about his own happiness that he did not even notice Lazarus lying outside his house.

What do *you* think the rich man should have done? – (Encourage the children to share their ideas.)

In this story Jesus wanted to show us that being well off and comfortable often makes us 'blind' to the needs of people around us. We can become selfish and self centred, caring only about our own happiness. We should not forget that our words and actions in life will decide whether we share God's everlasting happiness or like the rich man pay for our greed and selfishness.

ACTIVITY
Copy and cut out the two figures, the house, path and some palm trees. After colouring these separately stick them onto a large sheet of paper and encourage the children to fill in the background.

CREED

CLOSING PRAYER
Father in Heaven,
bless all the homeless people in our world,
and those who have to beg for their food.
Open our eyes to their needs
so that we can help them
in whatever way we can.

Twenty-seventh Sunday of the Year
Have faith

INTRODUCTION
When people believe in the power of Jesus, extraordinary things can happen because nothing is impossible for God.

SIGN OF THE CROSS

LIGHT THE CANDLES
Say together:
May the light of Jesus shine in our lives.

SORRY
Because we trust in God's goodness and his love for us, we are not afraid to come before him to admit our mistakes and ask for his forgiveness as we sing Sorry Song 5.

GLORIA

GOSPEL ACCLAMATION
To welcome today's Gospel sing Acclamation 4: *Praise the Lord.*

GOSPEL (cf Luke 17:5-6)
One day the apostles said to Jesus, 'Master make our faith grow.' Jesus said to them, 'With just a little faith you can do marvellous things. If you truly believe in me then nothing is impossible.'

DISCUSSION
Do you know what the word faith means? – It means to have complete trust in something or someone, to believe in that thing or person completely.

Can you think of some people in the Bible who had great faith in God?
– Noah built an ark even though others laughed at him; he believed and trusted in God.
– Abraham's trust in God was so great that he is often called our 'Father in Faith'. He was ready to sacrifice Isaac his son because God asked him to.
– a Roman centurion believed that Jesus could cure his servant with a simple command.

There are many examples of people's faith throughout the Old and New testament. Each of them had *complete* trust in God and believed that he would always take care of them and do what was best.

Listen to this story about a woman who had complete faith in Jesus.

A large crowd of people surrounded Jesus as he walked along. Many had come to see him; others wanted to talk to him or listen to his words; one woman in the crowd just wanted to touch him. She had been ill for twelve long years, and no-one could make her better. 'If I can get close enough just to touch his cloak,' she thought, 'then I believe that Jesus will cure me.' She pushed her way through the bustling crowd, and stretching out her hand, she managed to touch Jesus as he passed. At once she knew that she was cured! Then Jesus asked Peter, 'Who touched me?' and Peter answered, 'Master, in such a crowd many people have touched you.' 'I felt my power leaving me,' Jesus said. Then the woman stepped forward and said, 'I touched you because I believed that you would cure me and you have!' Jesus said to the woman, 'Because you believed in me, your faith has made you well. Go in peace!'

What did the woman believe would happen if she managed to touch Jesus? – She believed that Jesus had the power to cure her illness, and this power was so great that one touch was enough.

What did Jesus say to the woman at the end of the story? – 'Because you believed in me your faith has made you well.' Faith is a gift from God; it helps us to pray and to believe. There are many things we do not know or understand about God, but with faith we can put our trust in God and his word.

ACTIVITY
Photocopy the series of pictures telling the story of the faithful woman and help the children to arrange them in the correct order. Staple the pictures together to make a small booklet.

CREED

CLOSING PRAYER
Send your spirit Lord,
to increase our faith in you,
and to work through the hearts
of all those who believe.
Help us to believe in your goodness,
and to always trust
in your love for us.

The Woman who HAD FAITH

A crowd of people surrounded Jesus.

A sick woman said, "If I can touch Jesus cloak!"

She pushed closer and just managed to touch the cloak.

"Who touched me? asked Jesus. "I don't know", said Peter.

Jesus said, "Your faith has made you well!"

Twenty-eighth Sunday of the Year

Thank you Jesus

INTRODUCTION

As children we are taught to say 'thank you' when we are given something, but how many times do we forget to thank God for all his goodness.

SIGN OF THE CROSS

LIGHT THE CANDLES

Sing together: *See the light.*

SORRY

Each one of us is filled with God's spirit.
If we have acted selfishly or unkindly
towards someone else,
we have done the same to God
As we sing our song together, we ask God
to forgive us, and to fill our hearts and our
lives with his love.
Sing Sorry Song 1.

GLORIA

GOSPEL ACCLAMATION

Alleluia, alleluia.
Give thanks to God for all his love.
Alleluia.

GOSPEL (*cf Luke 17*)

On the way to Jerusalem, Jesus drew near a village where he found ten lepers waiting to meet him. Keeping their distance they called out to him, 'Jesus of Nazareth, have pity and help us!'

Jesus saw their suffering and said, 'Go and show yourselves to the priest.'

They set off to see the priest and on the way they realised that their leprosy had disappeared and they were cured! As the others ran to find the priest, one of the ten went back to find Jesus. He threw himself down before him, praising God and thanking Jesus for his kindness. 'Were the others not cured too?' Jesus asked. 'Yet only one has bothered to thank God for his goodness.' Then he said to the man, 'Now go and see the priest, your faith in God has made you well.'

DISCUSSION

In what ways did lepers suffer? – They suffered from the disease of leprosy which causes deformity with the loss of limbs and sometimes blindness. They also suffered because they were outcasts who were driven away from their homes and families, to live far away from villages and towns. They had to warn people that they were 'unclean' by ringing a bell or shouting, because they were afraid of catching their disease. Their lives were miserable and their suffering was very great.

What did Jesus do when they asked for his help? – Jesus took pity on them and told them to go and show themselves to the priest. The priest was the person who decided whether their leprosy had gone and gave them permission to live with their families again. They showed how much they believed in Jesus because they set off at once, and trusted him to cure them.

What did one of the lepers do when he realised that he had been cured? – He remembered to go back to Jesus and say thank you. The others had rushed off to see the priest and be reunited with their families and friends again.

Do you think that Jesus was pleased that one said 'thank you'? – Jesus was very pleased with the one leper who had remembered to say thank you but was disappointed that the other nine did not. People often forget to thank Jesus when something good happens. All too often we take things for granted and forget to thank God for all his kindness.

ACTIVITY

Photocopy the picture onto some stiff paper to make a card. Fold a 4cm wide strip of paper and stick one end inside the card, and the other end onto the 'Thank you Jesus' badge. Encourage the children to write something that *they* want to thank Jesus for.

CREED

CLOSING PRAYER

Lord Jesus,
the lepers asked for your help
and you gave them new life and new hope.
Thank you for all the love
and kindness you give to me.

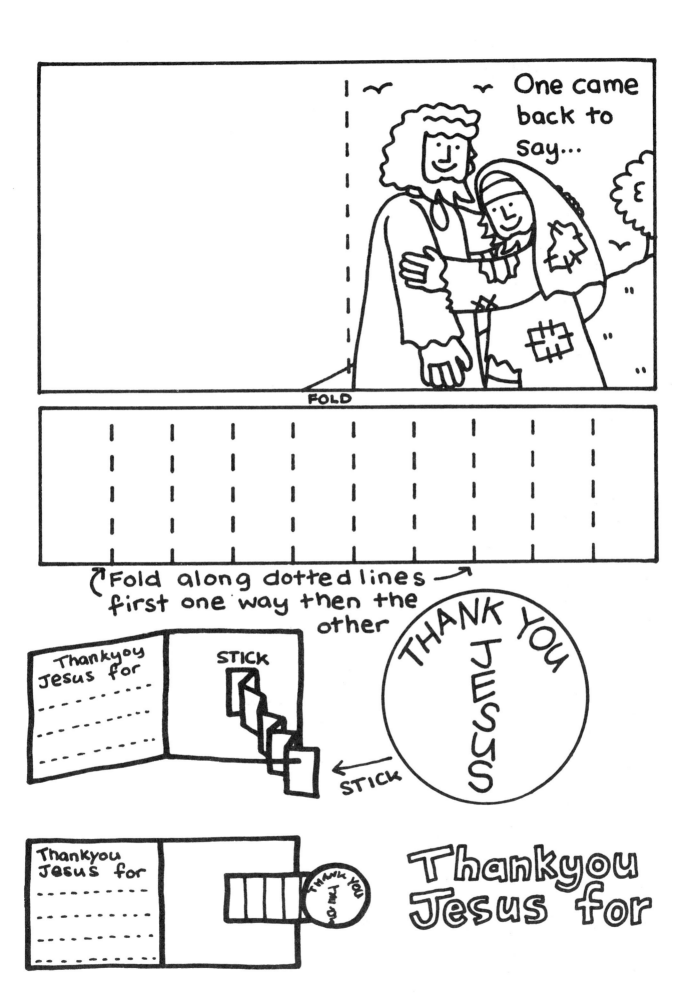

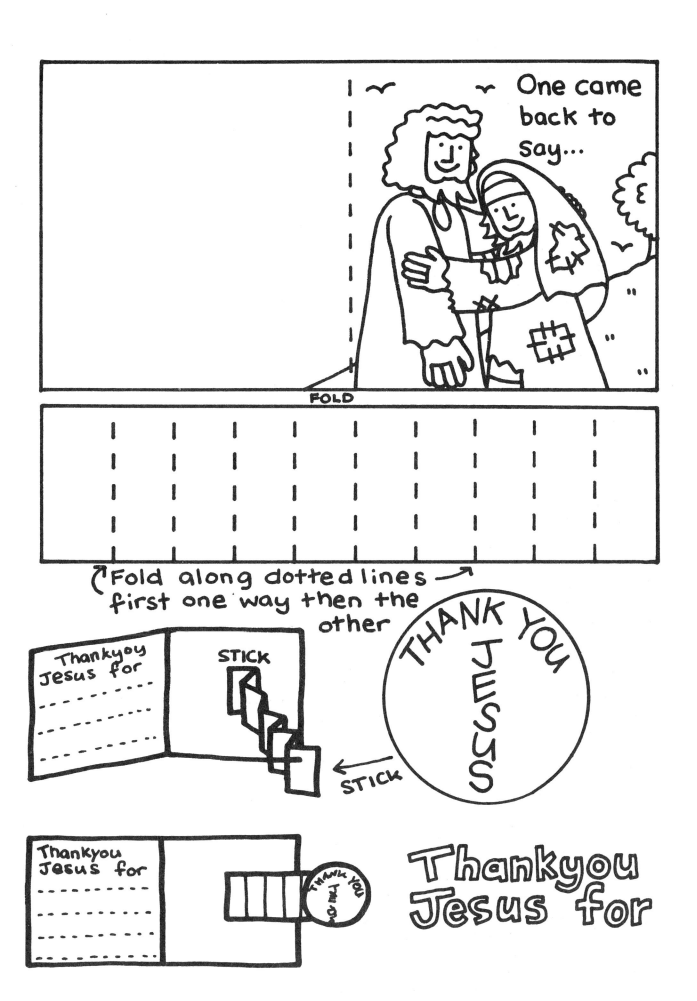

Twenty-ninth Sunday of the Year

Don't give up

INTRODUCTION
Jesus told a parable to show that we shouldn't become disheartened but should keep on asking for what we want because God will hear and answer our prayers.

SIGN OF THE CROSS

LIGHT THE CANDLES
Make your thoughts only kind ones,
and others will see your goodness
in the things that you do.
Hold your head high
and keep walking towards the light,
and you will never
lose your way.

SORRY
Jesus taught us that God will forgive us, just as we are ready to forgive others. One day Jesus told this story (cf Matthew 18:23-35):

There was once a servant who owed his master lots of money. His master took pity on him and cancelled all his debts. Now the servant had a friend who owed him a small amount of money which he could not pay, so he had him thrown into jail. When his master heard this he sent for his unforgiving servant. 'Could you not forgive others as I forgave you?' he asked. Then he threw him into jail until he could repay all that he owed.

Help us, Lord,
to remember this story
so that we are always ready to forgive others
just as you are always ready to forgive us.

GLORIA

GOSPEL ACCLAMATION
To welcome today's Gospel sing Acclamation 3:
Alleluia, alleluia.

GOSPEL (cf Luke 18:1-8)
Jesus told this story: In a certain town there was a judge who was often unjust and unfair. A woman in the town asked the judge to help her settle a quarrel with her neighbour. The judge was not interested in the woman's problem and sent her away. The woman did not give up! She came back every day, day in and day out, until the judge could not stand being pestered any more. 'I must give this woman what she wants,' he said, 'or she will never give me any peace.'

Then Jesus said, 'If such a man can finally listen and do what is asked of him, how much more will my heavenly Father do for you if you keep on asking.'

DISCUSSION
Why did the woman keep on pestering the judge? – She was determined that the judge would hear her request, listen carefully to what she wanted and then respond.

Did the woman's persistence pay off? – No-one likes to feel pestered or nagged and after a while the judge finally agreed to what the woman wanted.

Have you ever pestered anyone for something you really wanted? What happened?
(Encourage the children to reflect on their own experiences.)

What was Jesus trying to tell us in this parable? – That if we ask God for something he will hear our prayers and answer them. Because we do not understand God or his plans for us, sometimes we feel disappointed when he doesn't seem to give us what we want or need, but we must not give up or stop asking, instead we must learn to put our trust in God because he will always do what is best for us.

ACTIVITY
Photocopy the activity sheet and see if the children can discover the woman's message to them!

CREED

CLOSING PRAYER
Let us say together the prayer which Jesus himself taught us: Our Father . . .

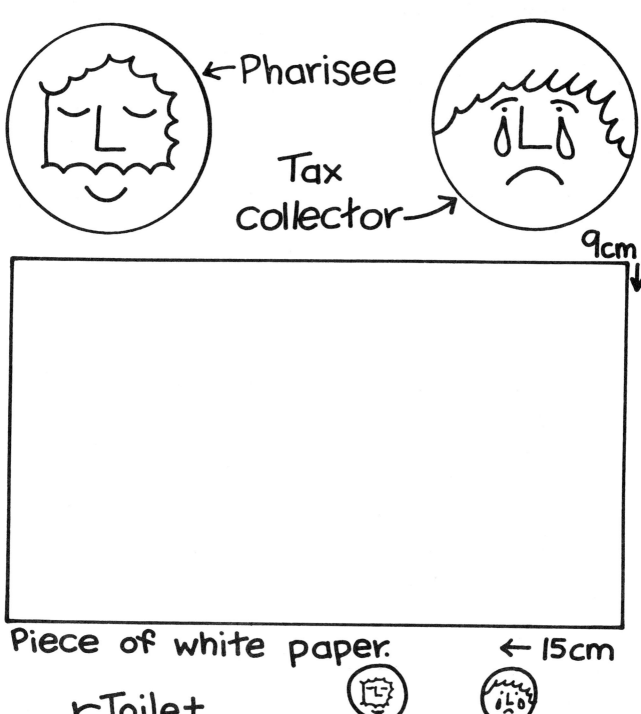

Pharisee

Tax collector

9cm

Piece of white paper. ← 15cm

←Toilet roll tube or roll of paper

I am so good

Forgive me Lord

Thirty-first Sunday of the Year
The story of Zacchaeus

INTRODUCTION
Have you ever been in a crowd where you could not see? Perhaps someone lifted you onto their shoulders to get a better view! In today's Gospel we hear how one man climbed a tree to see Jesus clearly.

SIGN OF THE CROSS

LIGHT THE CANDLES
Light the candles and say aloud:
'Your words, Lord, are a light in the darkness. Help us to listen carefully.'

SORRY
Ask one of the children to choose a sorry colour and together read the corresponding prayer aloud.

GLORIA

GOSPEL ACCLAMATION
Alleluia! Alleluia!
Jesus came to change our hearts.
Alleluia!

GOSPEL (cf Luke 19:1-10)
Jesus went to a town called Jericho, where a man called Zacchaeus lived. Nobody liked Zacchaeus because he was a tax collector who cheated people to make himself rich. When Jesus arrived, crowds gathered to see him and Zacchaeus was among them. Zacchaeus was very small and could not see Jesus because of the crowds, so he climbed a tree to get a better view. As Jesus passed by, he looked up and said, 'Come down Zacchaeus! I want to visit your house today.'

Zacchaeus almost fell out of the tree with surprise. Hearing this, the crowd began to grumble and complain. 'How can Jesus speak to such a wicked man!' they said.

Then Zacchaeus turned to Jesus and said, 'Lord, I know that I am a dishonest cheat, but I want to change and put things right! I will give half of everything I own to the poor, and pay back everything I have stolen four times over.' Jesus smiled at Zacchaeus and said, 'I have come to find and save anyone who has lost their way. Now change your heart and make a fresh start.'

DISCUSSION
Why did the people think that Zacchaeus was wicked? – Zacchaeus was the chief tax collector in Jericho. (Recall last week's discussion about how the tax collectors grew rich by charging extra taxes and cheating the people out of their money.)

Why did Zacchaeus end up sitting in a tree? – Zacchaeus was a very short man, and could not see Jesus because of the crowds around him. Zacchaeus climbed the tree to get a good view.

What did Jesus do as he walked by? – Jesus called Zacchaeus to come down and take him to his home.

The crowds, and Zacchaeus himself, were shocked when Jesus did this. Why were they so surprised? – The crowds did not think that Jesus should have anything to do with such a dishonest man. None of them liked Zacchaeus, and he had no friends until Jesus offered his friendship. Jesus was willing to forgive and forget what Zacchaeus had done, and to give him the chance to make a fresh start.

Jesus came to call all sinners back to God's love and away from selfishness and greed. What did Zacchaeus promise to do to show that he had truly had a change of heart? – He promised to be generous and to give back everything he owed and more. Jesus loved Zacchaeus despite his faults, and because of this love Zacchaeus turned back to God. We all make mistakes and Jesus calls each one of us to turn back to his love, and change our hearts. He is full of forgiveness, and will fill us with his love and goodness to help us make a fresh start.

ACTIVITY
Cut out a tree shape with branches and the figure of Zacchaeus. After colouring, place Zacchaeus 'in' the tree and attach it to a sheet of paper. The children can glue on leaves made from tissue paper or real leaves if preferred. Add the caption, 'Zacchaeus finds a friend!'

CREED

CLOSING PRAYER
Lord Jesus,
make our hearts more loving
and ready to forgive others
just as you forgive us.

Zacchaeus finds a friend!

Thirty-second Sunday of the Year

Imagine Heaven

INTRODUCTION
The Sadducees were a group of priests who held the most important positions in the Jewish church. They did not believe in life after death, and were displeased that so many people were listening to Jesus, and believing what he told them.

SIGN OF THE CROSS

LIGHT THE CANDLES
Light the candles and sing the Candle Song.

SORRY
God is our Father and we are his children. He is slow to anger and always ready to forgive us. Close your eyes and listen carefully to the words of this prayer:
Do not be afraid,
God will always love you.
Whatever you have done,
God will always love you.
As a Father loves his child,
He will always love you.
Come back to him and know,
God's love lasts forever.

Now spend a few moments speaking to God in our hearts and making our peace with him.

GLORIA

GOSPEL ACCLAMATION
To welcome today's Gospel sing Acclamation 1: *Share your word with us.*

GOSPEL (cf Luke 20:27-36)
The Sadducees wanted to trick Jesus so they asked him this question. 'If a woman's husband dies, and she marries his brother who also dies, which man will be her husband when she is dead and they all meet again in the next life?'

Jesus answered them, 'In this life they may have been husband and wife, but in the next life they will all be children of God. After the resurrection from the dead, those who are chosen will never die again, and they will share everlasting life and happiness together with the angels in Heaven.'

DISCUSSION
Why did the Sadducees ask Jesus such a difficult question? – The Sadducees were very harsh towards Jesus and disagreed with most of his teachings. They did not believe in the resurrection or life after death. They asked this question to try to make Jesus look foolish.

What does the word 'resurrection' mean? – Resurrection means to rise again and come back to life.

Whose resurrection do we celebrate every Sunday and in particular every year on Easter Sunday? – Christians celebrate the resurrection of Jesus every Sunday. Jesus rose from the dead on Easter Sunday, and so we celebrate his resurrection in a special way on that day.

What will happen at the end of time to everyone who has died? – Because Jesus conquered death and rose from the dead, everyone who has died will be brought back to life. Jesus explained to the Sadducees that our heavenly lives will be very different to our lives on earth. Anyone chosen to share everlasting happiness with God in Heaven, will become a child of God, and will not be concerned with the worries of their earthly lives.

Does anyone know what Heaven will really be like?

Sometimes people feel afraid of the unknown, but Jesus has promised us that Heaven is a place of eternal peace and happiness, close to God our Father. Perhaps we find it difficult to imagine, but if we think of that place we would most like to be, doing what makes us happiest, then maybe we can imagine a little bit of Heaven.

ACTIVITY
Ask the children to spend a few moments thinking about their idea of Heaven and what would make them happiest. Ask them to draw a picture of their idea. Pin the pictures on a board with the caption 'Heaven is . . .' and encourage each child to explain their picture to the rest of the group.

CREED

CLOSING PRAYER
Jesus said:
'I am the resurrection and the life.'
Let us pray for all those who have died,
that they will be raised
to everlasting life and happiness.

Thirty-third Sunday of the Year

Believe in me

INTRODUCTION
Jesus expects each one of us to share his message and the gift of our faith with other people. He will send the Holy Spirit to give us strength and courage, and will remember our goodness when he returns at the end of time.

SIGN OF THE CROSS

LIGHT THE CANDLES
Light the candles and read *(cf John 8:12)*:
Jesus said, 'I am the light of the world. Whoever follows me will have the light of life and will never walk in darkness.'

SORRY
Jesus taught us how we should lead our lives and treat other people. In this reading from St Luke, he reminds us that God will forgive us as easily as we forgive others. *(cf Luke 6:37-38):*
Do not always believe that you are right and others are wrong, but treat people the way you would want to be treated. If you are full of forgiveness for others, then God will be full of forgiveness for you.

(Sit quietly for a few moments of reflection.)

GLORIA

GOSPEL ACCLAMATION
To welcome today's Gospel sing Acclamation 6: *Jesus here we are.*

GOSPEL *(cf Luke 21:5-7, 12-19)*
Jesus was at the temple in Jerusalem when he overheard some of the crowd talking.
    'This temple was built to last forever!' they said.
    But Jesus told them, 'One day, everything, including this temple will be destroyed.'
    'When will this happen?' they asked him.
    'Do not be afraid,' said Jesus, 'the time for all this to happen is still a long way off. Before then many will suffer because they are my followers. I will give them courage and strength, and they will be rewarded for their faith and goodness by my heavenly Father.'

DISCUSSION
What did Jesus mean when he said that one day everything, including the temple would be destroyed? – Jesus was talking about the end of the world, when he will return in power and glory.

Buildings and possessions will not last forever, but love and goodness can never be destroyed.

Did Jesus tell the people when this would happen? – Jesus did not tell them an exact day or time, but that the end of the world would not come until many people had suffered because they believed in him.

Why is being a Christian not always easy? – As Christians we believe in Jesus and everything he taught us. We share one faith which is a gift from God. Jesus expects us to share that faith with others, through our words and by the lives we lead. Many of the early Christians suffered and died for their faith, because others would not believe in Jesus. Today it is not always easy to follow Christ's way of love, and to build our lives around his teachings, but Jesus promised to give us the strength and courage that we need.

How will Christians be rewarded for their faith? – If we choose to follow Jesus and to live as he taught us, then we will be rewarded for our goodness by sharing everlasting happiness with God at the end of time.

ACTIVITY
Cut an oval shape from card for each child, and punch two holes opposite each other at the ends of the oval. Write 'Believe in' on the top half of one side above the holes. Turn the oval over so that the words are upside down and face down. Write 'Jesus' above the holes as before. Loop elastic bands or pieces of wool through the holes. After colouring in the letters and decorating the ovals, the children can wind the ovals to twist the bands. Then pull apart and see the message they have written.

CREED

CLOSING PRAYER
Heavenly Father,
thank you for the gift of faith
which each of us has been given.
Help us to share it
with whoever we meet.

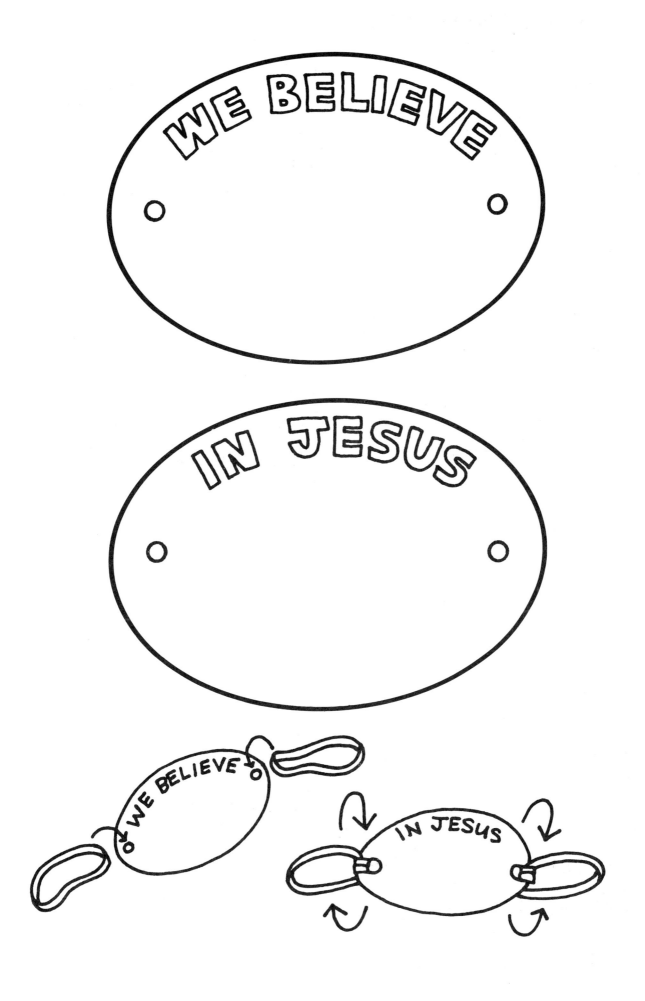

The Feast of Christ the King
King of the Jews

INTRODUCTION

Today is the last Sunday of the Church's year, when we celebrate the Feast of Christ the King. Jesus had been sentenced to die on the cross and the soldiers and crowds who had gathered to watch his suffering jeered and made fun of the 'King of the Jews'.

SIGN OF THE CROSS

LIGHT THE CANDLES

Sing together: *See the Light.*

SORRY

Jesus came to show us how to be loving and forgiving. Even as he was being nailed to the cross he prayed to his heavenly Father, 'Forgive them because they do not understand what they are doing'. Together we ask Jesus to forgive us and to make *us* more forgiving towards others as we listen to the words of this prayer:

Teach us your ways, Lord,
and make them known to all your people.
Show us how to walk in your truth,
because you are our saviour
and we can always trust
in your love and forgiveness.

GLORIA

GOSPEL ACCLAMATION

To welcome today's Gospel sing this Acclamation (to the tune of *Hickory, Dickory, Dock.*)
Christ is the king of the world,
One day he will come back
And we will see his full glory,
Christ is the king of the world.

GOSPEL (*cf Luke 23:35-43*)

The soldiers nailed Jesus to the cross and above him hung a sign which said: 'This is the King of the Jews.'

A crowd had gathered to watch and they laughed and made fun of him saying, 'If you are so great, save yourself now!'

At the same time two thieves were crucified with Jesus, one on either side. One of the thieves jeered, 'Call yourself a king! If you had any power you could save yourself, and us as well!'

But the other thief said, 'Leave him alone. We deserve to be punished but he has done nothing wrong.'

Then he said to Jesus, 'Lord, do not forget me in your kingdom,' and Jesus answered, 'Today we will be together in Heaven.'

DISCUSSION

The soldiers and the crowd teased and made fun of Jesus. What did the sign which hung above him say? – 'This is the King of the Jews'. Earlier, some of the soldiers had made a 'crown' from thorny brambles, and had wrapped a red cloak around him to make fun of him.

How would you describe a King to someone? – They often live in a palace; they have servants to take care of all their needs; on grand occasions they wear a crown; they own jewels and treasures and are very wealthy; they rule over their kingdom, and their people do as they command.

Was Jesus a typical king? – People laughed at Jesus when he called himself a king. He had no wealth, no fine palaces or servants; he ruled over no country and he had no army to save him. Jesus had told them, 'My kingdom is not of this world,' but people did not understand. His kingdom is not a country or place, it is the sharing of God's love with each of us. Anyone who puts their love for God and their neighbour before anything else is a part of the kingdom. The kingdom of God grows in people who love Jesus, and as they grow in love, kindness and forgiveness so God's kingdom grows too.

Who was crucified on either side of Jesus?

What did Jesus promise the good thief? – That he would not forget his faith and trust, and that he would be welcomed into the kingdom of Heaven.

ACTIVITY

Cut out the three crosses and a sun with rays, and ask the children to colour them. Ask some of the children to colour the banner background before gluing the crosses and sun in position. Add the title, 'Christ is our king.'

CREED

CLOSING PRAYER

Lord Jesus,
you come to share the Good News
of God's Kingdom
with the whole world.
May your love reign
in our hearts always.
We ask this through Christ our Lord.

Songs

Candle Song

We should be like little candles
To the tune of Bobby Shaftoe

We should be like little candles,
brightening up the world around us.
Helping everyone to see
how we can all love Jesus.

Smiling, happy, full of love,
with the help of God above,
Shine out, shine out help them see,
That we all love Jesus.

Alternative Candle Song

See the Light
To the tune of Hot cross buns

See the light.
See the light.
How a little candle flame can shine so bright.

Chase away the darkness,
fill the world with light.
Be a little candle flame and shine out bright.

Candle Prayers

1. Flicker, flicker little candle,
   in the corner of the room,
   as your flame grows ever stronger,
   darkness flees and so does gloom.
   Amen.

2. Show me, show me little candle,
   just how much a little light,
   shining out with warmth and brightness,
   chases off the darkest night.
   Amen.

3. The light of God shines on us,
   to help us do things right,
   If we do wrong we turn away,
   from the light of God.
   As we look at these candles
   help us to remember this.
   Amen.

Sorry Songs

1. Dear Lord Jesus hear our prayers
To the tune of Twinkle, twinkle little star

Dear Lord Jesus hear our prayers,
as we bring to you our cares.
Please forgive us any wrongs,
as we sing our sorry song.
Help us to be kind each day,
in our thoughts and all we say.

2. We come to say we are sorry
To the tune of Lavender's blue dilly, dilly

We come to say we are sorry,
we come to pray.
We come to say we are sorry,
help us each day.

3. I want to say that I am sorry
To the tune of What shall we do with the drunken sailor

I want to say that I am sorry,
I want to say that I am sorry,
I want to say that I am sorry,
Help me dear Lord Jesus.

4. When we say that we are sorry
To the tune of When you're happy and you know it

When we say that we are sorry, God forgives.
When we say that we are sorry, God forgives.
When it's large or when it's small,
He will still forgive it all.
When we say that we are sorry, God forgives.

5. I have come to say sorry
To the tune of *There's a hole in my bucket*

I have come to say sorry,
Lord Jesus,
Lord Jesus,
I have come to say sorry,
and make a fresh start.

And to ask you to help me,
Lord Jesus,
Lord Jesus,
To be kind and forgiving,
with all of my heart.

Sorry Colour Prayers

S Lord, forgive us our impatience,
or when we've not been true,
for when we did not listen,
or turned away from you.
Give us lots of courage to make a fresh new start.
Help us to be sorry, we ask this from the heart.
Amen.

O Forgive me Jesus, for the things
I have done wrong.
Make my heart more loving
and help me to try again.
Amen.

R Lord, because you love me so much,
you are always ready to forgive me.
You offer me your love and friendship;
you give me your peace.
Help me to forgive others
and share this peace with them.
Amen.

R Father forgive me, when so often
I get things wrong.
Give me a pure heart and fill it with your love.
Help me not to 'look back', but to turn
towards the light of your goodness.
Amen.

Y Father in Heaven I give you my heart.
And ask for your help to make a fresh start.
Forgive all the things which I have done wrong.
Fill me with grace, so I will be strong.
Amen.

Gospel Acclamations
1. Share your word with us
To the tune of *London Bridge is falling down*

Share your word with us, O Lord,
us O Lord,
us O Lord.
Share your word with us, O Lord.
Help us listen.

2. Light up our hearts
To the tune of *Hickory Dickory Dock*

You light up our hearts with your love,
So we can see the way.
To follow you and all you do,
You light up our hearts with your love.

3. Alleluia, alleluia
To the tune of *If you're happy and you know it*

Alleluia, alleluia, praise the Lord,
Alleluia, alleluia, praise the Lord.
As we listen to the story,
Let us praise him for his glory.
Alleluia, alleluia, praise the Lord.

4. Praise the Lord
To the tune of *Row, Row, Row the Boat*

Praise, praise, praise the Lord,
Praise our Father dear.
As we listen to his word,
feel his Spirit near.

5. We have come to hear you

To the tune of *London Bridge is falling Down*

We have come to hear you Lord,
hear you Lord,
hear you Lord.
We have come to hear you Lord,
we are listening.

6. Jesus here we are

To the tune of *One man went to mow*

Jesus here we are,
gathered as your children.
To the word of God,
we have come to listen.

Glorias

1. Gloria (Song)

To the tune of *Here we go round the mulberry bush*

Let us all praise the Son of God,
Son of God,
Son of God.
Let us all praise the Father too,
And the Holy Spirit.

2. Gloria (Prayer)

Glory be to God the Father our heavenly King,
Glory be to Jesus his Son, who saved us from sin,
Glory be to the Holy Spirit, the giver of life,
We worship you and give you praise.
Amen.

3. Gloria (Prayer)

Glory be to God the Father, the creator.
Glory be to Jesus the Son, our saviour.
Glory be to the Holy Spirit, the breath of God.
Glory, glory, glory.
Amen.

4. The 'Gloria Be' (Prayer)

Glory be to the Father, and to the Son,
and to the Holy Spirit.
As it was in the beginning, is now,
and ever shall be,
World without end.
Amen.

The Little Creed

We believe in God the Father,
who made the whole world.
We believe in Jesus his Son,
who died on the cross for us,
and rose from the dead.
We believe in the Holy Spirit
who brings life and love to us all.
We believe that the Church is one family,
and that one day we will share everlasting life
with God in Heaven.
Amen.

Advent Song

To the tune of *Twinkle, twinkle little star*

Twinkle, twinkle little star,
Leading the wise men so far,
travelling both day and night,
guided by your light so bright.
Like the shepherds and the Kings,
We have come your praise to sing.